Aunt Jemima, Uncle Ben, and Rastus

Recent Titles in
Contributions in Afro-American and African Studies

Aunt Jemima, Uncle Ben, and Rastus)

Blacks in Advertising, Yesterday, Today, and Tomorrow

MARILYN KERN-FOXWORTH
Foreword by Alex Haley

Contributions in Afro-American and African Studies, Number 168

GREENWOOD PRESS
Westport, Connecticut • London

Library of Congress Cataloging-in-Publication Data

Kern-Foxworth, Marilyn.
    Aunt Jemima, Uncle Ben, and Rastus : Blacks in advertising,
yesterday, today, and tomorrow / Marilyn Kern-Foxworth ; foreword by
Alex Haley.
        p. cm. — (Contributions in Afro-American and African
studies, ISSN 0069-9624 ; no. 168)
    Includes bibliographical references and index.
    ISBN 0-313-26798-7
    1. Afro-Americans in advertising—United States—History.
I. Title. II. Series.
HF5813.U6K47 1994
659.1'089'96073—dc20   93-37507

British Library Cataloguing in Publication Data is available.

A paperback edition of *Aunt Jemima, Uncle Ben, and Rastus* is available from Praeger Publishers,
an imprint of Greenwood Publishing Group, Inc. (ISBN 0-275-95184-7).

Library of Congress Catalog Card Number: 93-37507
ISBN: 0-313-26798-7
ISSN: 0069-9624

First published in 1994

Greenwood Press, 88 Post Road West, Westport, CT 06881
An imprint of Greenwood Publishing Group, Inc.

Printed in the United States of America

∞™

The paper used in this book complies with the
Permanent Paper Standard issued by the National
Information Standards Organization (Z39.48-1984).

10 9 8 7 6 5 4 3 2

This book is dedicated to the
Memory of my beloved mother,
Mrs. Manella Lou Bertha Dickens Kern,
Who left this world hoping,
But not actually knowing,
That I would one day make a significant
Contribution to society
And to my race.

CONTENTS

Photo Essay follows Chapter 4

FOREWORD

On September 29, 1967, I stood on a dock in Annapolis, Maryland, where my great-great-great-great-grandfather had been taken ashore two hundred years earlier on September 29, 1767. It was one of the moments when I truly realized the importance of knowing one's history and the importance of documenting every facet of that history. Because for a long period of time it was against the law to teach slaves to read and write, much of black American history had to be documented by people other than blacks. As a result, much of our history has either been lost or severely distorted. Now that we have moved into a new era, there are many more opportunities for black Americans, and more and more books have been written that document the black experience. I am proud to say this is one of those books which offers a collection of information that is long overdue and chronicles the history of blacks in a critical area that has been previously under-recorded—advertising.

Advertising is an integral part of our lives, and we are constantly besieged by someone or some company urging us to buy this or that. It has been no secret that blacks in America have not been portrayed justly and fairly in advertising during the past decades. And the images of America's blacks perpetuated by advertising have not averaged very favorable. It is important for us to realize what effects such depictions have had on black people's self-respect, self-esteem, self-concept, and self-identity. We can't deny the importance of advertising and public relations in our lives as they are definitely a reality of human existence. I like the saying, "If you do not deal with what is truly the reality, then you can be certain that down the line the reality is going to deal with you."

I am aware that Dr. Kern-Foxworth has been researching this topic for years, and her diligence has paid off in the thoroughness of this book. All of the relevant areas are covered, and for those who still have questions, she has listed people and organizations which can assist in finding answers to those questions.

Appropriately, the book begins with slavery, which played a key role in the shaping of black America. Dr. Kern-Foxworth demonstrates graphically some of the psychological problems deeply embedded within the black community that descend from slavery.

This book is timely because African-Americans have begun to reexamine, investigate, analyze, and scrutinize their heritage more now than ever before. We have ceased shunning our past and are dedicating more time to understanding why and how slavery, Jim Crow, prejudice, discrimination, and bigotry became a part of the American way of life. As I travel from city to city in America, I see and hear people inquisitive about their "roots." I am asked by Americans of African descent about their heritage, legacies, and genealogy. I talk with black people who have acquired a greater appreciation for black artifacts and memorabilia, which is why there has been such a proliferation of interest in black collectibles, even those that are grotesque, demeaning, and denigrating to black Americans. This book provides a mirror of our past—a past that has been ignored or overshadowed for too long.

Alex Haley

PREFACE

The impetus for this project came in 1974 when I was doing research at Florida State University. While perusing index after index I stumbled across an article titled, "White Backlash to Negro Ads: Fact or Fantasy," by Carl Block (1967). The article made such an impression on me that most of what I have written from that period on has focused on this topic in one way or another. Hence, I have looked under dusty desks and searched every library accessible for information pertinent to blacks in advertising.

I have secured information from research centers, libraries, and antique shops and contacted over 400 organizations in an attempt to provide in-depth coverage on this topic. My annual vacations were not complete until I had found some information of interest or a clue that provided a vital link to the areas under investigation. At every conference and every meeting, whether in a social or academic setting, I cornered someone who could address the topics that I was researching. To those individuals who were responsive to my requests I will be eternally grateful. I am indebted, as well, to those organizations and businesses who responded to my letters of inquiry.

This book examines the stereotypical portrayals of blacks in advertising from the turn of the century to the present in television, magazines, newspapers, and newspaper inserts. Prior to this book no single literary work has provided a comprehensive report on the history and status of blacks in advertising. Advertising has mushroomed into an over $146 billion industry, which equates to approximately $584 spent annually to advertise to each man, woman, and child in America. It is an institution wielding a lot of influence and tremendously impacts every facet of our daily lives. Subconsciously, and sometimes consciously, advertising messages are major factors in formulating images of black Americans. In other words, the infiltration of this kind of money into the American economy buys influence and greatly dictates what is portrayed in the mass media.

Writing this book has indeed been an exceptional learning experience for me. One of the most valuable lessons has been in seeing how words, images, and nonverbal behavior influence the way we think of ourselves and the way others perceive us. On that same note, I would like to add that over the last couple of years while gathering information, I have felt "strange" each time I used or heard someone refer to black people as a minority. Having traveled to Africa and recognized that "people of color" are the dominant population in the world, I know that the word "minority" is a misnomer.

But even beyond that point, referring to ourselves as a minority is self-defeating and puts African-Americans and other races so often classified in this manner in a defensive posture and limits what we think we can do and what others' expectations of us are as well. With that thought in mind, I have purposely omitted the word minority from this book with the exception of direct quotations and titles of an organization or committee. Instead, I have opted to use multi-ethnics, people of color, or ALANA (African, Latin, Asian and Native Americans); nonwhites, African-Americans, and blacks interchangeably where I felt their use to be appropriate.

It is ironic that black involvement with advertising has escalated from the grotesque caricatures depicted as mammies, buffoons, and Uncle Toms around the turn of the century to an era in which Michael Jackson was once paid $10 million to advertise Pepsi Cola.

The book was written with the dire intention of filling an important void in American history by producing a written, as well as pictorial, documentation of blacks in advertising. Writing this book has been one of the most rewarding experiences of my life, if for no other reason than I finally learned what my mother was saying when she used to say, "Sit down, girl, looking like a Gold Dust Twin." At that time I had no earthly idea what a Gold Dust Twin was, but now, because of this book, I know, and the world can now learn everything there is to know about the Gold Dust Twins. Although some of the information uncovered was quite demeaning and caused me much dismay, I have grown from the experience and my horizons have broadened. As a result of writing this book, I have learned that through concerted efforts the negative images promulgated yesterday can be transformed into positive ones today, and that there is always hope for tomorrow.

It was often a painful experience at best to research, decipher, and record the omissions, the distortions, and the stereotypical depictions that confronted me as I plowed through an enormous amount of material. For the first time this material exists as one bound volume to be scrutinized, lambasted, and analyzed. Although painful to examine, it is indeed constructive that we disseminate this kind of information because it provides students, teachers, professionals, scholars, and laymen with a body of knowledge by which the future can be chartered. It does indeed help us to comprehend more fully the role of blacks in advertising, yesterday, today, and tomorrow.

ACKNOWLEDGMENTS

No project of this magnitude could be completed without the assistance of others. Some of the individuals who made this book a reality include: Grace Montemar, who served as my personal assistant and gave many hours to documenting sources; Gregory Foxworth (husband), whose computer acumen was a tremendous help in getting the manuscript into a publishable form; and Howard Eilers, who spent many unpaid hours photographing prints and slides.

I will forever be indebted to the American Association of University Women for awarding me an Agnes Harris Postdoctoral Fellowship. The award permitted me time from my hectic teaching schedule to finish the manuscript. My heartfelt appreciation is also given to Texas A&M University for the moral and financial support given during the entire process of writing and publishing this book.

I wish to thank the following for the assistance of their staff and use of their facilities: Tuskegee Institute, Moorland-Spingarn Research Center, The Poynter Institute for Media Studies, Gannett Center for Media Studies, American Society of Magazine Editors, American Press Institute, American Advertising Federation, and the Schomburg Center for Research in Black Culture.

The artwork is the dedication of William Joseph Wilborn, the best kept secret in the photography world. His work has brought this book to life and I can't say enough about his talents and his tenacity.

This book has been strengthened by the creative works shown and I am thankful to the following people for aiding me in this endeavor: Adrian

Piper, Naomi Long Madget, Sylvia Dunnavant, Murray N. DePillars, Maya Angelou, and John Onye Lockard. Appreciation is also extended to George W. Haley for granting permission to use the foreword by the late Alex Haley and to the following organizations for granting me permission to use certain information, materials, and illustrations: University of North Carolina Press, New York Telephone, Nabisco Brands Inc, University of Pennsylvania Press, Prentice Hall, Pepsi-Cola Company, Ralston Purina Company, John Wiley & Sons, Inc., Campbell Soup Company, Association for Education in Journalism and Mass Communication, The Broadcasting Education Association, TV Guide, Howard University Press, Procter & Gamble, and PO Boy Restaurants.

I thank Cynthia Harris, Nita Romer, and Maureen Melino at Greenwood Publishing for their patience with missed deadlines and for the time they spent talking through problems by telephone.

Many other family members offered support, guidance and encouragement during this process and although they have not been mentioned by name, their interest in my success meant more than I could ever say.

INTRODUCTION

This book chronicles an aspect of African-American history that has heretofore been ignored. Former slaves who were freed by President Lincoln's signing of the Emancipation Proclamation on January 1, 1863, were overjoyed in their newfound freedom. However, the legacy of slavery did not wash away as easily as snow does on a rainy day. Instead, the remnants of slavery clung to the liberal Northerners and the Southerners in the land of Dixie in the same way that Southern belles have become a staple of the Southern plantation. In other words, certain images that were dominant during slavery have been carefully transferred to contemporary society.

The concept of race and the stereotypes associated with it enabled the dominant group to view members of the subordinate group as inferior and to treat them accordingly. Stereotypes were used as a mechanism to reinforce and justify slavery.

In 1932 Katz and Braly (1933) conducted the first study of ethnic stereotypes at Princeton University. The paradigm created by these researchers has served as a model for most subsequent research in this area. To conduct the study 100 students were given a list of 84 traits and asked to select which they thought were typical of a particular ethnic group. Such traits as superstitious, lazy, dirty, and ignorant headed the list in frequency of attribution to African-Americans (Brigham, 1971).

William Van DeBurg (1984), in his work *Slavery and Race in American Popular Culture,* discusses the evolution of stereotypes associated with blacks from slavery into modern American society. "As outcasts in a white-dominated society, blacks alternately were portrayed as feeble-willed noble savages, comically musical minstrel figures, and dehumanized brutes" (p. xi). He meticulously outlines the interpretation of these stereotypes by American novelists, historians, dramatists, poets, filmmakers, and songwriters.

Appropriately, the beginning sections of this book investigate the advent of blacks in early American advertisements. There is an assessment of advertisements for the sale of slaves and for runaway slaves. A detailed analysis discusses the sociological implications of the wording of the advertisements and the psychological effects such advertisements had on slaves and their owners. Scrutinizing these advertisements provides a theoretical dimension to the discussion of slavery and details the impact that such advertisements had on the perpetuation and stability of this "peculiar institution."

Subsequently, manufacturers, advertisers, companies, and entrepreneurs who had to relinquish the rights to their "black mammies" and "black Sambos" declined to eradicate such images of blacks completely and very subtlely had such caricatures resurface on advertising trade cards, bottles, tins, dolls, and the like—thus reinforcing the stereotypes that had been forged during slavery and offering comfort to those whites who had exonerated slavery as a necessary trade. Not surprisingly, the early advertising paraphernalia featuring blacks was excessively demeaning and derogatory. Such portrayals served the same purpose as shackles during slavery, only this time the hands and feet were mobile and the mind was artificially imprisoned. George Fredrickson (1971) refers to this mentality as *The Black Image in the White Mind.*

From the end of the slave era to the culmination of the Civil Rights movement, early advertising artifacts ushered in the Aunt Jemimas, Uncle Bens, and Rastuses and helped maintain the status quo. The trade cards, advertising stamps, blotters, tins, and bottles displaying blacks with thick lips, bulging eyes, and distorted grimaces hung around the necks of blacks as chains had once in slavery. This situation created a paradoxical dilemma for all black Americans. They were faced with eradicating the fictitious black men and women who embodied eternal servitude. As such they also were forced to employ the brilliance of their heritage and inner depths of their intelligence to free themselves of psychological bondage.

Characters such as Aunt Jemima (pancake mix), Uncle Ben (rice), and Rastus (Cream of Wheat) have remained as constant reminders of the subservient positions to which blacks have been relegated over the years. Aunt Jemima was the first living trademark of a company and has been the impetus for an advertising strategy since 1889. Recognizable for over a century, her stability has caused some historians to refer to her as an American institution. Patricia Morton, (1991) in *Disfigured Images: The Historical Assault on Afro-American Women,* carefully illustrates the propensity of popular culture to perpetuate the mammy stereotype and the use of Aunt Jemima in that effort. "Providing a steady diet of mammies, the pancake-box

Aunt Jemima represents the modernization and yet continuity of this old-time figure. . . . Mammy remains a valuable emblem from a marketing perspective because of her image in the American popular mind" (p. xi). The popularity of Aunt Jemima, Uncle Ben, and Rastus transcended the plantation kitchen and entered the American psyche, and in so doing inadvertently circumscribed the aspirations and dreams of a whole race of people. Deeply rooted in slavery these stereotypes have persisted and continue to be perpetuated by mass media, including advertising.

A discussion of these symbols provides information pertinent to the psychological impact of stereotypical advertising, which was at its worst following the Great Depression. A listing of the various stereotypes that have been assigned to blacks is given. Some of the questions answered include: What were the psychological implications and ramifications of the denigration of blacks in earlier advertising and public relations campaigns? What effects did such blatant portrayals of blacks have on race relations and the economic stability of blacks during those periods?

Many of the changes that occurred in the portrayal and appearance of blacks in advertising were directly related to adverse reactions by them to such pejorative representations during the Civil Rights Movement. "Then came the late 1960s—the black nationalist period: dashikis, Afros, the clenched black power fist and the special handshake. Advertisers such as Kent and Newport cigarettes and Afro Sheen, with its Swahili slogan, 'Wantu wazuri' (beautiful people), began to target black consumers" (Sturgis, 1993, p. 22). A detailed account is given of those organizations that became involved in the elimination of such advertising, including the NAACP, CORE, and PUSH. The role of the Kerner Commission's Report on Civil Disorders is highlighted also. The commission recommended in 1968 that "Negro reporters and performers should appear more frequently—and at prime-time—in news broadcasts, on weather shows, in documentaries, and in advertisements."

In 1983 the Ad Watch Committee of the Black Media Association in North Carolina began monitoring the advertising industry. On a monthly basis they have written positive and negative responses to advertisers regarding the portrayals of blacks. They implemented guidelines, now being promulgated by the Better Business Bureau, that outline ways of eliminating stereotyping of multi-ethnic people in advertising.

The efforts of the organizations mentioned above were instrumental in getting more African-Americans included in advertising campaigns. The frequency of the appearance of blacks in advertising was an area often studied by mass communication and marketing scholars beginning in the middle of the 20th century. Scholars conducted research pertinent to the inclusion of blacks in newspaper, magazine, and television advertising. Research of this kind examined the number of blacks used, the product types and brands that most often used blacks as models, and the age of black models.

Over the years the researchers became interested in such issues as: What roles do the black models portray?, and Do black models serve primary or secondary functions within the advertising campaigns? These studies have been useful in determining that blacks were not used to advertise certain products, that black family life was not often portrayed, and that advertisers have always felt more comfortable using black children in advertising than black adults. Some advertisers have used the information disseminated in these studies to make necessary changes in their strategies directed toward the African-American market, while others have chosen to ignore the studies and this market or have continued to present blacks in unflattering situations.

During the 1970s and 1980s many of the studies focused on the occupations in which African-Americans were portrayed. They showed that, for the most part, the predominant images projected indicate that most successful blacks in American society are either professional athletes or entertainers. Over the years, the studies have documented increases in the appearance of blacks in advertising. The optimism that this information should bring is reserved, however, because the amount of advertising space bought in newspapers, magazines, and television has increased significantly over the years. This perhaps diminishes the notion that the use of blacks in advertising has increased as dramatically as some studies have noted.

Just as there were studies that documented the inclusion of more blacks in advertising, there also were studies that scrutinized the reactions of Americans to these changes. How did the country respond to black Americans coming into its homes by way of the daily newspaper, monthly magazine, and television, encouraging them to purchase Tide, Crest, Alka Seltzer and offering advice on whether a Kenmore or Maytag washer would prove more cost-efficient? One would assume that such studies would focus only on the reactions of white consumers, but this was not the case. Black consumer reactions also were surveyed and reported in magazines and scholarly journals. Contrary to popular thought, the studies indicated that most whites do not keep hidden in their memory banks the race or nationality of a person who advertises a product and then refuse to purchase that product when the information is recalled. The studies also indicated that blacks are more prone to pay attention to the race of the person advertising a product than whites, and they prefer to purchase products that use blacks to advertise them. Research also has shown that blacks are more attentive to advertising than whites. Although 26 percent of the general population said that they pay attention to advertising, 35 percent of black respondents indicated that they closely observe advertising (Holman, 1993, p. 11).

This book is completed with a listing of African-American museums and resources for those who would like to continue the expedition of garnering more information about blacks in advertising.

REFERENCES

Blassingame, John W. 1979. *The Slave Community: Plantation Life in the Antebellum South.* New York: Oxford University Press.

Brigham, John C. 1971. "Ethnic Stereotypes." *Psychological Bulletin* 76: 15–38.

Fredrickson, George M. 1971. *The Black Image in the White Mind.* New York: Harper and Row.

Holman, Blan. 1993. "Changing the Face(s) of Advertising: AAF [American Advertising Federation] and Its Members Seek Solutions to Advertising's Dearth of Diversity." *American Advertising,* (Fall): 10–13.

Katz, D., and K. Braly. 1933. "Racial Stereotypes in One Hundred College Students." *Journal of Abnormal and Social Psychology* 28: 280–90.

Morton, Patricia. 1991. *Disfigured Images: The Historical Assault on Afro-American Women.* Westport, Conn.: Greenwood Press.

Stephan, Walter G., and David Rosenfield. 1982. "Racial and Ethnic Stereotypes." In Arthur G. Miller, ed., *In the Eye of the Beholder: Contemporary Issues in Stereotyping.* New York: Praeger.

Sturgis, Ingrid. 1993. "Black Images in Advertising: A Revolution Is Being Televised in 30-Second Commercials." (September): 21–23.

Van DeBurg, William L. 1984. *Slavery and Race in American Popular Culture.* Madison: University of Wisconsin Press.

Aunt Jemima, Uncle Ben, and Rastus

Chapter 1

SLAVE ADVERTISEMENTS: A MIRROR TO THE "PECULIAR INSTITUTION"

> i have lived a million times,
> in a million different places
> in a million different faces
> i express myself falsely
> i live in constant fear
> i watched with tense and anxiety
>   as tears flushed my eyes
>   when they beat my father
>   bred my mother and
>   sold my brother!
>   i am not free,
>   i do not belong to me
>   i run away so i am hung
>   but i do not die because
> I AM THE REINCARNATION OF BLACK BOY.
>
> Kern-Foxworth

Slavery has always been and will continue to be one of America's greatest enigmas. "For centuries a 'peculiar institution' existed in the Americas, profoundly altering the lives of millions of Africans forced into bondage. The imposition of slavery altered the course of the nation's social and economic development, and ultimately led to the Civil War" (Fleming, 1992, p. 1). Throughout history researchers have sought to codify, identify, justify, and modify all materials that would assist in demystifying the people—slaves and slaveholders—involved in this institution. Slave advertisements have proven to be invaluable sources of information in this regard. They let us know who bought and sold slaves and what methods were used to buy them. On another dimension they offer us insights into those bondsmen and bondswomen who fled the grips of slavery to search for a better life for themselves—to search for freedom. The advertisements refute some of the notions we have formulated pertinent to slavery over the years. Serving as unofficial documents of slavery, they let us know that not all whites believed in the enslavement of other human beings. In fact, the editor of Wilmington's *Delaware Weekly Advertiser* refused to publish an advertisement offering a reward for the return of a runaway slave (Bergman, 1969, p. 129). However, it should be known that careful scrutiny has shown no general relationship between the editorial stance of a newspaper and the amount of slave advertising it carried (Bradley, 1987, p. 4).

Slave ads also let us know that many of the black Americans who were sold, bartered, raffled, chased, and sometimes apprehended were not illiterate, unskilled, and uneducated. From the legalizing of American slavery in 1611 until its closure in 1863 slave advertisements played an important role in uniting abolitionists and slaves toward its demise, and masters, bounty hunters, traders, and speculators in its continuity.

The first blacks traded to America settled in the English colonies at Jamestown in 1619. John Rolfe reported in his journal on August 20, 1619, "there came in a Dutch man-of-warre that sold us 20 negars" (Van DeBurg, 1984, p. 5.). The blacks were indentured servants, free to buy land. By 1650 "chattel slavery"—a system in which slaves were defined as property, not people—had been made legal, and among the most permanent historical documents available that describe the people and situations during that period are slave advertisements (Smith and Wojtowicz, 1989).

In 1776 the slave population of the 13 colonies was about 500,000, consisting of African Tribes of Ashanti, Bantu, Dahomean, Ezik, Fanti, Hausa, Ibo, Kru, and Mandingo. Between 1800 and 1860, another 250,000 were imported into the South, some after the practice had been banned (Beifuss, 1990). Recent historiographers estimate that approximately 10 million Africans made the journey safely to America. The pioneering work of Professor Philip D. Curtin (1969) suggests that 8 to 11.5 million slaves were imported over three and a half centuries: approximately 600,000 in the 16th century, 2 million in the 17th century, 5 million in the 18th century, and 3 million in the 19th century. Additionally, between 10 and 20 percent of those exported died during the "Middle Passage" from Africa to the Caribbean. Herbert Klein (1978) suggests that information pertinent to the "Middle Passage," or transoceanic crossing, has been the most controversial aspect of the entire trade: "Yet what the 'typical' voyage might have been in any trade or during any period is virtually unknown. Moreover, the age, sex, and mortality experience of the departing Africans and the manner in which they were transported is only partially understood" (p. xvii). A large number of slaves also died during "seasoning," the first year of settling in (Ploski and Williams, 1989). The death toll during transportation of slaves was more succinctly stated by Lorene Cary (1992) when she wrote, "First came at least a million and a half dead on shipboard, according to slave-trade historian Basil Davidson, and several millions from the beginning of the marches from the interior of Africa to final landing in the Americas" (p. 23).

Many people have probably never thought about the importance of advertising in the preservation of slavery. In fact, slavery—a practice by which human beings are owned by other human beings—would not have been such an effective institution without the vehicle of advertising. One author conjectured facetiously that slaves may, in fact, have had it better than black Americans in 1916. Using slave advertisements as a point of reference he wrote, "In some respects the eighteenth century slave was better off than the Negro of today. As a rule no Negro can now get his name into the leading newspapers unless he commits a heinous crime. At that time, however, masters in offering slaves for sale and advertising fugitives unconsciously spoke of their virtues as well as their shortcomings" (Greene, 1916).

Slave advertisements fell into two categories: those announcing the sale of slaves and those for runaways or fugitives.

ADVERTISING AND THE BUYING AND SELLING OF SLAVES

Findings show that advertisements emphasized the skillfulness of each individual slave. Posters in windows, flyers, and newspapers advertised slaves the same as inanimate objects are advertised today. *The Boston News-Letter,* the first continuing newspaper published in the American colonies, was founded September 25, 1690, and slave advertisements were often featured. The following is an example from March 21, 1734:

> A Likely Negro Man about Twenty two Years of Age, speaks good English, has had the Smallpox and the Measles, has been seven Years with a LIME BURNER: To be sold, Inquire of John Langdon, Baker, next Door to John Clark's at the North End, Boston.
>
> A Likely Negro Man about Twenty-five Years of Age, has had the Small Pox, and speaks pretty good English, suitable for a Farmer, &c. To be sold, Enquire of the Printers.

The slave trade was not totally dependent upon advertising, but ads served as a useful mechanism to let traders—those who had slaves to sell and those wanting to buy slaves—know when, where, the cost, and the quality to be bought or bartered.

Advertisements also served to let slave dealers or merchants know when a slave ship docked. "Whenever a slave ship sailed into a colonial port on the American mainland, its arrival was announced by a town crier or by an advertisement in the local newspaper" (Hughes, 1970, p. 14).

The slave trade was one of the most well-known businesses in America during the apogee of its existence. Slave owners and those who traded slaves used different methods of selling their "wares" and in some cases resorted to non–status quo means. Raffling was but one method used to make even the poorest individual a slave owner, as indicated by the following:

RAFFLE

Mr. Joseph Jennings respectfully informs his friends and the public that, at the request of many acquaintances, he has been induced to purchase from Mr. Osborne, of Missouri, the celebrated

DARK BAY HORSE, "STAR"

Aged five years, square trotter and warranted sound; with a new light Trotting Buggy and Harness also, the dark, stout

MULATTO GIRL, "SARAH"

Aged about twenty years, general house servant, valued at nine hundred dollars, and guaranteed

Will be Raffled for

At 4 O'clock P.M. February first, the selection hotel of the subscribers. The above is as represented and those persons who may wish to engage in the usual practice of raffling, will, I assure them, be perfectly satisfied with their destiny in the affair.

The whole is valued at its just worth, fifteen hundred dollars; fifteen hundred

CHANCES AT ONE DOLLAR EACH

The Raffle will be conducted by gentlemen selected by the interested subscribers present. Five nights will be allowed to complete the Raffle. BOTH OF THE ABOVE DESCRIBED CAN BE SEEN AT MY STORE, No. 78 Common St., second door from the Camp, from 9 o'clock A.M to 2 P.M.

Highest throw to take the first choice; the lowest throw the remaining prize, and the fortunate winners will pay twenty dollars each for the refreshments furnished on the occasion.

N. B. No chances recognized unless paid for previous to the commencement.

Joseph Jennings

Ulrich Bonnell Phillips (1966), in *American Negro Slavery: A Survey of the Supply, Employment, and Control of Negro Labor as Determined by the Plantation Regime,* suggests that in the cities a few slaves were sold by lottery, and he specifically notes an advertisement that appeared in the *Louisiana Courier* (New Orleans) on August 17, 1819, in which a man announced that he would sell 50 tickets at $20 each, the lucky drawer to receive his girl Amelia, 13 years old (p. 192).

Children of Slavery

During the times of slavery there were many more black children born in the South than in the North. Although farmers understood the marketing potential of slave children once they became older, most Northern owners viewed them as an extra expense and added burden. Consequently, most Philadelphia slave owners discouraged their female slaves from reproducing. One colonist was quoted in the local newspaper as saying, "In this city negroes just born, are considered as an incumbrance only, and if humanity did not forbid it, they would be instantly given away" (Smith and Wojtowicz, 1989, p. 8). As evidence of this situation, there often appeared advertisements announcing children for sale at a very young age, and many indicated that women were sold "for no fault but breeding!" (Smith and Wojtowicz, 1989, p. 8).

As Patricia Bradley (1987) notes, "Boston advertisements, however, provide the most compelling evidence that points to the vulnerability and isolation of the black child" (p. 13). Black babies were regularly "given away free." Between 1770 and 1774 the *Boston Gazette* and *The Boston News-Letter* carried 25 such advertisements for free babies, such as this one from the latter, January 30, 1773:

> To Be Given Away. A very, likely Negro Female Child, of as fine a breed as any in America. Enquire of the Printer.

According to Bradley advertisements for free black babies were found primarily in Boston newspapers. The practice of giving them away was apparently a long-standing Massachusetts tradition (Moore, 1866, p. 57). In other colonies advertisements offering free black babies were rare. As suggested earlier, Southern slaveholders were more prone to let their female slaves keep their babies, while Northern slave owners were not so readily accepting of these children. Researchers suggest that perhaps they placed them with other black families or found them homes through nonconventional networks. By the age of seven or eight children were able to work, and Northern slave owners found them more favorable as house or field hands.

Slave Traders

Slave trading was a very profitable business for some entrepreneurs during the pinnacle of its existence. There were those whose primary business ventures were as traders or speculators of slaves; "Negro traders" or "Negro speculators" were terms also used to describe these entrepreneurs. Advertisements have been used to discern some information about the traders and their modes of operations, but this method is limiting for two reasons: (1) Not all slave traders used advertising, and (2) the financial instability of newspapers in certain regions rendered them worthless to traders. Nonetheless, over the years researchers have been able to gather certain important information about this process for selling and buying slaves by closely scrutinizing advertisements. Moses Austin, a slave trader in Richmond, placed this advertisement in the local newspaper:

> One hundred Negroes, from 20 to 30 years old, for which a good price will be given. They are to be sent out of state, therefore we shall not be particular respecting the character of any of them—Hearty and well made is all that is necessary. (Tadman, 1989, p. 15)

It was usually easy to distinguish traders' advertisements because they began: "Cash for Negroes." Such advertisements typically gave an age range for the slaves wanted and usually requested groups of 25, 50, or even 100. One such advertisement, that of Clinkscales and Boozer, announced that "young and likely negroes between the ages of 12 and 25" were sought, and further noted that

> Those having such property to sell, will find it in their interest to bring them to us, or drop a line to us and we will come and see them. One of us can always be found at home, prepared to pay the highest prices for such negroes as suit us in cash. (South Carolina, *Laurenville Herald,* 1858)

Another speculator, A. J. Hydrick, advertised that

> Persons having . . . [suitable Negroes] and desiring to dispose of them, by addressing a line, at Poplar P.O., Orangeburg District, may do so to advantage. Such persons will please state the age, quality and price of the negroes, and if the stipulated figures are not above the CASH VALUE, I will in a short time after the receipt of their letter give them a call. (South Carolina *Sumter Watchman,* 1857)

The differences between advertisements of traders and non-traders were stark. First of all, non-traders rarely needed to advertise to purchase slaves, although they would sometimes advertise to sell them. Non-traders rarely bought large numbers of slaves at one time. Commonly, slave traders would purchase slaves by the pound and would note the poundage sought in the advertisement; non-traders did not use this measurement. Non-traders also usually bought on credit, promising to pay over several months.

Advertisements placed by Webb, Merrill & Company and Lyle & Hitchings, which supplied the sugar districts of Louisiana, notably New Orleans, and Nashville, Tennessee, in 1859 and 1860, stated that they "would at all times purchase NEGROES suited to the New Orleans market." At that same time N. B. Forrest in Charleston ran this advertisement: "500 Negroes wanted. I will pay more than any other person, for no. 1 negroes, suited to the New Orleans market." These announcements were atypical of the many offered by traders, as most of them "almost never specified the particular market for which they bought" (Tadman, 1989, p. 66).

Slave trading also opened avenues for other business ventures. Some slave agents used taverns or their own warehouses and stockades for the purpose of housing and viewing large numbers of slaves to be purchased or auctioned. However, as slave traders moved about from town to town, they needed holding pens in which to show off their wares and there were those entrepreneurs who supplied such facilities. Known as jails or slave pens, advertisements for such facilities are typified by this one placed by C. F. Hatcher of Gravier Street, New Orleans:

> Notice to Traders and Slaveholders
> Having built a large and commodius showroom, and otherwise improved my old stand, I am now prepared to accommodate over 200 Negroes for sale. The owners can have comfortable rooms and board in the same premises at reasonable terms.

Pens of this nature were common, and "in 1854, there were no fewer than seven slave dealers in a single block on Gravier, while on a single square on Moreau Street [New Orleans] there was a row of eleven particularly commodious slave pens" (Wade, 1964, p. 199).

Some slave speculators were unscrupulous in their trading and often used unorthodox methods of marketing. One case in point is substantiated by an item appearing in 1818 at Winchester in the Shenandoah Valley:

> Several wretches, whose hearts must be black as the skins of the unfortunate beings who constitute their human traffic, have for several days been impudently prowling about the streets of this place with labels on their hats exhibiting in conspicuous characters the words, "Cash for negroes." (Phillips, 1966, p. 192)

ADVERTISEMENTS FOR RUNAWAY SLAVES

Contrary to popular belief, blacks brought to America to become slaves were not quite so content with their fate as some researchers and historians have recorded. "An obvious indication of more or less common discontent and the non-acceptance of the slavery system is to be found in the number of runaways" (Moore, 1971, p. 133).

There were three categories of runaway slaves: (1) those who ran away in protest to a heavy beating or some loss of privilege, such as a reduction in rations or cancellation of a holiday, (2) those who fled to join separated families or to attain freedom in the North, Canada, or Mexico, and (3) recalcitrants whose desire for freedom would not let them rest until they were freedmen or until they had been maimed into submission or killed.

John W. Blassingame (1979) suggests that blacks were not so docile and easygoing as has been presented in some of the literature. Using the personal records of slaves, he observes that the black slave

used his wits to escape from work and punishment, preserved his manhood in the quarters, feigned humility, identified with masters and worked industriously only when he was treated humanely, simulated deference, was hostilely submissive and occasionally obstinate, ungovernable, and rebellious. (p. 216)

The intense desire for some slaves to regain their freedom can be observed in the following passage that recounts the relentlessness of Kunta Kinte, a central character in Alex Haley's *Roots* (1976):

The hero, Kunta Kinte, not long a slave, had fled: When he heard distant baying of the dogs, a rage flooded up in him such as he had never felt before. When they were but strides away, Kunta whirled and crouched down, snarling back at them. As they came lunging forward with their fangs bared, he too lunged at them. Springing away, Kunta began running again. Then there was another shot, and another—and he felt a flashing pain in his leg. Knocked down in a heap, he had staggered upright again when the toubob shouted and fired again, and he heard the bullets thud into trees by his head. Let them kill me, thought Kunta; I will die as a man should. Then another shot hit the same leg, and it smashed him down like a giant fist. [Kunta is caught, stripped and tied to a tree.]

The lash began cutting into the flesh across Kunta's shoulder and back, with the "oberseer" grunting and Kunta shuddering under the force of each blow. After a while Kunta could not stop himself from screaming with pain, but the beating went on until his sagging body pressed against the tree. His shoulders and back were covered with long, half-opened bleeding welts that in some places exposed the muscles beneath. Then everything went black. He came to in his hut, and along with his senses, pain returned. He boiled with fury that instead of beating him like a man, the toubob had stripped him naked. When he became well, he would take revenge—and he would escape again. Or he would die. (pp. 233–234)

Most researchers are in agreement that almost all slave owners had slaves run away. According to Winthrop D. Jordan (1968) there was "probably more time, more money and energy expended on the problem of runaway slaves by slaveowners, legislators, constables, jailers and newspaper printers than on any other aspect of administering the slave system" (p. 107). On some occasions the fugitives would set up their own colonies. Known as *maroons,* these runaways formed camps called *quilombos* (cabins) and lived in the woods on the outside of nearby cities (Hornsby, 1991, p. xix).

Most runaways were caught immediately because of the patrols accompanied by "nigger dogs" quickly mounted as soon as an escape had been noticed, but large numbers did manage to elude their captors. One historian estimates that by 1855, 60,000 slaves had successfully defected to the North (Everett, 1978, p. 122). Another researcher suggests that 40,000 slaves moved through Ohio between 1830 and 1860 (Everett, 1978, p. 162).

Notable Slaves Who Fled

With the help of more than 3,000 members of the Underground Railroad, it is estimated that approximately 75,000 slaves escaped to freedom in the decade preceding the Civil War. The mode and method of escape for the slaves varied, but generally they went on foot and ran into the deep forest to hide themselves, usually wading in streams and spreading pepper as often as possible to throw off their scent to the bloodhounds that were trained to hunt them down and viciously attack. In some rare instances a slave would steal his master's horse, and some even had the courage to ride the trains to freedom. Such was the case of Frederick Douglass, famed orator and abolitionist, who rode the train from Maryland to Philadelphia on September 3, 1838, in an effort to free himself of the chains of slavery which had constrained him since birth (Douglass, 1983).

Some other notable runaway slaves included Moses Grimes, who ran away repeatedly and was identified and apprehended for his unusual habit of walking on his hands, and Caesar, who escaped even though both his legs were cut off at the knee:

> Kingtown, Queen Ann's County, September 10, 1759
>
> RUN away the 8th of this Instant [month], a Negro Man, named Caesar, he has both his legs cut off, and walks on his knees, may pretend that he was Cook of a Vessel, as he has been much used on board of Ships; he was seen by New-Castle on Saturday last. Whoever secures the said Negroe in any Gaol or Work-house, shall receive Twenty Shillings Reward, paid by me SARAH MASSEY.
>
> N. B. He has been a Ferry man at Chester Town, Queen Ann's County, for many years. (Smith and Wojtowicz, 1989, p. 47)

Another runaway slave of notoreity was Crispus Attucks. Attucks was the first person to die on March 5, 1770, during the Boston Massacre and thus also became the first person to die during the American Revolution. It is believed that he was a runaway slave who had found work on a whaling ship after absconding from his master twenty years earlier. Evidence of this is based on an advertisement appearing in Boston on March 2, 1750 (Peters, 1974, pp. 13–14):

Ran-away from his Master William Brown of Framingham, on the 30th of Sept. a Molatto Fellow, about 27 Years of age, named CRISPAS, 6 Feet two Inches high short curl'd Hair, his Knees nearer together than common; bad on a light colour'd Bearskin Coat, plain brown Fustian Jacket, or brown all-Wool one, new Buckskin Breeches, blue York-Stockings, and a check'd woolen Shirt.

Whoever shall take up said run-away, and convey him to his above said master, shall have ten Pounds, old Tenor Reward, and all necessary charges paid. And all Masters of Vessels and others are hereby caution'd against concealing or carrying off said Servant on Penalty of the law.

Advertising Descriptions of Runaway Slaves

During the eighteenth and early nineteenth centuries, it was common practice for owners of runaway slaves to place classified advertisements in local and regional newspapers, in much the same way that ads for "lost" articles or items, particularly animals, are placed today. "Almost every issue of every newspaper published in the colonies contained such advertisements. Descriptions of runaway slaves were also posted in public places in towns and cities" (Jackson, 1970, p. 45). The missing slave was described, and a reward was offered for his or her return. Southern slaveowners, knowing the slave trade system as they did, were aware that more than anything else, a reward was a better guarantee of the return of the slave—provided that the reward was a much greater amount than the cost of returning the slave. To ensure the capture of their "property," slaveowners also made note of distinguishing characteristics in advertisements for the slaves to make them easier to spot and easier targets for bounty hunters and other slaveowners.

"Unbiased attempts of owners to recover property worth hundreds of dollars, the notices were carefully composed, dispassionate descriptions of the fugitives, indicating their character, clothing, motives, and identifying marks" (Blassingame, 1979, p. 201). The advertisements for runaway slaves generally emphasized any noticeable characteristics that would assist in identifying the runaway. The physical makeup of runaways were carefully detailed, including their age, sex, height, color, scars and any visible body markings, as well as the type of clothing they were wearing when they fled. Various features of their daily life-styles, from the kind of work they performed to the type of chains in which some were shackled, often were reported, along with their place of birth, musical and linguistic talents, speech impediments, number of previous owners, and frequency of escape attempts. The runaway's name, primary language, ritualistic African markings, religious inclinations, and information about relatives and friends were also typical of the kind of information an advertisement would contain. Slave owners were aware that the more descriptive the advertisement, the better the chances of capturing the runaway, as exemplified by the following from the *Pennsylvania Gazette,* July 17, 1776:

THREE POUNDS REWARD

RUN away from Birdsborough Forge, in Berks county, Pennsylvania on the 16th of June, 1776, a Negro Man, commonly called CUFF DIX; he is an active well made fellow, and most excellent hammerman; he is about 5 feet 5 or 6 inches high, fond of liquor, understands English well, though he stammers in his speech; there is an iron ring in one of his ears, which if he can take out, a hole will remain [in] it, large enough to receive the small end of a pipe stem, in which case he will probably endeavour to conceal the hole by filling it up; he wore, when he went away, a small old hat, light coloured homespun jacket, tow shirt and trowsers. He has often run away, changed his name, denied that the subscriber was his master, and been confined in several gaols in this province; he was employed the greatest part of last summer by a person near Dilworth's town, in Chester county. Any person who shall harbour said Negroe shall be dealt with as the Law directs, and his name not omitted in a future advertisement. As Negroes in general think that Lord Dunmore is contending for their liberty, it is not improbable that said Negroe is on his march to join his Lordship's own black regiment, but it is hoped he will be prevented by some honest Whig from effecting it. Any person who shall bring said Negroe home to his master, or secure him in any gaol, so that he may be had again, shall receive the above reward and reasonable charges, paid by

MARK BIRD

What Advertising Reveals about Slave Owners

Runaway advertising functioned as a means of binding slave owners into a cohesive unit, commensurate with trade associations that exist today. If an owner took a cavalier attitude and did not advertise for a healthy or useful slave, it would send a message to other owners that he or she did not take the business of ownership seriously and greatly undermined those who were adamant about the preservation of this "peculiar institution."

All slave owners did not advertise for their runaway slaves. Selectivity of those fugitives profiled in advertisements were based on certain factors: "the centralization or de-centralization of the slave population relative to the towns where newspapers were located and the value of the absconding runaway to his owner" (Algerna, 1974, p. 243). Some owners did not advertise because sometimes slaves returned on their own after days of running without food, water, and shelter. For this reason, careful observation of advertisements shows a tendency for slave owners to give their runaways a few days to return on their own before an advertisement was placed.

Some masters placed advertisements for runaway slaves more as a matter of principle than for recapture. In some cases advertisements were merely used as a warning to other slaves, to let them know that masters were serious about recapturing slaves who fled. The advertisements also served as a unifying force for all slave owners. In no uncertain terms they illustrate that whites were expected to ban together and were, therefore, obligated to help recapture runaway slaves. Those whites failing to do this or who aided or abetted the escape of a slave were subject to harsh punishment, as evidenced in the following advertisement from the *State Gazette of South Carolina*, January 26, 1786:

RUN-AWAY
From the Subscriber
The Following Negroes viz.

Moll, tall black wench, about 20 years old, is frequently seen in and about Charleston, and Stono, she has changed her name to Judah, and says she is free.

James, a short well made fellow, with a large scar on one cheek, has also a scar on one foot, with the loss of a part of his toes, is frequently seen in Charleston and at Mr. Manigault's plantation.

THIS IS THEREFORE TO FOREWARN ALL PERSONS FROM HARBOURING, OR MASTERS OF VESSEL FROM CARRYING OFF SAID NEGROES, AS THEY MAY DEPEND ON CONVICTION, TO BE TREATED WITH THE UTMOST RIGUOR OF THE LAW, BY

LEWIS DUTARQUE

By analyzing advertising we also learn that there were those who were not so proud of their ownership of slaves and chose not to advertise or not to release their names in such a public medium as the newspaper. Interestingly, "when one of George Washington's slaves ran away he advertised for his return, but did not allow his name to appear in the advertisement north of Virginia" (Bergman, 1969, p. 76).

Advertisements for slaves who were old, disabled, or otherwise unable to work were often never placed. Thus, the value of the slave became an important issue.

The value of slaves can be reasonably determined by the rewards offered for their recapture. Some slaves were more valuable than others, depending upon their acquired skills, English language proficiency, and health. Most of the time the reward ranged from $10 to $500 and in some rare cases higher. The following serve as examples:

TWO GUINEAS REWARD

RAN AWAY a Negro Man named Prince about twenty-three years old, and about five feet six inches high, small featured, of a dark complexion, has Guinea country marks on his face, SPEAKS VERY GOOD

ENGLISH, has a down look; had on when he went away a light coloured surtout coat, a pair of yellow stocking breeches, and a round black hat; he has been seen skulking about this city since Saturday last. Two Guineas reward will be given and all reasonable charges paid to any one delivering the said Negro to the Warden of the Work-house, or to the Subscriber, and the utmost rigour of the law will be inflicted on conviction of any person harbouring the said Negroe.

Charleston, July 6, 1784. SAMUEL BOAS, No. 5 Church Street. (*South Carolina Gazette and General Advertiser*, July 6, 1784)

RAN away on the 18th Instant [of this month] with the sloop Hopewell, belonging to the Subscriber, William Curtis, Master, the two following convict servants, and negro man, viz: . . .

Whoever secures the said sloop and Goods so that the Owner may have her again, and the three White Servants and two Slaves, so that they may be brought to Justice, shall have FIFTY PISTOLES[1] Reward, paid by Patrick Creagh. (*Maryland Gazette*, April 11, 1754)

It was common practice for owners to warn others of slaves' tendencies to run away in the advertisements they placed, as can be observed in the following (Greene, 1916, p. 213) from the *Carolina Gazette*, February 4, 1802:

TWENTY DOLLARS REWARD

For Jack who has again Run-Away

The Subscriber's Servant Jack, who calls himself John Leech, again absconded last night. He is a short well made young Mulatto, probably about five feet five inches high, about twenty-five years of age, and a plausible; he has a thick bushy head of hair, like a negro's thick lips, a film on his left eye, over which he sometimes wears a peace of green silk. He belonged when he as child, to the late Ephraim Mitchell, esq. deceased, and afterwards to Francis Bremar, esq. from whom the subscriber bought him.

Lewis Trezvant

What Advertisements Tell Us about Slaves

Two of the more definitive studies on slave advertisements are by Lorenzo J. Greene (1944) and Gerald W. Mullin (1972). Greene's article, entitled "The New England Negro as Seen in Advertisements for Runaway Slaves," provides one of the most complete profiles of runaway slaves. His study attempted to answer questions that other such works had simply ignored, such as: What kind of person was the slave who ran away? What were his/her physical characteristics? In what craft was the slave skilled? How educated were they? One of the major limitations of the study, however, was the small number of advertisements investigated, only 67. The author even notes this by observing that the conclusions reached were "neither complete nor definitive" (p. 146).

Mullin analyzed approximately 1,500 advertisements from various editions of the *Virginia Gazette* over the years 1736 to 1801. His observations center around the acculturation of the slaves. He contends that as slaves matured, they became outwardly rebellious and more difficult for whites to control.

These studies offer important profiles of slaves who fled their lives of bondage and help us see them more as individuals than as mere components in a system of permanent confinement.

One of the interesting side effects surrounding the advertising for fugitive slaves is that many blacks who were free were caught by bounty hunters, traders or jailers and sold back into bondage (Mullin, 1972, p. 44). In such instances jailers would place an advertisement similar to these from the *Virginia Gazette,* November 17, 1775 and October 31, 1779:

> COMMITTED to Norfolk county jail, on the 10th of September last, a slim negro man, who says his name is WILLIAM PARROT, that he is a freeman, and was born about a mile from Williamsburg; he is about 6 feet 2 inches high. His owner (if any) is desired to take him away, and pay charges.
>
> > SAMUEL PORTLOCK, Jailer

> Committed to the gaol of Westmoreland, on Monday, the 21st of October [1771], two Negro Men, that a yellow fellow, with a remarkable flat nose, the other black, with filed teeth, about 4 feet 8 or 9 inches high eac[h]. They are both Africans, and speak very little English, so they are not able to tell their master's name. They had with them two muskets, and two small books, in one of which is wrote Elijah Worden. They are supposed to have run from Maryland, as there was a strange canoe found near the place they were taken. The owner is desired to take them away and pay charges the law directs.
>
> > Edward Randsdell, jun. D. S.

In some instances it became necessary for slaves to solicit the aid of their owners. For example, Jerry Stevens, the slave of his free father, Lamb Stevens, a black planter of St. James and Goose Creek Parish in the Charleston District, was purchased by his father and permitted to live and work as a free person of color. On one occasion, when he traveled to Orangeburg County and attempted to establish himself as a free person, he was seized as a runaway and jailed on May 6, 1833. Fearing that he would be auctioned off to the highest bidder, he convinced the sheriff to place an advertisement for him. It is unique because it is one of those rare instances where a black person actually wanted an advertisement placed so that he could be returned to his owner. On May 28, 1833, the *Charleston Mercury* placed the following announcement:

> Committed to the Gaol of Orangeburg this day a Negro Man of dark complexion 5 feet 10 ½ inches high; calls his name Jerry, and says he belongs to his father, a free Negro, living in Charleston by the name of Lamb Stevens; and that his father bought him from Dennis Cain. He also states that a Mr. Riggs living near Cyrus is the Guardian of his father, Lamb Stevens. (Koger, 1985, p. 77)

Judging from the runaway advertisements, slaves acquired an array of skills, and owners were quick to stress them when they placed advertising for the return of their "property." Among some of the occupations mentioned in advertisements were carpenters, sawyers, brickmakers, butchers, blacksmiths, coopers, ministers, farmers, domestics, service workers, mariners, and tavern keepers. Slaves who had learned a craft were much more valuable, and owners made note of this in advertisements in the hope that such knowledge would help a speedy return (Smith and Wojtowicz, 1989, p. 1):

> RUN away the 27th of February [1731] from John England and Company, at Principle Iron Works, a Negro Man named Jack, formerly belonging to Sir William Keith, Bart at his Works in New-Castle County: He is an elderly Man, speaks thick, and generally pretty Sawcy; is a CARPENTER by TRADE, and has a Wife in New-Castle County. Whoever secures him, so as his Master may have him again, shall have Five Pounds Reward, and reasonable Charges paid, by
>
> John England

An excellent source of data for understanding the level of standard English, black American English, or West African pidgin English spoken by slaves between 1765 and 1800 is classified advertising. In other words, "classified advertisements in newspapers provided a primary source for determining English language proficiency of runaway slaves" (Brasch, 1981, p. xi).

Many Northerners turned to bounty hunting (capture and return of runaway slaves) as a form of supporting themselves and their families (Read, 1939). They used references to the speech of slaves as key factors since they were able to distinguish Southern speech patterns more easily than their northern counterparts. Because so many slaves who ran away could speak English, some researchers have suggested that they learned it in preparation for flight. Observe the following excerpts:

speaks very good English (*New York Gazette Revived in the Weekly Post-Boy*, November 28, 1748) talks very plain English (*Maryland Gazette,* July 4, 1754)

speaks very much broken English (*South-Carolina Gazette and General Advertiser,* July 10, 1784)

speaks remarkably good English for a Negro, and is exceedingly artful (*State Gazette of South Carolina,* August 21, 1786)

speaks very proper, and can at any time make out a plausible tale (*City Gazette and Daily Advertiser,* June 22, 1797)

speaks rather more proper than Negroes in general (*City Gazette and Daily Advertiser,* July 31, 1799)

speaks English, though somewhat Negroish (*City Gazette and Daily Advertiser,* Aug., 12, 1802)

The advertisements also dispel some of the myths that suggest that all slaves were uneducated and ignorant by showing that some were bilingual and in some cases multilingual, and in addition to English were fluent in Dutch, French, Swedish, and/or German:

> RUN away from William Bird, Esq; a Negroe Man, named Hercules, about 26 years of Age, has a Blemish in one Eye, and a remarkable Eye Lid. Whoever brings the said Negroe to Jacob Kern, in Reading [Pennsylvania], shall have Forty Shillings Reward. It is thought secreted, in Lancaster County, among the Germans, as he speaks that Language well. (*Virginia Gazette,* November 17, 1775)

Female Slaves Who Stole Themselves

As some historians have noted, the plight of female slaves has not been given the same amount of attention given to male slaves. The battle to address issues affecting black female slaves was fought wholeheartedly by black females who spoke vociferously about the inhumane treatment suffered by them at the hands of their masters and mistresses. One black female who had a profound impact on making sure the story of the black female slave was not swept under the carpet was Maria Stewart.

The African-American Female Intelligence Society of Boston made history in 1832 when it sponsored a young abolitionist's speech before an audience of men and women in Franklin Hall. The society made history because it had invited a woman to lecture, and a black woman at that! During that time women were forbidden from public speaking, and black women's views on any serious matter were never disclosed. Ironically, opposition to public speaking by black women received tremendous support from black men. Four months prior to Stewart's address *The Liberator,* published by Frederick Douglass, advised, "The voice of woman should not be heard in public debates, but there are other ways in which her influence would be beneficial" (Giddings, 1984, p. 50). Stewart did not heed this advice, "thus becoming the first American-born woman to give public speeches and leave extant texts of her addresses" (Quarles, 1969, p. 7).

Stewart assailed the subjugation to which blacks had been subjected, mainly discrimination in the North and slavery in the South. She also chastised free blacks for not doing enough to help themselves. She counseled black women to commit themselves to being the best mothers possible, and finally she challenged the "better than thou" attitude of the white women in the audience:

O ye fairer sisters whose hands are never soiled, whose nerves and muscles are never strained, go learn by experience! Had we the opportunity that you have had, to improve our moral and mental facilities, what would have hindered our intellects from being as bright, and our manners from being as dignified as yours? Had it been our lot to have been nursed in the lap of affluence and ease, and have basked beneath the smiles and sunshine of fortune, should we not have naturally supposed that we were made to toil? (Loewenberg and Bogin, 1976, p. 194)

Stewart's public speaking career, although short-lived, formed the foundation upon which black female activists would build for years to come. This foundation was important because female slaves were subjected, in many cases, to the same brutality as their male counterparts. Johnnetta Cole (1978), president of Spelman University, echoes this sentiment in the article "Militant Black Women in Early U.S. History," in which she wrote, "When it came to oppressiveness, slavery was an 'equal opportunity employer' with respect to black men and women. Sisters too had to bear the whip and hoe the fields." In discussing the harsh treatment of female slaves, almost all historiographers are quick to point out the sexual offenses suffered at the hands of white masters.

Gerda Lerner (1972) capsules the harsh realities of slave life for black women by explaining:

In general, the lot of black women under slavery was in every respect more arduous, difficult and restricted than that of men. Their work and duties were the same as that of the men, while childbearing and rearing fell upon them as an added burden. Punishment was meted out to them regardless of motherhood, pregnancy or physical infirmity. Their affection for their children was used as a deliberate means of tying them to their masters, for children could always be held as hostages in case of the mother's attempted escape. The chances of escape for female slaves were fewer than those for males. Additionally, the sexual exploitation and abuse of black women by white men was a routine practice. (p. 15)

Female slaves were prone to resist this harsh treatment, and such resistance came in many forms. Because "there was not only repression by those who owned and ruled, there was resistance by those who worked and suffered. And black women, like black men, worked and suffered" (Cole, 1978, p.

40). Consequently, there are cases cited in many books where female slaves poisoned or fed glass to their masters, and even struck them during an attempted rape. As Paula Giddings (1984) notes, "Black women proved especially adept at poisoning their masters, a skill undoubtedly imported from Africa. Incendiarism was another favorite method. . . . But black women used every means available to resist slavery—as men did—and if caught were punished as harshly" (p. 39). As a final resort, some did in fact flee.

We do know that men were more prone to run than women. Betty Wood (1986) points out that women constituted only 24 percent of all runaways during the Revolutionary period, and Eugene Genovese (1974) suggests that at least 80 percent of the slaves who fled were men between 16 and 35 years of age. There have been several reasons offered for why more men ran away than women.

Women were generally less likely to flee because of their attachment to their young, as well as being responsible for caring for siblings and other family members. Although some women had babies while on the run from their masters, many chose not to run while pregnant because of illness or fear of harming themselves and their unborn children. According to Algerna (1974, p. 66), other possible explanations for females being reluctant to run include: (1) women lacked the physical stamina necessary to run away, (2) the female's position as a house servant in the intra-plantation setting reduced her chances of escaping due to closer surveillance, and (3) suspicion surrounding a Negro female traveling alone was much greater than for a Negro male traveling alone. This is why it makes a lot of sense that William Gowdey of South Carolina included the following in an advertisement for a runaway female slave named Molly which he placed in the *Charleston South Carolina Gazette,* December 24 to December 31, 1763: "reason to think she will scruple to disguise herself as a man, in order to get on board some vessel."

An analysis of advertisements in the *Pennsylvania Gazette* (Smith and Wojtowicz, 1989, p. 13), revealed that "males accounted for about nine of every ten runaways in the Mid-Atlantic region and Virginia, although females absconded in higher proportions in the Lower South" (see Table 1.1). Additionally, 18th-century advertisements for runaways include more references to men than to women. More specifically, in South Carolina about 25 percent of the advertisements for runaways during the middle decades of the century were for women; in Virginia 11 percent were for women between 1736 and 1801; and in Georgia 13 percent during the 13 years before the Revolution (Fox-Genovese, 1988, p. 304). Yet the ratio of male to female runaways cannot reasonably be ascertained by examining advertisements because "slaveholders, for reasons best known to themselves, were much less likely to advertise for [women] than for men" (p. 320). Many researchers have surmised that slaveholders did not advertise for female

Table 1.1
Runaways in the Mid-Atlantic Region, Virginia, and South Carolina

Characteristics of Runaways	Mid-Atlantic (%)	Virginia (%)	South Carolina (%)
SEX			
Male	91	88	77
Female	9	12	23
AGE			
1–19	14	17	26
20–29	54	46	43
30–39	23	26	20
40–49	8	10	9
50+	1	2	1
BIRTHPLACE			
American Continent	55	62	38
Africa	13	*	*
West Indies	12	*	*
Not American Continent	20	38	62
PHYSICAL TRAITS			
Smallpox-pitted	6	6	1
Whip scars	2	3	1
"African marks"	2	*	*
Branded	1	2	3
ITEMS STOLEN			
None noted	72	70	88
Extra clothes	20	26	8
Horse	2	3	1
Cash	3	1	0
Gun	3	1	0
NUMBER OF CASES	1,323	1,276	2,424

*Data not available.
Sources: Billy G. Smith and Richard Wojtowicz, 1989. *Blacks Who Stole Themselves: Advertisements for Runaways in the* Pennsylvania Gazette, *1728–1790.* Philadelphia: University of Pennsylvania Press. Lathan Algerna Windley. 1974. "A Profile of Runaway Slaves in Virginia and South Carolina from 1730 through 1787." Ph.D. diss., University of Iowa.

slaves as readily or as often because they assumed that female slaves had gone to visit kin in the neighborhood or children who had been sold to other masters. There is also evidence that women ran away to avoid work or punishment or simply to have some time alone, and often returned after a few days (p. 320).

There was little or no distinction made between advertisements for female and male runaways. There was also very little distinction in advertising for slaves and for horses (Smith and Wojtowicz, 1989, pp. 26–27)

Philadelphia, October 8, 1747

RUN away from Francis Mines, in Appoquinimy, Newcastle county, a servant woman named Ann Wainrite: She is short; well-set, fresh colour'd of a brown complexion, round visage, was brought up in Virginia, speaks good English and bold. Had on when she went away, a blue linsey-woolsey gown, a dark-brown petticoat, and a Bath bonnet. She hath taken with her a striped cotton shirt, and some white ones, a drab-colour'd great coat, a silver-hilted sword, with a broad belt, and a cane; with a considerable parcel of other goods: Also a large bay pacing horse, roughly trimm'd, shod before, and branded on the near buttock SR. There went away with her a Negro woman belonging to Jannet Balvaird, named Back; she is lusty, strong, and pretty much pocket broken; had on when she went away, a brown linen gown, a striped red and white linsey-woolsey petticoat, the red very dull, a coarse tow petticoat, and callicoe one, with a great piece tore at the bottom, and stole a black crape gown: Also a bay horse, with three white feet, a blaze down his face, and a new russet hunting saddle. Whoever takes up the above mentioned women and horses, and secures them, so as they may be had again, shall have Four Pounds reward, and reasonable charges, paid by

Francis Mines [and] Jannet Balvaird.[2]

Quite often the women in advertisements were called wenches, a term used to refer to a young woman, a female servant, or a lewd woman or prostitute. It is generally assumed that such references were more likely associated with the latter definition offered, reinforcing a common theme, or stereotype, that many plantation mistresses thrust upon their black female slaves in retaliation for bearing the children of their husbands, brothers, and fathers. Such disdain is clearly apparent in the following (Smith and Wojtowicz, 1989, pp. 33–34):

New York, February 7, 1751

Run away last Sunday night, from Judah Hays, a Negro wench, named Sarah, aged about 30 years; she is a likely wench, of a Mulatto complexion, was brought up at Amboy, in Col. Hamilton's family, and has had several Masters in the Jerseys: She dresses very well, has a good parcel of clothes, and speaks good English. Whoever takes up the said wench, and brings her to her said master, or secures her in any county gaol, so that he may have her again, shall receive Forty Shillings reward, and reasonable charges. Whoever entertains said wench, shall be prosecuted with the utmost riguor of the law. All masters of vessels, boatmen, &c. are forewarned of conveying said wench away, as they shall answer the same.

JUDAH HAYS

N. B. Said wench has robb'd her said master, in apparel, &c. upwards
of Fifty Pounds.

Among the most popular advertisements for a runaway female slave were
announcements for the capture of Harriet Tubman. Called the "Moses" of
her people, she made 19 journeys south and led 300 slaves to freedom in
the Underground Railroad. Advertisements bought by slave owners offered
$40,000 for her capture, dead or alive. She boasted that she never lost a
single passenger. She always carried a pistol, with which she offered fellow
slaves who were thinking of quitting the option: "You'll be free or die"
(Lerner, 1972, pp. 63–64). She would usually make her journey on a Saturday night so that masters would have to wait until Monday to place advertisements in newspapers for slaves who had fled with her (Moon and
Mathis, 1991, p. 19).

INTERESTING FACTS REVEALED THROUGH ADVERTISEMENTS

Investigation of slave advertising was a useful tool for abolitionists to document the brutality of slavery. Slaves, fearful of retaliation from their owners,
refused to disclose the physical violence against them by their masters and
overseers, and no other documents were available.[3] Abolitionists read the
newspapers and collected advertisements that were proof of how brutally
some slaves were treated in general and how they were inhumanely punished
when they failed to pick 200 pounds of cotton a day or were indolent or
insubordinate. Theodore Weld (1971), a well-known abolitionist and slavery
historian, collected evidence of violence such as whipping scars, gunshot
wounds, and a variety of physical mutilations, primarily from Southern
sources, in *American Slavery as It Is: Testimony of a Thousand Witnesses*.
Not all advertisements placed pertinent to slaves were for their sale or
recapture. One in the *Genius of Universal Emancipation* sought 8 or 12
slaves and their families to be educated for freedom under the auspices of
the Emancipation Labor Society of Kentucky (Bergman, 1969, p. 123). And
some advertisements placed for runaway slaves encouraged that they be
killed; in fact, the reward for some runaways was much higher if they were
returned dead. Such advertisements were particularly prevalent for slaves
who had lived on the outskirts of a town for a while and had threatened
the security of homes. Labeled as "outlying" or "outlawed" slaves, their
killing was permitted by law, as illustrated in this advertisement from the
Virginia Gazette, April 16, 1767:

RUN AWAY from the subscriber in Norfolk about the 20th of October last, two young Negro fellows, viz. WILL, about 5 feet 8 inches
high, middling black, well made . . . PETER, about 5 feet 9 inches high

. . . They are both outlawed; and TEN POUNDS a piece offered to any person that will kill the said Negroes, and bring me their heads, or THIRTY SHILLINGS for each if brought home alive.

JOHN BROWN

Not all advertisements placed were for slaves of good quality, either. Note this advertisement in an 1839 issue of the *Kentucky Gazette:*

> To planters and owners of slaves! Those having slaves rendered unfit for labour by Yaws, Scrofula, Chronic Diarrhea, Negro Consumption, Rheumatism, etc., and who wish to dispose of them on reasonable terms will address J. King, No. 29 Camp Street, New Orleans. (Coleman, 1940, p. 188)

Tadman (1989) conjectures that something dishonest would take place regarding these slaves or that they may have been used as guinea pigs in medical experimentation. He further notes that in his reading of hundreds of advertisements, he had never seen another advertisement in which the buyer was interested in inferior-quality slaves (p. 190).

Advertisements for runaway slaves also tell us that some blacks gained the impeccable trust of their masters and that they were allowed to pursue and return other slaves who had run away. A South Carolina slave owner in 1786 highlighted this trust when he advertised that one of his fugitive slaves was:

> sensible and artful, speaks quick, and sometimes stutters a little; HE MAY POSSIBLE HAVE A TICKET THAT I GAVE HIM TWO DAYS BEFORE HE WENT AWAY, DATED THE 6TH OF APRIL, MEN-TIONING HE WAS IN QUEST OF A RUNAWAY, AS I DID NOT MENTION WHEN HE WAS RETURN, HE MAY ENDEAVOUR TO PASS BY THAT. (Blassingame, 1979, p. 205)

Another advertisement that implied that slaves were entrusted to capture other slaves is (Starobin, 1974, p. 30):

$100. Reward.

Runaway from the subscribed on the night of the 6th Nov. negro man, Frank. He is about 5 ft. 9 inches in height, 37 years of age, weigh-ing about 140, of a dark mulatto color, not fleshy, some of his teeth rotten in front, with a small scar on his forehead, over one eye, caused by a kick from a horse when a child, and very polite in his manners when an end is to be gained. He is a carpenter. I am informed he has in several instances, since making his escape from my plantation, informed persons whom he has met on the road that he, himself, had been sent by me in search of a runaway. This mentioned that persons may be on their guard against his art & cunning. Previously to having made his escape, he, by means of false keys, robbed my house of $160. in gold & silver—most of which was of gold.

Any one delivering said man to me, or depositing him in jail, or elsewhere, so that I can obtain possession of him shall have the above reward.

William S. Pettigrew
Scuppernong, Washington Co. N. C.
November 13, 1857

The fact that free blacks were slaveowners is an often overlooked phenomenon in discussing the "peculiar institution," but at one time or another, free black slaveowners were recorded in every Southern state which sanctioned slavery, as well as Northern states. "In Louisiana, Maryland, South Carolina and Virginia, free blacks owned more than 10,000 slaves, according to the federal census of 1830" (Koger, 1985, p. 1).

Free black slaveowners also placed advertisements in the local newspapers for the return of their runaway slaves. In an advertisement placed in the *Charleston Courier* on August 20, 1836, Sarah Johnson, a black seamstress, alerted the public of a black female who had absconded in the following (Koger, 1985, pp. 91–92):

Servant Hester went away on Tuesday Morning. She is small stature a little pitted with small pox her front teeth much decayed had on when she went away a striped blue frock. It is suspected that she will try to go into the country. I will pay any reasonable reward.

No. 95 Wentworth Street
Sarah Johnson

There also were advertisements denouncing slavery and the legislation that would perpetuate its continuity. One such advertisement was placed regarding the Dred Scott case. In 1857 the U.S. Supreme Court handed down a decision that seemed to make open warfare between the North and South inevitable. Dred Scott, a Virginia-born slave, sued for his freedom after living for four years in free states. The Court ruled against him, ordered that he be returned to his master, and stated that Negroes had "no rights which the white man was bound to respect." A handbill advertising black opposition to the Dred Scott decision, circa 1856–57, announced a meeting on that topic (Hornsby, 1991, p. 29):

A PUBLIC MEETING
will be held on
. . .
to consider the atrocious decision
of the Supreme Court in the

DRED SCOTT CASE,
and other outrages to which the colored
people are subject under the
Constitution of the United States
C. L. Remond,
ROBERT PURVIS
and others will be speakers on the occasion. Mrs. Mott, Mr. M'Kim and
B. S. Jones of Ohio have also accepted invitations to be present.
All persons are invited to attend.
Admittance free.

And in one of the most unusual advertisements placed during slavery in
1854 the New Orleans *Delta* advertised a description of a white man who
had allegedly stolen a slave. The advertisement closely resembled advertisements for runaway slaves and according to the *Delta*, the white man "speaks
slowly, [and] has a sly countenance" (Blassingame, 1979, p. 204).

SUMMARY

The advertising documents for the sale of slaves and for runaway slaves
were quite descriptive as has been notably documented in the above pas-
sages. Information given in the advertisements also highlighted the mental
disposition of some blacks toward their bondage and their bondsmen. Although not offered here in any great length, an analysis of these advertisements also offers much insight into the psychological and sociological forces
that drove slaveowners during that period in history.

The analysis of slave advertisements offers a definitive account of the status
of blacks during that time period. It is important to disclose information of
this type because of the social and cultural ramifications that they suggest
about the existence of blacks during the eighteenth and nineteenth centuries. Historiographers in this area have provided evidence that some slaves
were privy to information and lifestyles that eluded other slaves. In other
words, not all slaves were dependent on society and their owners for their
livelihood. "To see slaves as a 'society of helpless dependents' is to make a
judgment that ultimately rests on one's view of the relationship of slavery
to the rest of society" (Mullin, 1972). The documentation suggests that in
addition to being slaves some of them made valuable contributions to society and lived lives similar to some of the lower-class whites. As one writer
stated:

We observe that the eighteenth century slave was rapidly taking over modern civili-
zation in the West Indies and in the thirteen colonies on the American continent.
The blacks were becoming useful and skilled laborers, acquiring modern languages,
learning to read and write, entering a few of the professions, exercising the rights of

citizens, and climbing the social ladder to the extent of moving on a plane of equality with the poor whites. (Greene, 1916, p. 163)

A thorough investigation of slave advertisements, especially those for runaway slaves, tells us that although everyone was affected in one way or another, some were affected differently and more severely than others. In scrutinizing such advertisements, it is also important to remember that they were all written from the standpoint of the slaveholder and therefore certain inherent biases are observed. Notably, for obvious reasons slave owners were more obliged to present favorable characteristics of slaves to be sold and unfavorable characteristics of those who had run away. Advertisements are critical documents in trying to put together the puzzle of slavery—a puzzle that would otherwise remain incomplete if not for their existence.

Patricia Bradley (1987) suggests that slave advertising during the colonial period provides a "mirror to the dilemma"—a mirror that more and more African-Americans are examining because they realize what an integral part slavery plays in the recovery of their past and how much its scrutinization will play in their future.

Whereas there was a period in history when blacks wanted to forget that slavery ever happened, they now realize that instead they should read, analyze, and document everything remotely related to slavery[4] as well as those atrocities that followed: namely, Jim Crow, discrimination, segregation, racism, prejudice, racial bias, and bigotry. The legacy of slavery did not wash away as easily as snow does on a rainy day. Instead the remnants of slavery clung to the liberal Northerners and the Southerners in the land of Dixie in the same vein that the image of the Southern Belle has become a staple of the Southern plantation. In other words, certain images that were dominant during slavery were carefully transferred into contemporary society.

NOTES

1. Pistoles were Spanish coins often used in the specie-poor American colonies. One pistole was equal to slightly more than one Pennsylvania pound during the middle decades of the 18th century.

2. The majority of people who placed advertisements for runaway slaves were men, but this shows that some were placed by women.

3. Even if it were possible to examine all of the advertisements for runaway slaves, it would be difficult to determine that those scars or other visible signs of mutilation mentioned occurred at the hands of their masters or overseers or those law officials who imprisoned them. All the abolitionists or, for that matter, we can assume is that some slaves were severely beaten, branded, or treated in an exceptionally cruel manner by someone.

4. One group of African-American citizens wants to ensure that the plight of slaves will live in infamy. African-Americans for Humanism, based in Buffalo, New York,

has begun a national campaign for a Washington-based *Monument to the Slaves* to be much like the Vietnam Memorial.

The National Afro-American Museum and Cultural Center, located in Wilberforce, Ohio, sponsored a 1992 exhibit entitled "Before Freedom Came: African-American Life in the Antebellum South," the most comprehensive ever organized on the topic of slavery. Coordinated by the Museum of the Confederacy in Richmond, it reflected virtually every aspect of African-Americans' life in the South from 1790 to 1865: the work they did, what they owned, their relationships among themselves and with whites, the ways in which slaves resisted the system and participated in the Civil War. A 219-page catalog, fully illustrated and annotated, contained essays by scholars in history, material culture, folklore, and archeology. For more information, call 1-800-BLK-HIST.

REFERENCES

Adler, Mortimer J., ed. 1969. *The Negro in American History: Slaves and Masters 1567–1854.* Chicago: Encyclopedia Britannica.

Algerna Windley, Lathan. 1974. A Profile of Runaway Slaves in Virginia and South Carolina from 1730 through 1787. Ph.D. diss., University of Iowa.

Beifuss, John. 1990. "Organizers Say Study of Slavery Benefits All." *Commercial* (Tenn.) *Appeal,* July 7.

Bergman, Peter M. 1969. *The Chronological History of the Negro in America.* New York: New American Library.

Blassingame, John W. 1979. *The Slave Community: Plantation Life in the Antebellum South.* New York: Oxford University Press.

Bradley, Patricia. 1987. Slave Advertising in the Colonial Newspapers: Mirror to the Dilemma. Paper presented at the annual meeting of the Association for Education in Journalism and Mass Communication, San Antonio, Texas, August 1–4.

Brasch, Walter M. 1981. *Black English and the Mass Media.* Amherst: University of Massachusetts Press.

Cary, Lorene. 1992. "Why It's Not Just Paranoia: An American History of 'Plans' for Blacks." *Newsweek,* April 6, p. 23.

Cole, Johnnetta. 1978. "Militant Black Women in Early U.S. History." *Black Scholar* (December): 38–44.

Coleman, J. Winston. 1940. *Slavery Times in Kentucky.* Chapel Hill: University of North Carolina Press.

Curtin, Philip D. 1969. *The Atlantic Slave Trade: A Census.* Madison: University of Wisconsin Press.

Douglass, Frederick. 1983. *Life and Times of Frederick Douglass.* Reprint. Secaucus, N.J.: Citadel Press.

Everett, Susanne. 1978. *History of Slavery.* London: Magna Books, 1978.

Fleming, John. 1992. "NAAMCC to Host Major Slavery Exhibit." *National Afro-American Museum and Cultural Center Newsletter* 3 (Spring).

Fox-Genovese, Elizabeth. 1988. *Within the Plantation Household: Black and White Women of the Old South.* Chapel Hill: University of North Carolina Press.

Genovese, Eugene. 1974. *Roll, Jordan, Roll: The World the Slaves Made.* New York: Pantheon Books.

Giddings, Paula. 1984. *When and Where I Enter: The Impact of Black Women on Race and Sex in America.* New York: Bantam Books.

Greene, Lorenzo J. 1916. "Eighteenth Century Slaves as Advertised by Their Masters." *Journal of Negro History* 1 (April): 163–216.

———. 1944. "The New England Negro as Seen in Advertisements for Runaway Slaves." *Journal of Negro History* 29 (April): 125–145.

Haley, Alex. 1976. *Roots.* Garden City, N.Y.: Doubleday.

Hornsby, Alton. 1991. *Chronology of African American History: Significant Events and People from 1619 to the Present.* Detroit: Gale Research.

Hughes, Langston. 1983. *A Pictorial History of Black Americans.* New York: Crown.

Jackson, Florence and J. B. Jackson. 1970. *The Black Man in America 1619–1790.* New York: Franklin Watts Inc.

Jordan, Winthrop D. 1968. *White Over Black: American Attitudes Toward the Negro, 1550–1812.* Baltimore: Penguin Books.

Katz, William Loren. 1968. *Teachers' Guide to American Negro History.* Chicago: Quadrangle Books.

Kern-Foxworth, Marilyn. 1988. "The Reincarnation of Black Boy." *Ebonessence: Expressions of a Black Woman through Verse.* Unpublished book of poetry.

Klein, Herbert. 1978. *Middle Passage: Comparative Studies in the Atlantic Slave Trade.* Princeton, N.J.: Princeton University Press.

Koger, Larry. 1985. *Black Slaveowners: Free Black Slave Masters in South Carolina, 1790–1860.* Jefferson, N.C.: McFarland.

Lerner, Gerda, ed. 1972. *Black Women in White America: A Documentary History.* New York: Pantheon Books.

Loewenberg, Bert James, and Ruth Bogin, ed. 1976. *Black Women in Nineteenth Century American Life: Their Words, Their Thoughts, Their Feelings.* Philadelphia: Pennsylvania State University Press.

Moon, Clinton, and Renita Mathis. 1991. "Visionaries." *Upscale* (February/March): 19.

Moore, Wilbert E. 1971. *American Negro Slavery and Abolition: A Sociological Study.* New York: Third Press.

Mullin, Gerald W. 1972. *Flight and Rebellion: Slave Resistance in Eighteenth-Century Virginia.* New York: Oxford University Press.

Peters, Margaret. 1974. *The Ebony Book of Black Achievement.* Chicago: Johnson Publishing.

Phillips, Ulrich Bonnell. 1966. *American Negro Slavery: A Survey of the Supply, Employment, and Control of Negro Labor as Determined by the Plantation Regime.* Edited by Eugene D. Genovese. Baton Rouge: Louisiana State University Press.

Ploski, Harry A., and James D. Williams. 1989. *The Negro Almanac: A Reference Work on the African American.* Detroit: Gale Research.

Quarles, Benjamin. 1969. *Black Abolitionists.* London and Oxford: Oxford University Press.

Read, Walter Allen. 1939. "The Speech of Negroes in Colonial America." *Journal of Negro History* 24 (July): 247–58.

Romero, Patricia W. (ed.) 1969. *I Too Am America: Documents from 1619 to the Present*. New York: Publishers Company.

Smith, Billy G. and Richard Wojtowicz. 1989. *Blacks Who Stole Themselves: Advertisements for Runaways in the* Pennsylvania Gazette, *1728–1790*. Philadelphia, Pa.: University of Pennsylvania Press.

Soderlund, Jean R. 1985. *Quakers and Slavery: A Divided Spirit*. Princeton, N.J.: Princeton University Press.

Starobin, Robert S. 1974. *Blacks in Bondage: Letters of American Slaves*. New York: New Viewpoints.

Tadman, Michael. 1989. *Speculators and Slaves: Masters, Traders, and Slaves in the Old South*. Madison: University of Wisconsin Press.

Van DeBurg, William L. 1984. *Slavery and Race in American Popular Culture*. Madison: University of Wisconsin Press.

Wade, Richard C. 1964. *Slavery in the Cities: The South, 1820–1860*. New York: Oxford University Press.

Weld, Theodore. 1839. *American Slavery as It Is: Testimony of a Thousand Witnesses*. New York: American Anti-Slavery Society, 1971.

Wood, Betty. 1986. Some Aspects of Female Slave Resistance to Chattel Slavery in the Georgia Low Country, 1736–1815. Paper delivered at the annual meeting of the Society for the History of the Early Republic, Knoxville, Tennessee, July.

Chapter 2

MEMORIES OF THE WAY WE WERE: BLACKS IN EARLY PRINT AND ELECTRONIC ADVERTISING

Dear Friend,

I am black.

I am sure you did not know this when you made/laughed at/agreed with that racist remark. In the past, I have attempted to alert white people to my racial identity in advance. Unfortunately, this invariably causes them to react to me as pushy, manipulative, or socially inappropriate. Therefore, my policy is to assume that white people do not make these remarks, even when they believe there are no black people present, and to distribute this card when they do.

I regret any discomfort my presence is causing you, just as I am sure you regret the discomfort your racism is causing me.

Sincerely yours,
Adrian Margaret Smith Piper
My Calling (Card) #1, 1986[1]

Racist overtones in advertising were the norm before the Civil War ended. After the Civil War blacks were free to begin their own communities, own their own homes, open businesses, and become members of the buying public—a viable consumer market. Their status in society changed, but this was not reflected in the advertising prevalent during the period. Most advertisers created campaigns targeted toward white audiences; they used blacks in their advertising, but in demeaning and stereotypical postures that appealed to the white majority.

During the 19th century advertising prospered. The Industrial Revolution had a great impact on the advertising trade. A plethora of products was being produced by factories, and advertising was used to move those products off the shelves and into consumers' homes. Magazines and newspapers proliferated and helped in the selling of goods from community to community, city to city, and state to state. Advertising helped manufacturers and retailers tell the world about new inventions, new products, and convenient services.

The courting of black consumers began with black-owned newspapers, which also began buying advertising. Advertisers who bought space in these papers knew that the majority of the readers would be black. They also knew that the black consumer market was smaller, and so the dollars budgeted for advertising were not commensurate with the big amounts targeted for the general-circulation national magazines and newspapers (Reno, 1986, p. 1). The significance of such placements in African-American media was that the courting of blacks was as that of a servant, as a faithful porter on an army train or as a chef in a military camp. "To be sure the image of black as servant continued for years after the war, even in the advertising for such liberal and sophisticated magazines as *The New Yorker*" (Atwan, 1979, p. 86).

Some of the earlier advertising featuring blacks was highly offensive and greatly exaggerated physical features. The mouth was opened unusually wide and filled with very large and/or carnivorous white teeth encased by exceptionally large, thick, ruby-red protruding lips. The eyes in these advertisements were most often seen bulging uncontrollably with ecstatic fright. Adjectives such as "saucer" lips and "banjo" eyes were often used to describe blacks with a negative connotation.

The derogatory nature of these advertisements did not end with the images they so meticulously portrayed. The words used to describe blacks also were defamatory. Throughout history the word "nigger" has been offensive to blacks. It is probably the most powerful shorthand verbal symbol used by whites to humiliate. "For black people the word nigger symbolizes almost four hundred years of anti-African racism and cultural repression" (Wilson, 1980, p. 16). Yet around the turn of the century and after it was common to see products bearing the name "nigger" blatantly advertised:

- Nigger Head Brand canned fruits and vegetables (1905)
- Nigger Head stove polish (1920)
- Nigger Head tees (1920)
- Nigger Head tobacco
- Nigger Head oysters

The Poster, a magazine for artists published around the turn of the century, used the word "nigger" when trying to find good-quality trade cards (discussed later). This is from the April 1900 issue:

Since we have devoted a few pages of *The Poster* each month to show [trade] cards, we have commented on the dearth of originality in the designs, and now that we have gone farther afield we are struck with the absence of good drawing in the majority of the show cards that have come under our observation. The only perfect show card that we have come across emanates from France, and as we do not wish to reproduce it until we have exhausted the English field in our search for our ideal, we may state at once, what we consider the essentials of an artistic trade advertisement. We are seeking a good drawing with an idea in it, illustrating the article advertised, and coloured to perfection.

The nearest approach we have found this month is the show card for Stower's Lemon Squash. Against a light blue background stands a NIGGER boy with an expressive smile on his copper-coloured countenance, which is shaded by a straw hat with a red ribbon round it.

African cannibalism also was prominently displayed in many early advertisements. African tailors constantly measured whites for the stew pot that brewed over roaring flames. One advertisement that served as a calling card for the Scioto Sign Company during the 1930s shows a white male sitting in a huge pot of hot steaming water while an African male, complete with bone through his hair, looks at him the way one looks at Sunday dinner; the caption read: "If you don't know that you are over your head by now, you need help." Another advertisement in 1938 for Cannibal, a drainpipe cleaner manufactured by the John Sunshine Chemical Company of Chicago, featured a black male captioned with the slogan, "Eats Everything in the Pipe." Typical of the period between the turn of the century and the 1930s this African connection was a not-so-subliminal threat to whites, a connection that stirred up subconscious anxieties of black retaliation.

The labeling of black children as pickaninnies was commonplace from the end of the Civil War until the 1930s. One product popular in the 1920s, Pickaninny Brand peanut butter, was decorated with a black girl on the front of the can. There also were blatant references to the eating of black children by alligators. A cigar company titled its 1890s card "Little African" at the top and "A Dainty Morsel" at the bottom; in between were a snapping alligator coming ashore and a naked black baby crawling away. This idea, in addition to playing on the African theme, also gave in to the notion viciously promulgated by Southerners that black children were only suited for "gator bait."

Another common advertising theme during this period was that blacks were so disgusted with their plight that they really wanted to be white. It was not uncommon to pick up a publication and see an advertisement claiming that a product had the power to cleanse the black skin of Negroes and miraculously change it to white.

"Washing blacks white has been a popular motif in the advertising of soap. Playing on connotations of the distinction black/white, such as dirty/clean, dark/light, it gets at the foundations of racial thinking" (Pieterse, 1992, p.

195). The concept was skillfully reinforced by a Pears' Soap advertisement published in the September 30, 1899 issue of *Harper's Weekly* that proudly proclaimed, "The first step towards lightening the White Man's Burden is through teaching the virtues of cleanliness." Also note this text for Kirkman's soap:

TWO LITTLE NIGGER BOYS

There were two little nigger boys,
Two little nigger boys
Whenever they were sent to bathe
They made a dreadful noise
Because their mother did believe
That white they could be made
So on them with a scrubbing brush
Unmerciful she laid.
She tried a combination of
Many kinds of soap;
But the result of all her labor
Gave her but scanty hope
Although the lather that she got
Was very soft and white
It did not make her offspring so,
Though she scrubbed with all her might.
So she got Kirkman's Wonder Soap
Composed of rare ingredients
Sweet and clean her sons became—
It's true, as I'm a workman—
And both are now completely white,
Washed by this soap of Kirkman.

Such also was the case with the soap manufactured by Lautz Brothers. The advertisements showed a black baby turning white through the powerful cleansing properties. And in 1923 Herry E. Howind of Chicago advertised the Athenia Wonder polishing cloth, treated for cleansing metal. The ad shows a very dark black male who has turned one area of his hand completely white by using the cloth. With an expression of disbelief and amazement, he appears to be delighted with being able to switch from one race to another at the swish of a tiny cloth.

Another advertisement using the same theme was for Pear's soap. The ad shows one black child in a bathtub and another offering him the soap. The caption reads, "For the hands and complexion, I Prefer it to any other." The next frame shows that after using the soap, the black child's body had turned white. The caption for the second picture reads, "I have found it matchless for the hands and the complexion" (Everett, 1978, p. 232). Nonetheless, the use of black children in advertisements for soap was not always so blatantly offensive. In *The History and Development of Advertising* by Frank Presbrey (1929, p. 396) the advertising savvy of Ivory soap is noted, and few are aware that the debut appearance of the slogan "It Floats" featured a small black girl (Printer's Ink, 1963). As the story goes, up to 1879 Procter and Gamble, established in 1837, sold a pure white soap they simply called "White Soap." With the need for a distinctive name in mind, Harley Procter was inspired when he heard read at a church service a passage from the Forty-fifth Psalm: "All thy garments smell of myrrh and aloes and cassia out of the ivory palaces whereby they have made thee glad" (Presbrey, 1929, p. 396). From that moment on the product was called Ivory, and the first cake under its new name was sold in October 1879. Ivory was a leader in advertising in its formative days, and by 1890 the company was selling over 30 million bars annually. As Presbrey notes, "The Ivory advertisement, always containing an idea, and illustrated as attractively as the methods of the period permitted, was ever one of the most interesting pages in the magazines of the 1880s" (p. 396). Widely known for its catchy slogans, in 1891 the company introduced the "It Floats" slogan with a young black girl marveling over a small sailboat she has made using Ivory and a sail made from a torn piece of paper. Her round, brown face smiles proudly over her accomplishment.

Advertising featuring blacks began before the Civil War and continued through the 1940s. Faces of blacks were prominently displayed on all forms of advertising available during that period, including trade cards, advertising cards, advertising stamps, blotters, bottles, boxes, and tins.

ADVERTISING FEATURING BLACKS

Trade Cards

African-Americans began appearing regularly in advertising during the 1870s when color lithography was originally used to print trade cards. The cards varied greatly in size and color contrast, as well as subject matter, although sports figures and ethnic humor were the two most popular motifs (Congdon-Martin, 1990, p. 55).

The cards were given to the purchasers of articles such as shoes, thread, and other household items, especially during the Victorian era. The cards became valuable collectibles, and sometimes family members would paste them into albums like photos. The subjects varied, with sports figures and black humor being two of the most popular topics. The first large-scale use of blacks in advertising actually came with the introduction of trade cards. Ranging from wallet size to postcard size and larger, trade cards featuring blacks surfaced in the early 1800s as lithographers in Boston, New York, Philadelphia, and Baltimore began printing cards for nearly every product manufactured. Enjoying their greatest popularity between 1870 and 1900,

some of the cards depicted blacks in a positive manner, but others were
blatantly racist. One of the most defamatory showed Frederick Douglass
with his second wife, a white woman, taking Sulpher Bitters to lighten her
skin (Reno, 1986, p. 5). Another card for Ariosa coffee, manufactured by
the Arbuckle Brothers, was one in a series of 50 providing a pictorial history
of the sports and pastimes of various nations. It was used to introduce international customers to the American Negro and was exceptionally degrad-
ing. The copy, in addition to supplying information about Ariosa coffee,
offered the following:

American Negroes

The American negro is a child of nature, and one of the most entertaining, interesting and happy of beings. His disposition is sunny, he is
a born humorist, and has an inexhaustible fund of good-nature and spir-
its. There is infection to laughter even in the unctuous tones of his rich
voice. He is fond of display, gorgeous in his choice of colors and happy-
go-lucky.

'Possum hunting is much practiced in the warmer portions of this
country by the negroes. The opossum is the daintiest of dishes to their
taste. To catch one requires great skill for these animals are very tricky,
and even simulate death so well, when caught, as to deceive the novice.
It is the object to capture the opossum without injuring his hide, as this
has market value. 'Possums are oftenest "treed," but they are also caught
in traps, the former method is sportsman-like and generally requires an
arduous chase.

The cake-walk is one of the most original and entertaining of amuse-
ments. This is an exhibition participated in by as many couples as may
choose to compete. The idea is based upon the simple desire of being
pronounced the most graceful and best of walkers. Human nature is so
constituted that this challenge is accepted by most of the young negroes
of a community. Judges are appointed, and before them pass in serious
and sober fashion to the accompaniment of music, couple after couple.
They award the prize, a cake, to the best deserving, to the envy of the
rest.

The banjo is the favorite instrument of the negro and adds to gayety
of his home life in his cabin. Here while thrumming the notes, and
beating time with his foot, he teaches his young pickaninnies to make
their crude steps in harmony with the music. The bones and the tam-
bourine, rude and elementary as they are, played by negroes as accom-
paniments to their vocal music, add much that is pleasing to the effect.

Over the years trade cards using blacks have become collectibles, and their
value has increased significantly. The more insulting they are to blacks, the
higher their value. The cards show them in compromising positions, and
the visages are often overly exaggerated with large heads, thick lips, pop
eyes, and huge teeth. Rising Sun stove polish made a series of comical trade

cards depicting the devastating hazards a home would suffer without this product. One shows a black woman exclaiming:

Look yere old man! What kind o'stove blacking you call dat? I'se been rubbin' on dat stove all mornin' an it don't gib it a polish worf a cent. You jest git de Rising Sun Stove Polish right away or dar'l be trouble. You think I got time to 'speriment with such mud?

The bottom half of the card shows the woman gladly beckoning her man:

Come in, Ephraim! I'se not mad with you dis time, case yer sent de genuine Rising Sun Stove Blacking; an it shines de stove in good shape. An' here's yer dinner all ready. Somethin' agin ye? No, deed I haven't; yer tink I'se an anjul to get along without good stove polish? (Reno, 1986, p. 5)

Used to build brand and store recognition, trade cards served as mirrors of American social attitudes and prejudices. The use of blacks, whether for local, regional, or national distribution, in many cases exceeded "the bounds of good taste, offering the foulest kinds of racist appeals" (Stern, 1984, p. 5). Trade cards lost their momentum with the advent of national magazines, but the use of blacks continued. The image of black people in magazine advertising was quite different from that of trade cards, and the ethnic humor prevalent in the cards had lessened. Advertising around the turn of the century featured blacks most often as porters, chefs, maids, and butlers.

Advertising Cards

During the first year of its use, the postcard also served to advertise products and services. A picture was supplemented with details of use and functions on one side; the other was reserved for the address. Eventually, the two formats were separated, and the advertising card, although retaining the original size and appearance of the postcard, became a distinct product with its own purpose, and assumed its own place within the commercial business world and popular culture. Myriad businesses and products were introduced through this medium to customers, who were reminded as well to purchase again. Despite the cost incurred by postage, almost every consumer-oriented company used the card extensively in the decades before and after the turn of the twentieth century (Boskin, 1986, p. 135).

Advertising Stamps

The advertising stamp, placed on the back of an envelope, was one of the earlier formats used to perpetuate the image of blacks. The stamps evolved as an ingenious means of securing more printing revenue at a time when advertising as a means of selling goods and services was in its infancy.

Also referred to as poster stamps, advertising stamps were a tremendous tool for promoting the business of advertising. An array of products, services, and events made use of this innovative practice: food companies, insurance companies, hotels, electric companies, banks, tobacco products, and clothing stores also were all loyal users. One of the stamps' greatest selling points was their well-produced, high-quality looks, attained because most were merely full-size posters or point-of-purchase displays photographically reduced. "Even the most cliché ridden image was curiously transformed into a striking miniature. People have irrepressible fondness and illogical tolerance for all things miniature" (Heller, 1990, p. 33).

The use of blacks on all advertising paraphernalia was in vogue during the time of the advertising stamp. Therefore, it was commonplace to receive an envelope bearing the image of a black "pickaninny," "auntie," or "uncle." Such a stamp was distributed by the Armour meat company in 1915–1916. Against a brilliant "Star Ham" emblazoned on top was a smiling black chef in an immaculate white hat and coat, holding a large ham in one hand and pointing to it with the other. In the slogan used exclusively by the company, the chef acclaimed, "The Ham What Am" (Heller, 1990, p. 33).

Strict postal regulations that legislated what was proper and improper to affix on envelopes, coupled with the rise in more visibly competitive advertising tactics requiring more copy, stifled the production and distribution of advertising stamps. Moreover, the process depended upon consumers to subsidize merchants by affixing unpaid advertising to their mail. By the 1940s their use was virtually extinct. Junk mail has replaced the advertising stamp as the most popular means of invading a consumer's privacy and consciousness.

Blotters

Prior to the invention of ballpoint pens, pen and ink was the writing instrument used most often. Dip and fountain pens often made quite a mess, and the residual ink was usually absorbed with blotting paper. As a marketing strategy businesses began the practice of giving away blotters with their company or product trademarks visibly marked on each one. As with all forms of early advertising, the use of blacks was common for all types of products and services, including whiskey, paper products, life insurance, peanut butter, and coal. Some companies capitalized even more on the concept and actually developed advertising slogans that incorporated the use of the blotter (Thalberg, 1990, p. 38). Note, for example, this advertisement for Green River whiskey which featured an elderly black gentleman clad in a "Sunday" suit and black top hat, holding the reins of a horse with a jug of Green River slung over its back:

GREEN RIVER
The Whiskey Without A Headache
BLOTS OUT ALL YOUR TROUBLES
A Straight Whiskey That Has No Equal
KEPT POPULAR BY QUALITY

Bottles and Boxes

The earliest advertising boxes were of painted or stenciled metal. Nicolas Appert, a Paris confectioner, was the first to succeed in using glass bottles to preserve foods in 1810. It was not until 1850 that the Somers Brothers of Brooklyn invented a method of lithographing a design onto a metal box. The most common collectible bottles depicting blacks were not made until the turn of the century, with the bulk produced in the 1920s and later. Utica Club ale bottles show a young black waiter; other bottles, especially liquor bottles, show blacks in similar subservient positions (Reno, 1986, p. 3). Cardboard boxes to hold soap powder or spices also began to be produced after the Industrial Revolution. Some of the more popular ones that used blacks were for Gold Dust (discussed in a later section) and Fun-to-Wash (Reno, 1986, p. 3).

Tins

Roly-poly tins were made to resemble people. One was a massive black woman called "Mammy," made between 1913 and 1915, of which there were at least two versions. Coffee cans often had black figures in their advertising. It was very common during this period to show blacks from the Caribbean with turbans wrapped around their heads and brightly colored clothes. When trying to date these cans it should be noted that the words "java" and "mocha" were used prior to 1906, but after 1906—the year the Pure Food and Drug Act was passed—all claims had to be true, so these words disappeared from packaging. Luzianne coffee is perhaps the most well-known of these cans. Today they are sought as a black collectible and command prices ranging from $50 to over $100, depending on size (Reno, 1986, pp. 3, 7).

Television: Advertising in Black and White

When television became the dominant advertising medium within American society, replacing radio, newspapers, and magazines, advertisers were confronted with enormous problems and the use of blacks would prove to be the tip of the iceberg. Because television is such a visual medium, it posed particular restrictions, especially when people of different skin tones, complexions, and facial features figured so prominently into the total scheme of programming. Television programs were interrupted by commercials at first on a gradual basis, then more consistently. Programming content had to be acceptable to an array of sponsors and their advertising agencies. Consequently, television, like radio, was subjected to the same social issues that confronted society. Thus, racism and discrimination were rampant when the magical instrument of television made its debut. Moreover, television was sold to many of the same audiences who had accepted, and perhaps even expected, demeaning and derogatory images of blacks in popular culture (MacDonald, 1983, p. 8).

SOUTHERN REACTION TO THE USE OF BLACKS IN ADVERTISING

There was resistance against the use of Negroes in advertising nationwide, but it was greatest in the Southern states. It was a known axiom in the advertising industry that Southern whites would not tolerate positive images of blacks on television. Because advertising is the economic backbone of the mass media, agencies trying to sell airtime in the South were fearful of white backlash should blacks be showcased in commercials in roles that were not minstrel or comedic in nature. As an ad executive explained to black actor Frank Silvera, a company such as Pillsbury could not afford to become associated too closely with black Americans or black issues. "If it became a popular perception that a Pillsbury product was a 'nigger flour,' the company would be severely hurt in sales" (Edmerson, 1954, p. 354). Despite the argument that speculation about the white Southern market was actually a myth, to the advertising industry it was a reality worth considering. Television executives and advertisers feared alienating consumers and therefore avoided programming and commercials that were too flattering or egalitarian toward blacks.

These fears were not unfounded, and during the 1950s boycotts by Southern consumers adversely affected large corporations in more than one incidence. For example, when a black girl won a Chicago beauty contest, Southern whites boycotted the sponsor of the contest, Philip Morris. The fear of such reprisals was what writer Rod Serling termed "a wrathful wind to come up from the South" (Serling, 1957).

There were, however, some successes in this scenario, and in the fall of 1952 "The Billy Daniels Show," a quarter-hour musical series, aired Sunday evenings on ABC. It became the first black show to be broadcast nationally by a single sponsor—Rybutol vitamin supplement. Although the show lasted only 13 weeks, it became an important breakthrough in the ability of black celebrities to secure sponsors. The success, however, was short-lived, and securing sponsors for shows featuring blacks remained a major problem for television executives, as evidenced by the demise of the "Nat King Cole Show" on NBC in 1957. Occasionally the quarter-hour show was sponsored by Arrid deodorant and/or Rise shaving cream, but the majority of the time the program was financially backed by NBC. Cole voiced animosity toward the advertising industry for the show's failure. He contended that executives never seriously tried to sell his show to national accounts. He was quoted in *Ebony* as saying: "Madison Avenue, the center of the advertising industry, and their big clients didn't want their products associated with Negroes. Madison Avenue said I couldn't be sold, that no national advertiser would take a chance on offending Southerners" (MacDonald, 1983, p. 62).

CIVIL RIGHTS MOVEMENT

The civil rights movement was critical in changing the way blacks were presented in American mass media and ultimately in American advertising. The news director of a Southern television station noted that during the civil unrest of the 1960s, television advanced the cause of racial equality by giving many poor blacks a chance to ameliorate their life-styles and improve their economic conditions. Southern conservatives charged, however, that the media "served as instigators of the turbulence rather than as a vanguard of change in society" (Monroe, 1967).

The Kerner Commission Report issued after riots occurred in Watts, Newark, and Harlem noted the affects of the mass media on the sociological and psychological disposition of the dominant and subordinate cultures (Baker and Ball, 1969). The daily repetition of commercials and programs has impressed on Negro families that they are the have-nots in our society. Television has helped intensify their yearning not only for basic dignity and equality, but for the material things identified with status, with the way "white" people live (Monroe, 1967, p. 89). Armed with this knowledge blacks demanded depictions of themselves that more resembled reality and portrayed them in real-life situations such as wives, husbands, fathers, mothers, workers, and family members—people equipped with the same ambitions, desires, and needs of the dominant group.

In 1963 blacks were eyewitnesses to what they thought was the end of the stereotypical portrayals of blacks in advertising, especially print advertising. On Wednesday, May 7, 1963, an advertisement for the New York Telephone Company that featured a black male appeared in general circulation publications. Because the advertisement was news itself, newspapers carried stories about the historic event. The lead for one read:

What might well be the first use of a Negro model in general circulation publications was published in this and other metropolitan area newspapers yesterday by the New York Telephone Company. Whether it was actually the first would be almost impossible to determine out of the millions of advertisements run over the years, but no one could recall having seen one before. (Kaselow, 1963)

The advertisement showed a well-dressed model about to enter a sidewalk telephone booth and had the headline, "A man of action knows—you get action when you telephone." A spokesperson for the telephone company commented, "We took a couple of pictures, one with a white model and the other with a Negro model, and of the two pictures the one we used was the better one. It was more dynamic and fitted the headline better." Although company officials and the advertising agency responsible, Batten, Barton, Durstine and Osborn, argued that the advertisement was really no big deal, it did appear at a time when the Urban League of Greater New York issued a study condemning the advertising industry for not hiring more Negroes.

Television was not as quick to react to change as the print media. In fact, in 1969 local stations reported diminishing advertiser interest in programs featuring blacks or focusing on black issues. "It just isn't chic anymore," said a spokesperson for WNEW-TV, New York, "for advertisers to sponsor a black show" (*Variety*, 1969, p. 27).

Ironically, a bold headline in the *New York Times* painted a much different picture during January 1969. The headline, "For Advertising, Signs of Change," actually says it all. In the article the writer reminisced about the major changes that had occurred in 1968, noting two that were significant, one in the area of race relations: "With governmental prodding agencies became aware of the need not only to hire the disadvantaged but also to feature Negro and Puerto Rican talent in their advertising" ("For Advertising," 1969, p. C129). As an example of how things had changed, the newspaper displayed a storyboard of a television commercial by Young and Rubicam which featured a black person but which could have used a person of any race. (The advertisement was for Bufferin.)

The situation did not get much better, however, despite protests by many civil rights organizations to improve the depictions of blacks in advertising. The New York Ethical Society published the results of a second television survey to determine black representation. The first report was issued in 1962 and recommended that improvements be made in the use of blacks in advertising and public service announcements. The second report was issued in December 1964, and the society noted that where there had been an average of two blacks in such spots every five hours in 1962, there were 36 in 1964. Yet, the society concluded "that the industry was not keeping abreast of national political and social developments and that continued glaring deficiencies outweigh the few improvements" (*Variety*, 1964, p. 28).

From the turn of the century to the mid-1960s negative advertising images of blacks were pervasive throughout America. Some became American icons and permanent staples in most homes. It was difficult to prepare a meal without using food products featuring a stereotypical pickaninny, black mammy, or black Sambo.

In other words, the use of blacks in pejorative and stereotypical advertising kept them emotionally bound to the idiosyncratic whims of their former masters. With advertising, former slaveowners became masters over different objects. They made them subservient. They made them docile. They made them act stupid. They made them appear ignorant. They made them ugly. They made them grotesque. They made them want to be white. If it were domestic work or menial labor, blacks could do it the best. Blacks could bake it, shake it and make it the best. Blacks could wash it the cleanest and then they could press it the smoothest. Blacks could serve anyone, anytime, anywhere, anything the best. Sometimes they polished it so well that they rubbed the black right off their charcoal black skin the best and lo and behold they became white. And advertisers discovered that blacks advertised their subservience the best. Advertisers used little black pickaninnies with braids and spindly legs, tar black Sambos with oversized rubbery red lips and large bugging eyes and overweight mammies to sell everything from cigarettes to cereals.

These symbols not only continued but proliferated around the turn of the century with the overwhelming success of Uncle Ben, The Gold Dust Twins, Rastus and Aunt Jemima.

NOTE

1. Lucy R. Lippard, *Mixed Blessings: New Art in a Multicultural America*. New York: Pantheon Books, 1990, p. 236.

REFERENCES

Atwan, Robert, Donald McQuade, and John W. Wright. 1979. *Edsels, Luckies and Frigidaires: Advertising the American Way*. New York: Dell Publishing Company.

Baker, Robert, and Sandra Ball. 1969. *A Staff Report to the National Commission on the Causes and Prevention of Violence*. Washington, D.C.: U.S. Government Printing Office.

Boskin, Joseph. 1986. *Sambo: The Rise and Demise of an American Jester*. New York: Oxford University Press.

Congdon-Martin, Douglas. 1990. *Images in Black: 150 Years of Black Collectibles*. West Chester, Pa: Schiffer Publishing.

Edmerson, Estelle. 1954. A Descriptive Study of the American Negro in United States Professional Radio, 1922–1953. Master's thesis, University of California, Los Angeles.

Everett, Susanne. 1978. *History of Slavery*. London: Bison Books.

"For Advertising, Signs of Change." 1969. the *New York Times*. January 6, p. C129.

Heller, Steven. 1990. "Advertising Stamps." *U & LC* (Winter): p. 33.

Kaselow, Joseph. 1963. "A Bellwether Ad for Negro Models." *New York Herald Tribune*, May 8.

Lippard, Lucy R. 1990. *Mixed Blessings: New Art in a Multicultural America*. New York: Pantheon Books.

MacDonald, J. Fred. 1983. *Blacks and White TV: Afro-Americans in Television since 1948*. Chicago: Nelson-Hall.

Monroe, William B. 1967. "Television: The Chosen Instrument of the Revolution." In Paul L. Fisher and Ralph L. Lowenstein, eds., *Race and the News Media*. New York: Frederick A. Praeger.

Pieterse, Jan Nederveen. 1992. *White on Black: Images of Africa and Blacks in Western Popular Culture*. New Haven, Conn.: Yale University Press.

Presbrey, Frank. 1929. *The History and Development of Advertising*. Garden City, N.Y.: Doubleday, Doran and Company.

Printers' Ink. 1963. *Advertising: Today, Yesterday, Tomorrow*. New York: McGraw-Hill.

Reno, Dawn. 1986. *Collecting Black Americana*. New York: Crown.

Serling, Rod. 1957. *Patterns: Four Television Plays with the Author's Personal Commentaries*. New York: Simon and Schuster.

Stern, Gail. 1984. *Ethnic Images in Advertising*. Philadelphia: Balch Institute for Ethnic Studies.

Thalberg, Jan. 1990. "Black Advertising: Blotters." *Black Ethnic Collectibles*, Fall, p. 38.

Variety, December 9, 1964, p. 28.

Variety, December 24, 1969, p. 27.

Wilson, Geraldine L. 1980. "Sticks and Stones and Racial Slurs Do Hurt: The Word Nigger Is What's Not Allowed." In *Children, Race and Racism: How Race Awareness Develops Interracial Books for Children*. New York: Racism and Sexism Resource Center for Education.

Chapter 3 ————————————————————

MYTHS, LIES, AND STEREOTYPES: BLACK ADVERTISING SYMBOLS, CHARACTERS, AND MODELS

> The American white man today subconsciously still regards the black man as something below himself. And you will never get the American white man to accept the so-called Negro as an integrated part of his society until the image of the Negro the white man has is changed and until the image the Negro has of himself is also changed.
>
> Malcolm X

The characters, the models, and the symbols that represent blacks in advertising have always been important to blacks, because they are aware that they determined how they feel about themselves and their race and how others perceive them as well. Some contemporary writers have theorized that this is the age of symbol manipulation. "In our grandfather's day, most people earned their living by manipulating things, not by manipulating symbols," wrote David Berlo (Broom, Center, and Cutlip, 1985, p. 281). An example of how symbols can be used to influence culture can be seen in the proliferation of the black power symbol during the civil rights movement. "Black power is a powerful symbol because it condenses an enormous amount of information and experience into a little bit—there or not there, for me or against me, right or wrong" (p. 281). Another writer attests to the strengths of symbols within the black community by asserting, "In the service of black morale, symbols are immensely important. . . . Symbols can bring change. They have real powers in the world" (Morrow, 1984, p. 84). John Henrik Clarke, a well-known historian, very eloquently and succinctly states the importance of imagery and symbols relative to the African-American presence in our society:

Because what we see about ourselves often influences what we do about ourselves, the role of images and the question of how they control our minds are more important now, in our media-saturated society, than ever before. For the last 500 years, the history of African people throughout the world has been told through the slavery experience—only a short period in our life, considering that we are the oldest of the world's peoples. (Clarke, 1989, p. 158)

Symbols like Aunt Jemima, Rastus, and Uncle Remus have transcended the traditional definitions of symbols and evolved into icons, and in so doing have become integral components of American culture. These icons are important in molding and perpetuating perceptions of other peoples and other cultures. As Herbert M. Cole, a leading art historian at the University of California–Santa Barbara so eloquently states, "Icons are powerful because they encapsulate ideas and actions of central importance in human life" (Kaplan, 1989).

No one can attest to the power of symbols within the black community more fervently than the former owners of Sambo's restaurants. When the partners opened them, they never envisioned that the name "Sambo" would be so condescending to the black community and eventually contribute to the chain's demise. The name for the restaurants was actually derived by joining together parts of the names of its founders, Sam Battistone and Newell Bohnett. The chain developed a close association with the book *Little Black Sambo* in its publicity campaigns and later closed because of the negative connotations associated with the book. The controversy had become intense when in 1977 some residents of Reston, Virginia, protested when the group planned to open one of its restaurants there. There were no claims that the chain discriminated against anyone, but the name, as a symbolic reference to blacks, was totally objectionable.

William Raspberry, columnist for the *Washington Post* got in on the act on November 14, 1977, and wrote: "If Alan King and Gene Kelly opened a restaurant, they wouldn't call it Kike's Kitchen. If Daniel Inouye and Henry Gonzales went into the fast-food business, they wouldn't call it Dago's Diner. If Bruce Nigel, Germaine Greer, and Jimmy Stewart started a franchise, they wouldn't call it Nigger Jim's." He contended that the name "Sambo" was taken as an insult by black Americans nationwide, and that it was difficult to imagine that the owners of the chain were not aware of this fact (Hay, 1981, p. 163).

Ironically, before attaining such a high negative profile within the black community, Sambo's sought to increase its staff by advertising in black publications. One ad in the March 1977 issue of *Ebony* stated: "Sambo's is looking for Manager Partners. One of the nation's leading chains of family restaurants offers talented, hard-working people a tremendous opportunity to earn what they're worth." The advertisement continued by challenging readers to consider the rewards of managing a $500,000-a-year restaurant with an opportunity to become a partner and share in the profits.

The symbols that have stood for and defined blacks in advertising over the years have varied. Some have been real people, some have been fictitious. Nevertheless, whether real or artificial they have forged permanent images of blacks into the American psyche.

BLACK SYMBOLS IN ADVERTISING

Rastus: The Cream of Wheat Chef

As a result of having acquired some machinery at a fire sale, George Bull, Emery Mapes, and George Clifford of Grand Forks, North Dakota, began operating the Diamond Milling Company in 1890. Thomas Amidon, Diamond's Scottish-born head miller, was often seen taking a concoction home that he called "middling" (what we would refer to as farina today) to be made into a tasty breakfast porridge. It took a year of constant pressure and persuasion, but Amidon finally convinced the owners to sell some of the packaged "middling" to grocery wholesalers. Mapes, formerly a printer, obtained a small supply of cartons into which the product could be packaged. He also searched around a print shop that he owned until he found an old woodcut of a Negro chef emblazoned on a skillet. Using the skillet as a mold, he reproduced a small supply of labels, and after much thought chose the name "Cream of Wheat," because only the best and whitest parts of the grain were used. Then, without giving the broker any advance notice, he carefully loaded ten cases of the new product into a carload of flour being shipped to New York wholesalers, Lamont, Corliss and Company. Much to his surprise, he never received any of the irate responses he had envisioned, but instead was elated to receive a telegram that said, "Forget the flour. Send us a car of Cream of Wheat" (Sacharow, 1982, p. 66). The mill switched over entirely to the production of Cream of Wheat, and from that point on the product continued to gain momentum as a breakfast food.

The original chef trademark survived until 1925, when it was replaced by the more realistic version we know today. While dining in a restaurant in Chicago, Kohlsaat's, Mapes noticed the broad smile of his Negro waiter and instantly saw his image as a replacement for the antiquated woodcut. The waiter was persuaded to pose in a chef's cap for a full-face snapshot and was paid five dollars for his services. Little did he know that his face would become as familiar to American families as that of George Washington as it toured the country on bags and boxes of Cream of Wheat.

Although his face has adorned Cream of Wheat boxes for over 70 years, neither the waiter nor any of his relatives has ever received any further remuneration for the picture. Throughout the years, many blacks have tried to win monetary compensation by posing as the chef or a relative of the chef, but they were proven to be imposters by company officials. G. Barnard Clifford, treasurer and sales manager of the Cream of Wheat Company, commented, "Up until a few years ago hardly a year passed that we were not approached by various gentlemen claiming to be the original chef. However, Colonel Mapes had a secret way of identifying the original man and we have never found him. Perhaps he is gone to his reward these many years" (Watkins, 1949).

The smiling chef was given the name Rastus, and although the company has made several changes during the 100 years of his existence, officials have not made dramatic changes in his appearance. The demand for the product outgrew the producing capacity of the mills in Grand Forks, and the business was relocated to Minneapolis in 1897. In 1936 the company offered a stuffed, 18-inch Rastus doll that sold for $10. Today that same doll sells for $65 to $100 (Thalberg, 1989).

One of the ads featuring Rastus was included in the book *The 100 Greatest Advertisements,* written in 1949. The author observed, "You'd think perhaps that the Cream of Wheat chef has long ago lost his identity in the constant boil of change, yet a recent survey showed that this famous Negro is still one of the first three or four best-known trademarks in the country" (Watkins, 1949, p. 21).

The company had one of its most memorable moments in 1929 when it was listed on the New York Stock Exchange. Cream of Wheat is now a division of Nabisco.

Gold Dust Twins

Gold Dust washing powder was introduced by the N. K. Fairbank Company of Chicago during the 1880s. It was so called because of its color and exceptional fineness. The product was heavily advertised and originally sold for 25 cents in a four-pound package. By 1898 a larger selection of sizes was available, with prices starting as low as five cents.

The idea for the Gold Dust Twins came from a cartoon in the English humor magazine *Punch,* showcasing two black children washing each other in a tub. The caption read, "Warranted to wash clean and not fade." A company executive thought the idea presented a funny concept and instructed an artist to draw the twins for the washing powder package in 1887 (Morgan, 1986, p. 52).

The Gold Dust Twins were the creation of E. W. Kembel, a staff artist for the *Daily Graphic.* The Fairbank Company compiled a number of Kemble's drawings and published them in a booklet, *Fairbank's Drawing and Painting Book Showing the Gold Dust Twins at Work and Play as Sketched by the Famous E. W. Kembel* in 1904. Composed of seven color and black-and-white sketches, it was created as a coloring book for children to be given away with the purchase of the soap and also to be sold separately (Martin, 1976, p. 55).

In 1902 during a trade convention in Chicago, two black children, David Henry Snipe and Thomas (last name unknown), were selected to pose as the Gold Dust Twins.

Snipe was born on October 24, 1896, in New York. He traveled throughout the United States and Europe with the vaudeville team Harvey and DeVore and remained with them until 1921. Snipe made his debut as a Gold Dust Twin during the 1904 St. Louis World's Fair, along with Thomas (Reed, 1991, pp. 28, 29).

What is really fascinating is that Snipe was the original blackface comedian. To make it in the competitive world of entertainment, he appeared as "a Black imitating a white, imitating a Black. The Al Jolsons and Eddie Cantors picked up his performance and copied it" (Reed, 1991, p. 29).

The St. Louis fair was the high point of the Gold Dust Twins' career. The Fairbank Company maintained a rather large exhibit, and atop stark white columns were many statuettes of the twins. A pair of real-life Gold Dust Twins, dressed in red and blue skirts, handed out booklets to all visitors (Sacharow, 1982, p. 57), but the use of live trademarks beyond that point was limited.

Through the years the twins were featured in magazines, on billboards, and on other promotional items ranging from hand-held mirrors to thermometers. One of the billboards using the image of the twins was recognized for being the "greatest commercial poster ever placed on the bill-boards." The headline read, "Roosevelt scoured Africa—The Gold Dust Twins Scour America." Accompanied by the slogan for which they became so well known, "Let the Gold Dust Twins do your work," the poster was beautifully lithographed and appeared in all large cities just a week prior to Theodore Roosevelt's return to America. The timing and the connection to American patriotism made for a very good advertising campaign, and the poster became the most talked about during that time.

The Gold Dust Twins were also popularized in 1925 through a radio show of the same name: a format similar to the "Amos 'n' Andy Show" featuring two white performers, Harvey Hindermyer and Earl Tuckerman. By the 1930s both the radio show and the soap were no longer national attractions, but as symbols of one of the most heavily advertised products after the turn of the century, the Gold Dust Twins have remained a part of American popular culture through the collectibles on which their images have been forged, including 1904 World's Fair items, tin containers, calendars, signs, trade cards, buttons, and various size washing powder and scouring powder boxes.

For nearly 50 years women in America relied on Goldie and Dustie, the Gold Dust Twins, to do their cleaning for them. Easily recognized were the small boys with their jet-black skin, naked except for tiny skirts, with their arms wrapped lovingly about each other against a yellowish-orange back-drop. Over the years their skin was lightened and their broad African facial features became more European, but their impact and image remained emblazoned in the minds of consumers and also in the minds of those they were supposed to represent.

G—Stands for Gold Dust,
    Of cleaners the prize,
  All folks who use
    Praise it up to the skies.

O—Is for oilcloth
    On tables or shelf;
  Keep bright with Gold Dust,
    Apply it yourself.

L—Is for laundry
    Place clothes in a tub
  Gold Dust will clean them
    With scarcely a rub.

D—Is for dishes
    Cleaned three times a day
  Use Gold Dust and drive
    Half the labor away.

D—Is for dirt,
    Likewise dust and decay,
  With Gold Dust it's easy
    To keep them away.

U—Is for utensils
    Pot, kettle and pan;
  In a second with Gold Dust
    They're made spick and span.

S—Is for scrubbing
    Woodwork, door and floor;
  Gold Dust works like lightning—
    Your back won't be sore.

T—Is for Twins,
    Ne'er known to shirk;
  Make housework so easy—
    Let them do your work.

Uncle Ben

The original Uncle Ben, from whom Uncle Ben's Converted Rice derived its trademark, was a rice farmer in Houston. "It was said that Uncle Ben harvested his rice with such care that he repeatedly received honors for full kernel yield and quality" (The Story of Uncle Ben, 1988). Other rice growers tried relentlessly to duplicate his success but usually fell short.

The Uncle Ben saga actually begins during the 1940s when Gordon L. Harwell, eventually president of Uncle Ben's Converted Rice, and his partner were having dinner in their favorite Chicago restaurant. They both agreed that they wanted to bring American consumers the same high-quality rice as had been given to soldiers during World War II. They ultimately decided that the quality of the famed Uncle Ben's rice that they had heard so much about was what they were seeking. It was in the restaurant that they also decided to call the product Uncle Ben's Converted Brand Rice and to manufacture it in the area around Houston known for producing high-quality rice. The original Uncle Ben had died some years before, but both men felt he would be an excellent symbol to represent their product.

The restaurant's maître d', Frank Brown, had been a close friend of both men for many years, and they asked him to pose for the picture that would appear on boxes. When first introduced, the portrait of Uncle Ben was featured over the entire front of the box, but in later years it was reduced to a small oval located on the upper right-hand side. According to a market research survey, Uncle Ben's Converted Rice is purchased by 13 percent of black families and 23 percent of white families (Assael, 1987, p. 333).

BLACK CELEBRITIES IN ADVERTISING

Most of the blacks used in advertising during the early years were based on the imagination of advertisers. It was not until the 1950s that real-life blacks were used on a small scale to advertise products. The use of blacks in advertising was heightened in the 1980s by the success of Michael Jackson's *Thriller* album and Bill Cosby's television situation comedy, "The Cosby Show," which was the top-ranked program for several consecutive years following its 1984 debut.

Some advertisers use African-American superstars that have mass audience appeal in their ads, like Jackson, Cosby, and athlete Michael Jordan. By doing this they are catering to both African-Americans and whites in promoting their products (George, 1991, p. 20). Writing in *Black Enterprise* Jube Shiver explained that "black celebrities have become seemingly ubiquitous in television commercials; in addition their appearance has increasingly become more strategic and less symbolic" (Shiver, 1988, p. 51).

Michael Jackson

Michael Jackson is one of the celebrities who has been able to cash in on his popularity and has parlayed his success into a several-million-dollar jackpot. He was named the top recording artist in the world by the *Guinness*

Book of World Records. Forty million copies of Jackson's *Thriller* album, released in 1982, have been sold worldwide.

In 1984 he was paid $6 million to make two commercials for Pepsico. They featured The Jacksons accompanied by Michael's Grammy-nominated "Billie Jean," adapted with Pepsi lyrics. Because of his mass appeal with young teenagers throughout the country, the commercials were very successful and offered the star an opportunity to rock and roll his way into more mega deals with Pepsico.

March 2, 1988, marked the debut of another highly publicized four-part commercial series featuring Jackson, who received more than $10 million for his work. Called "Chase," the spots aired consecutively as a fantasy adventure that had Jackson miraculously escaping from throngs of adoring fans by parachuting, skiing, and leaping tall buildings. Each of the segments, produced by the ad agency Batten, Barton, Durstine and Osborn (BBDO) Worldwide, based in New York, was designed to be used separately in future campaigns. Barbara Lippert's *Adweek* critique of the performance was:

> Given the response to his tour, this Pepsi commercial can't really lose. For Jackson to sing "I'm bad, and Pepsi's cool" is a perfect '80s-style blend of innocence and cynicism.
> This four-part extravaganza plays off his fear and conflicts about fame and the pursuit of the press and crowds; it shows him in concert and doing daredevil feats. We see him (actually his double) leap off a building and a helicopter, and slide down a metal wire with the grace and athleticism of Fred Astaire and Spiderman. There's a shot of him driving a car that's strangely humanizing (I never pictured him driving, although he lives in California) and flying through the air with the greatest of ease. (Lippert, 1988, p. 22)

Pepsico has shied away from Jackson in more recent years because black youths have voiced disapproval of his plastic surgery and injections to change his facial appearance and lighten his skin tone. Some blacks view this as an attempt to deny his heritage and become more European. The rationale is that his publicists advised him to take such actions as a means of becoming a crossover artist. His appeal has always been to both black and white teenagers, but with the changes made to his appearance, his acceptance has become phenomenal. In 1990 he was named Entertainer of the Decade by the Capitol Children's Museum.

Pepsi-Cola USA paid $5 million to be the official sponsor of Jackson's Victory Tour and used this connection to tout the Pepsi name, logo, and slogan on tickets, T-shirts, posters, balloons, and in skywriting escapades. The tour was an overwhelming success.

In 1991 Sony gambled that Jackson had a $1 billion net worth appeal. Jackson signed a multimedia contract with Sony's music president Tommy Mottola which experts proclaimed as the biggest show business deal ever.

Sony entered into the contract encouraged by the fact that Jackson's *Thriller* and *Bad* albums made about $700 million in retail sales alone (Scott, 1991).

Because of their success with Michael Jackson, Pepsi Cola signed other black celebrities as endorsers. In 1985 the company initiated an $8 million campaign which featured Lionel Richie and included a tour, a major television special, and a film project. Mike Tyson and his former wife, actress Robin Givens, tried to cash in on their popularity when they appeared on television proclaiming the good taste of Diet Pepsi. Pepsi dropped the twosome after their divorce was turned into a circus by the press.

Unfortunately, the relationship between Jackson and PepsiCo did not end on a good note. On November 14, 1993 the company severed its nine-year relationship with the pop star after he announced he was breaking off his *Dangerous* tour on November 12 to seek treatment for addiction to painkillers. The medication was prescribed for burns suffered while filming a 1984 Pepsi ad (Gundersen, 1993, 1D). According to a PepsiCo spokesman the company had agreed to sponsor the tour until it ended and when Jackson cancelled the tour prematurely that action simply meant, "we no longer have a relationship" (Yancey, 1993, p. 1A).

The tour, worth an estimated $7–10 million, which had stopped in Europe, Asia, Australia, and Latin America, was cancelled when allegations surfaced during the fall of 1993 that Jackson had molested a 13-year-old boy (della Cava, 1993, p. 1A).

Coca-Cola, Pepsi's strongest competitor, has also used black celebrities to sell its soft drinks: Vanessa Williams, the first black Miss America; Shari Belafonte Harper; Julius Erving (Dr. J); and Marcus Allen.

Bill Cosby

One of the most successful black actors to be cast in major ad campaigns has been Bill Cosby. During the 1970s the advertising industry began to use black Americans on television and in print advertisements, and Cosby became the spokesperson for the Del Monte Corporation. He performed an indistinguishable voice-over, using his warm, whimsical humor to make the product name well recognized. General Foods hired Cosby as a spokesperson for Jell-O in 1973, and in that capacity he has made some highly memorable commercials. Using adorable kids to spoof the Mafia, Western shoot-outs, and national political conventions, Cosby has given Jell-O extremely high recognition and recall. In 1976 he was retained to shoot commercials for Ford. Cosby was selected by these companies "because research had proven that he exuded an unusual amount of believability and warmth" (Dates, 1990, p. 435). Said Cosby in 1980:

When Coca-Cola first proposed that I make a commercial for them, I thought, "These people are going to pay me to say that I love to drink this, when it's what

I drink anyway." And then came the Jell-O pudding ads. My mama used to make that for our dessert. These products are bigger than life to you, because you see them advertised as a child. To me, it's like meeting a celebrity. (Hill, 1986)

Cosby's phenomenal success with commercials for Coca-Cola, Jell-O, Texas Instruments, Ford, Del Monte, Merrill Lynch, Kodak, and Dutch Master has some people calling him the "king of commercials."

Telling the truth is the primary reason Cosby believes his commercials are so successful. "If I didn't believe in a product, I wouldn't touch it. I want people to truly understand that I'm not throwing something to them so that they can buy it. Anytime I say 'please buy,' I'm on the record" (Hill, 1986, pp. 103–104). Cosby's appeal in commercials was one of the ingredients that made him highly marketable as a television series commodity and gave him lots of creative leverage for producing "The Cosby Show."

In 1986 E. F. Hutton, a securities firm, commissioned Cosby to help revive its public image after the company was rocked by scandal. Its highly successful commercials, known nationwide for their theme, "When E. F. Hutton talks, people listen," were discontinued after Hutton pleaded guilty to mail and wire fraud and paid a $2 million fine for illegalities committed by company officials. Cosby was hired because of his believability factor. The commercials performed by Cosby featured statements that were very easy to understand. In one he told viewers that when he was a child, he had not needed a company to handle his money because he had none. Now, however, "I trust E. F. Hutton with *my* money." The scenario was quite believable, considering that Cosby at that time had a reported multimillion-dollar annual income.

Through his commercial ventures and his television show, Cosby has achieved higher ratings than any other performer in the past decade. Six thousand Americans were polled in May and June of 1988 by Marketing Evaluations/TV *Q* and asked to rate how much they liked 1,450 television and movie actors, authors, businessmen, and other personalities (see table below). The recognizability score tells what percentage of people recognized the performer. The *Q* score tells what percentage of people recognizing the performer rated him or her as one of their favorites. Bill Cosby was known by 96 percent of all participants, and 57 percent said he was one of their favorite performers (he set an all-time record a few years ago with a *Q* score of 71) (Hurley, 1988, p. 3).

The 10 Most Popular Performers in America, 1988

Rank	Performer	Recognizability	Q Score
1.	Bill Cosby	96	57
2.	Michael J. Fox	90	47
3.	Clint Eastwood	89	46

4.	Katharine Hepburn	81	45
5.	Paul Newman	84	42
6.	Robin Williams	80	41
7.	Estelle Getty	75	41
8.	Carol Burnett	92	40
9.	Tom Selleck	87	40
10.	Betty White	82	40

Source: *TV Guide,* December 10, 1988

Michael Jordan

Of all the popular black athletes, Michael Jordan, basketball player for the Chicago Bulls, has managed to garner more advertising endorsements than any. His popularity and genuine concern for mankind has made him a multimillionaire, and his unbelievable skill as a basketball player hasn't hurt either. Known as Air Jordan by his adoring fans, he is only the second player to score more than 3,000 points in a season (Wilt Chamberlain was the first); he led the National Basketball Association during the 1986–1987 season with an average of 37.1 points per game; he made the All-Star team in the first four years of his professional career; and he helped win a gold medal in the 1984 Olympics.

ProServ, a professional athlete management organization, is responsible for all of Jordan's endorsements, from negotiating his contracts to investing his millions. ProServ signed Jordan with Nike in September of 1984, before he had even reported to the Bulls' rookie camp. The deal amounted to an unprecedented $2.5 million over five years. With additional royalties, this increased to more than $1 million a year for Jordan. ProServ was also successful in signing McDonald's, Coca-Cola, and Chevrolet during Jordan's first year of professional basketball; Wilson sporting goods, Excelsior International, a watch manufacturer, and Johnson Products were signed later. Jordan was eventually added to the Wheaties honor roll and has had his picture placed on the box and a souvenir calendar.

Willie Tyler and Lester

In an unprecedented move the advertising agency of Stern/Monroe chose a black "dummy" to advertise one of its clients, Rent-a-Center. During 1987 the well-known ventriloquist Willie Tyler and his wooden dummy, Lester, signed a contract to star in four television spots for the Wichita, Kansas–based company. Each of the 30-second ads focused on different aspects of a Rent-a-Center store, including appliances, furniture, and electronics. The first, aired in November 1987, was a national Christmas pro-

motion that ran through the end of the year; the other spots were aired in
1988. The team was hired to add a comedic touch to the everyday problems
encountered by the audiences targeted by Rent-a-Center (Gerdemann,
1987, p. 16).

Since few black artists reach the white audiences targeted by major companies, only a few can survive on only advertising contracts. The success of
black celebrities to secure work in advertising depends upon their ability to
appeal to multi-ethnic and mainstream consumers. And even when some
black celebrities have that kind of appeal, they opt not to do commercials.
Eddie Murphy disclosed his reluctancy to do commercials on the "Arsenio
Hall Show" (February 10, 1989) by stating: "It's such a precious thing to
do films. If they see you every five minutes on television, why come and see
you at the movies? But if the bottom falls out, I'll be a Coors beer drinking
fool." But the tides are turning, and in the 1990s black actors are no longer
being cast only in supplemental or ethnic advertising, and "are now often
used by major companies in crucial marketing situations to introduce products to the mass market or to review a flagship brand" (Shiver, 1988, p.
51).

BLACK FEMALE MODELS

Black models have often had a difficult time tearing down racial barriers
that either told them that they were too dark or not dark enough. Thus, it
was very rare to see black models telling us that "gentlemen prefer Hanes."
During the latter 1950s *Ebony* noted that "big business was beginning to
use an increasing number of brown models to sell its products" (Lewis,
1981, p. 70). It was a breakthrough that would be short-lived, as advertisers
limited their use of black models and only a few were able to make enough
money to sustain themselves.

There are some blacks who have been able to work in the advertising
industry on a consistent basis as models, but more often than not, "the
black model, like many other successful blacks, struggled for many years in
a society that chose to ignore her" ("Have Black Models," 1970, p. 158).
Unless they were hired by black magazines, they generally could not find
work. For many years, advertisers shied away from using black models, particularly, in advertisements for cosmetics and health and beauty aids (Kern-
Foxworth, 1989c, p. 18). Naomi Campbell notes that, "There has never
been a [major] cosmetic contract for an ethnic girl—Hispanic, Asian or
black" (Yang, et al.). And that remained true until 1992, when Cover Girl
signed its first African-American model to an exclusive mainstream market
cosmetics contract (Sturgis, 1993, p. 22). The most notable black models
of that time were Janie Burdett from Los Angeles, Mease Booker, a native
of Waco, Texas, Marlene Fitzhugh and Josie Cain from Chicago and Joyce

Jones of New York. You could see them acclaiming the good qualities of soft drinks, toothpaste, rice, radios and cosmetics (Lewis, 1981, p. 350).

Diahann Carroll, recently named by *Ebony* as one of the ten most beautiful women in the world, tried to make it as a model in the 1950s but failed miserably. When she did find work it was usually for *Ebony* or *Jet* and was paid only $10 or $15 per hour, versus the $35 to $40 made by white models. "Until 1945 virtually no black faces appeared in ads. Then they began to appear regularly in the black publication *Ebony* but only to tout hair products and eventually cosmetics, cigarettes and liquor" ("Black Models," 1969, p. 36). It was not until 1964 that the first black female model graced the cover of a nonblack fashion magazine. Donyale Luna of Detroit arrived in New York and within three months had her face on the cover of *Harper's Bazaar*. With that photo, she also became the first black model to earn top fees ("Did You Know. . . ?," 1989, p. 142).

Before Luna was Helen Williams, the first really successful black model. Dubbed "the black model of the 1940s," she was identified in 1959 as the most photographed black model in the country, but she was primarily limited during most of her career to black magazines because she was "too dark." Hailing from Riverton, New Jersey, she began modeling as a child in New York ("Black Look," 1969). An article about her notes that she was "every black girl's dream come true in their aspirations to model. She [was] the first dark model to gain acceptance in the industry and has opened the doors for all women of darker than olive complexion" (Murphy, 1975, p. 33). Her well-known Budweiser and Modess ads became her trademarks.

In 1975 Williams had this to say about her career:

When I started modeling, I was out there alone. It was fun for me, a challenge. Every time a door closed, I wanted to find out why until it opened. I kept on fighting. The industry just wasn't ready to accept the idea of a dark-skinned model. Over the years, more doors have opened, but it is still a constant struggle for our women. There are too many beautiful black women to give one as an example for the black race. We should have more beauty commercials, be on the covers and in more publications. (Murphy, 1975, p. 33)

Following the assassination of Dr. Martin Luther King, Jr., in April 1968, there appeared to be a greater number of requests for black models. The general sentiment was that "some advertisers are using Negroes in ads because they now feel guilty if they don't" (Levine, 1968, p. 6). At that time casting director Elaina Brooks estimated that 15 percent of black models were employed full-time, and the rest had other means of support.

Indisputably, three of the most successful black female models have been Naomi Sims, Beverly Johnson, and Iman.

Naomi Sims

Scholarships from the Fashion Institute of Technology and New York University (psychology) prepared Sims for a career in modeling. She eventually became one of America's leading fashion models and was the first black model to appear in a television commercial and on the cover of a major women's magazine, *Ladies Home Journal.* She has also appeared on the cover of *Life* and in 1969–1970 was voted Model of the Year by International Famous Mannequins. Today Sims is the owner of her own company, which specializes in wigs and cosmetics for women of color (pp. 1014–1015).

Beverly Johnson

One of the most talented and energetic black models of this generation is Beverly Johnson. Although she won a full academic scholarship to Northeastern University, she was strongly encouraged by friends to withdraw following her freshman year and head to New York. After two years in the city she penetrated the difficult high fashion industry, and in August 1974 became the first black model to grace the cover of *Vogue.* Since 1974 it has been virtually impossible to pick up a magazine, catalog, or newspaper insert and not see her advertising some article of wearing apparel. When a radio talk-show host once commented that she was the "biggest black model in the business," she replied: "No, I'm not. I'm the biggest model, period" (Ploski, 1976, p. 1009).

Iman

Iman has been dubbed "supermodel" because of her insatiable beauty and widespread appeal. She has been featured in numerous magazines and is constantly used to display the fashions of all the top designers.

Iman burst upon the American scene in 1976 after spending most of her childhood in Somalia. In the latter 1980s she became one of the principal models in a major campaign for Revlon. Her career has suffered because of some major personal crises, but despite these obstacles she has become one of the highest paid models in the world. In an *Essence* interview she attributed her stamina, fortitude, and perseverance to this philosophy: "It's like a duck swimming in a pond. The surface looks so calm and beautiful, but under the water the duck's feet are paddling like hell" (Garth-Taylor, 1988, p. 64–65).

BLACK MALE MODELS

Black male models have been used to advertise products for over four decades. Their debuts came primarily in black publications and for the most part they were pigeonholed, just as black female models were, into advertising a small category of products. According to Ophelia DeVore, founder of Grace Del Marco, a black modeling agency in New York, "They were used basically in cigarette ads" (Lewis, 1977, p. 82). This occurred because no women, black or white, were used during that time to advertise cigarettes. In fact, this was during a time when women thought twice about smoking a cigarette in public.

In a 1977 issue of *Ebony*, Shawn Lewis provided the following synopsis of the black male model's plight:

Whether they are smiling at you from a cigarette billboard, munching hamburgers in a television commercial or modeling skin-tight jeans in a magazine advertisement, there is no denying that they are indeed a salable product.

They are black male models and although they may look like a million bucks in idyllic advertisements, many are often broke and disillusioned. (p. 71)

In an effort to explain the hard road traveled by black models, George Patterson asserted that "in descending order of earning power, and gaining exposure, it goes like this: white women, white men, black women and finally black men" (Lewis, 1977, p. 71). To substantiate his claim, Patterson conjectured that while white female models commanded salaries of over $100,000, black men at that time could expect to earn $15,000 to $20,000.

The tides did turn, and during the latter 1970s and early 1980s more black male models surfaced in one fashion or another. "Ten years ago, you would not have seen black men frolicking with white women across the pages of a slick fashion magazine. And the chances of seeing a black man on television agonizing over 'ring around the collar' would have been slim," wrote Lewis (1977, pp. 71–72). In addition to cigarettes black male models were also seen advertising liquor, clothes, and music. The rationale for the use of black male models with these products was offered by Barbara Proctor, owner of the Proctor and Gardner agency in Chicago, who suggested that "there are psychological categories awarded to blacks in which we are supposed to have expertise in this country" (Lewis, 1977, p. 82). She further elaborated that black men were often used to advertise clothes because "they are the catalysts in fashion trends that are eventually copied by the masses." However, the optimism she expressed was overshadowed by the fact that the increase in black male model talent was a by-product of the civil rights movement, and closer scrutiny actually showed a significant drop in the use of professional male models, with firms opting to hire inexperienced models at a lesser rate. Dori Wilson, a former model and former director of fashion and casting at the Foote, Cone and Belding ad agency in Chicago, summarized the situation best when she stated:

During the Johnson administration, the ad agencies had to turn in reports concerning how many blacks were being used in ads and commercials, but as soon as his term ended, that requirement was no longer in effect and we don't have to turn in those reports any longer. (Lewis, 1977, p. 72)

Ron Gardner, Charles Williamson, and Justin Lord were among the most recognized black male faces during the latter part of the 1970s. Richard Roundtree, whose *Shaft* movies made him a household word, was another. Most black male models, however, were not as fortunate and did not get the opportunity to cash in on their looks at the box office. Through the years black male models, even those who manage to appear on the covers of fashion magazines, have not been able to support themselves without other jobs. Some are doing better today than their earlier counterparts by modeling for newspaper inserts and catalogs, but those who are able to make modeling a full-time career are still few and far between.

Using blacks to sell products has always been a strategy employed by advertisers. From the historical beginnings of advertising blacks were portrayed in demeaning situations to appease white consumers. Such presentations were eventually eradicated but were replaced by overt stereotypes. When these were targeted by civil rights activists during the 1960s, changes were made and some of the stereotypes became more subtle. "During the sixties we were finally allowed to demonstrate that we too washed our dirty drawers with detergent" (Allen, 1980, p. 19). But throughout all the transitions fictitious black characters have made more indelible impressions than real models. Drawing on the image of slave cooks on Southern plantations, advertisers have never been reluctant to use black caricatures and symbols to advertise food products. This association has always enhanced sales, and Barbara Proctor reinforced this by adding, "That's why products like Uncle Ben's Rice and Aunt Jemima Pancakes are doing well" (Lewis, 1977, p. 82).

Aunt Jemima, more than any other black caricature or model, has been wholeheartedly embraced by the American consumer. At various points in history she has been dubbed "the most famous colored woman in America," and today she may in fact be the most well-known African-American female.

REFERENCES

Allen, Bonnie. 1980. "In Focus: Blacks in Ads." *Essence* (February): 19.
Assael, Henry. 1987. *Consumer Behavior and Marketing Action.* Boston: Kent Publishing.
"Black Look in Beauty." 1969. *Time,* April 11, pp. 72–74.
"Black Models Take Center Stage." 1969. *Life* (October): 36.

Broom, Glen, Allen Center, and Scot Cutlip. 1985. *Effective Public Relations.* New York: Prentice-Hall.

Clarke, John Henrik. 1989. "In Our Own Image." *Essence* (September): 158.

Dates, Jannette L., and William Barlow. 1990. *Split Image: African Americans in the Mass Media.* Washington, D.C.: Howard University Press.

della Cava, Marco R. 1993. "Grand Jury Gets Molestations Case." November 24–25, p. 1A.

"Did You Know. . . ?" 1989. *Essence* (February): 142.

Garth-Taylor, Mikki. 1988. "Iman: By Her Own Rules." *Essence* (January): 64–65, 97.

George, Lori A. A Study on the Effectiveness of Target Marketing to the African-American Market. Master's thesis, American University, 1992.

Gerdemann, Gary. 1987. "Showbiz Spots Make Room for Mom, Dad." *Adweek,* December 21, p. 16.

Gundersen, Edna. 1993. "Jackson Not Dodging Law, Lawyers Say." *USA Today,* November 16, p. 1D.

"Have Black Models Really Made It?" 1990. *Ebony* (May): 158.

Hay, Elizabeth. 1981. *Sambo Sahib: The Story of Little Black Sambo and Helen Bannerman.* Totowa, N.J.: Barnes and Noble.

Hill, George, ed. 1986. *Ebony Images: Black Americans and Television.* Los Angeles: Daystar Publishing.

Hurley, Dan. 1988. "Those Hush-Hush *Q* Ratings—Fair or Foul?" *TV Guide,* December 10, pp. 3–6.

Johnson, Robert E. 1987. "Michael Jackson Comes Back." *Ebony* (September): 143–44, 146, 148–49.

Kaplan, Janice L. 1989. "African Art Comes from Everyday Life." *Hammond* (La.) *Daily Star,* November 24, p. 4B.

Kern-Foxworth. 1989. "Ads Pose Dilemma for Black Women." *Media and Values* 49 (Winter): 18–19.

Kiefer, Michael. 1988. "Air Attack: Flying High in Points and Profits, Michael Jordan Is the Jam Master of the N.B.A." *Playboy,* (April): 80–83.

Levine, Jo Ann. 1968. "Look for Penny Bogan and John Johnston." *Christian Science Monitor,* August 19, p. 6.

Lewis, Alba Myers. 1981. "Beauty, Culture, Fashion and Modeling." In Marianna Davis, ed. *Contributions of Black Women to America.* Columbia, S.C.: Kenday Press.

Lewis, Shawn D. 1977. "More than Just Handsome Faces." *Ebony* (March): 70–72, 82, 84, 86.

Lippert, Barbara. 1988. "Pepsi's 'Chase' Shows Jackson Is a Bad Act to Follow." *Adweek* 10 (March 14): 22.

Martin, Francis, Jr. 1976. "Edward Windsor Kemble, A Master of Pen and Ink." *American Art Review,* (January/February): 55, 57.

"Michael Jackson: Choice of the New Generation." 1984. *Tony Brown's Journal* (April/June): 13.

Morgan, Hal. 1986. *Symbols of America.* New York: Viking Penguin.

Morrow, Lance. 1984. "The Power of Racial Example." *Time,* April 16, p. 84.

Murphy, Frederick. 1975. "Black Models Have Their Say." *Encore,* April 7, p. 33.

Noel, Pamela. 1984. "TV Ad Wars' Newest Weapon: Use of Black Celebrities Plays a Big Role in the Wooing of American Consumers." *Ebony* (July): 81–82, 84.

Ploski, Harry A. 1976. *The Negro Almanac: A Reference Work on the Afro American.* New York: Bellwether.

Reed, Robert. 1991. "Gold Dust Twins Still Golden." *Black Ethnic Collectibles* 4 (Spring): 28–34.

Sacharow, Stanley. 1982. *Symbols of Trade: Your Favorite Trademarks and the Companies They Represent.* New York: Art Direction Book Company.

Shiver, Jube. 1988. "Star Struck: The Magical Attraction of Celebrity Families Has Madison Avenue under a Spell." *Black Enterprise* (December): 51.

The Story of Uncle Ben. 1988. Memo distributed by Uncle Ben's, Inc., Houston.

Sturgis, Ingrid. 1993. "Black Images in Advertising: A Revolution Is Being Televised in 30-Second Commercials." *Emerge* (September): 21–23.

Thalberg, Jan. 1989. "Cream of Wheat." *Black Ethnic Collectibles* (January/February): 15.

Watkins, Julian Lewis. 1949. *The 100 Greatest Advertisements: Who Wrote Them and What They Did.* New York: Moore Publishing Company.

Winters, Patricia. 1987. "Pepsi to Use Jackson in 4-Part Spot." *Advertising Age* 58 (September 14): 1, 112.

Yancey, Kitty Bean. 1993. "Pepsi Ends 9-year-Tie to Jackson." *USA Today,* November 15, p. 1A.

Yang, Jeff, Angelo Ragaza, Grace Suh, and Rodney Gonzalez. "The Beauty Machine: The U.S. Is Getting Darker, but the Standard of Beauty Is Still White." *Asian-American Quarterly.*

Chapter 4 —————————————————————————

AUNT JEMIMA: THE MOST BATTERED WOMAN IN AMERICA RISES TO THE TOP

> The myth of the strong black woman is the other side of the coin of the myth of the beautiful dumb blonde. The white man turned . . . the black woman into a strong self-reliant Amazon and deposited her in his kitchen—that's the secret of Aunt Jemima's bandanna.
> Eldridge Cleaver (*Soul on Ice,* 1968, p. 162)

Aunt Jemima has been invited to have breakfast with millions of families all over the world, and in 1989 she had been doing so for 100 years.

As a trademark, Aunt Jemima has been a familiar part of American culture and has been woven into the mainstream of the American advertising industry. Traditionally, Aunt Jemima and other blacks were depicted in very stereotypical advertising modes, none more pervasive than that of servant and caretaker. "There was Old Uncle Tom or Uncle Remus, Aunt Jemima or Mandy the maid, Preacher Brown and Deacon Jones, Rastus and Sambo, and the ol' mammy" (Lemmons, 1977).

Ever since advertising became instrumental in the selling of ideas, services, and products, blacks have been used to increase their recognizability. Steven Heller (1982, p. 102), author of *Racist Ephemera: The Melting Pot Reconsidered,* describes the integration of blacks into American society following the abolishment of slavery well:

The growing pains of this young nation—exacerbated by the very melting pot policy it encouraged—were manifest in a populace uncomfortable with the new foreign inhabitants and in a government undeniably ill-equipped to deal with an alien native population and with new freed slaves.

Nowhere are these upsetting chapters of history and the emotions it conjures up revealed more profoundly than in the mass-produced popular art of the period—advertising, trade cards, posters, product labels, trademarks. Through commonplace, highly visible, graphic, racial and ethnic stereotypes a vivid picture—sometimes precarious, often comic—materializes of a country fraught with class, religious and racial prejudice.

Verta Mae (1972) offers a historical viewpoint relative to the concept of Aunt Jemima as a servant and suggests that the foundation for her birth dates back to ancient Rome and Europe. She defines Aunt Jemima within the context of the preparation and serving of foods by blacks to whites from a historical context and suggests that it was common practice for royalty to have black male and female servants. Consequently, the price of black slaves in Rome was higher than for whites sold at slave markets. She also maintains that in the 1600s European women walked young blacks like they now walk poodles. This assumption is corroborated by Rogers (1952), who wrote the following: "Ladies of fashion appeared in public each with a monkey dressed in an embroidered jacket and a little black slave boy wearing a turban and baggy silk pantaloons."

Verta Mae further maintains that the Moors or people of color have historically been valued by whites as servants: "Black women have been preferred as wet nurses to the big boys as well as the babies; and the Roman women resented that fact to the extent that there were many abuses to the Moorish women by the Roman ladies." Within this frame of reference she suggests that the placing of blacks, both Aunt Jemima and Uncle Ben, on the boxes of various food products is a "cultural hangover from this earlier era" (Jewell, 1976, p. 113).

Blacks were used extensively during the post-slavery era because they reinforced the stereotype of the docile servant who was always ready to serve humbly. Whether consciously or unconsciously conceived, advertising was a structured mechanism that eroded the self-esteem of blacks and kept them powerless. "Early advertising was the strongest medium through which American white businessmen could express their feelings toward American blacks and seek to keep control over those people they considered their slaves" (Reno, 1986, p. 1).

Arthur Marquette (1967) notes, "The American Negro has always represented in American life the acme of the culinary arts, respected as in France are the chefs who belong to the Société Gastronomique." He further asserts that Southern hospitality during slavery was defined and influenced by black cooks and chefs and that "blacks become enmeshed in the folklore in America as the ultimate experts in cookery." Jewell (1976, p. 138) suggests that "it is from this legend that Aunt Jemima pancake flour capitalized upon and exploited black women" (p. 114).

Another theory posited offers a different reason for why blacks were the central figures in so much advertising from the end of the Civil War to the early 1940s:

Blacks in advertising soon became a sales gimmick, a device to improve sales; they were the come-ons in ads to promote the sales of gardening or farming tools, janitorial equipment, and foods.

It was an often-inbred belief among whites that because of their antebellum experience, blacks were the master gardeners, farmers, unskilled laborers, and cooks. If a black said such a product was good, the white Northerner reasoned it must be so. From such thinking there emerged Aunt Jemima and Uncle Ben. (Brasch, 1981, pp. 114–115)

By the turn of the 20th century Aunt Jemima and other stereotypes were an integral part of American culture. They were so familiar and so accepted that few people, black or white, protested how denigrating they were to black Americans, especially to black women. "Most people thought the caricatures were simply funny. They laughed with good humor, but their sense of humor revealed a pervasive lack of sensitivity. The images were spread and maintained in advertising cards, songs from Tin Pan Alley, phonograph records, children's books, cartoons, magazine ads, Valentine's and postcards" (Lemmons, 1977, p. 103). All of these items were used to promote the image of blacks as docile, subservient, and laughable characters.

A thorough examination of images like Aunt Jemima provides not only a kaleidoscopic look into American commercial culture, but illustrates the relationship between minority and majority societies. Although scholars have theorized that the subordinate position into which blacks have been categorized is rooted in an ideology of black inferiority, "what is less well known is that American popular culture has been an important vehicle transmission of those ideological notions" (Barnett, 1982, p. 42). Images reflecting blacks in docile and servile roles included Rastus (Cream of Wheat), Uncle Ben, and the Gold Dust Twins, but none was more pervasive than Aunt Jemima. "Whether as a mammy doll or as an advertisement for pancake batter, these artifacts and adornments entered the homes of America and became a part of the American way of life" (Henderson et al., 1982, p. 19).

THE BEGINNING OF AUNT JEMIMA

The Aunt Jemima trademark had its beginnings in Missouri. Chris L. Rutt, a reporter for the *St. Joseph Gazette*, and Charles G. Underwood, a mill owner, purchased the Pearl Milling Company in 1888. They then began a relentless search for a product all America would eat (Morgan, 1986, p.

55). "They needed something exclusive and novel. What did almost everybody eat? Pancakes. What consumed a lot of flour? Pancakes. What was difficult to mix with any consistency from one batch to the next? Pancake batter" (Marquette, 1967, p. 140). They also chose pancakes because of the festive spirit that had always been associated with them.[1]

Rutt and Underwood experimented with a combination of various ingredients such as hard wheat flour, corn flour, phosphate of lime, soda, and salt such that when milk was added and the batter cooked, pancakes resulted. They finally perfected the product for which they had been looking, and within a year they produced the first pancake mix (Campbell, 1964, p. 40).

Eager to get the opinion of someone more objective than themselves, they solicited comments from Purd B. Wright, the town librarian. That event was later described like this:

One afternoon, as Wright described the event later, he was escorted by Underwood to the Rutt kitchen. A ready mixed concoction lay in a bowl. As Wright and Underwood watched, Rutt added milk and beat the mixture quickly into a batter. By now the griddle was hot, and circles of bubbly yellow batter were ladled out and browned evenly on both sides. A neat stack, laced with melted butter and sugar syrup, was set before the tester.

"I ate the first perfected Aunt Jemima pancake," Wright reported, "and pronounced it good" (Marquette, 1967, p. 141). His enthusiasm was so overwhelming that they brought out a bottle of Missouri corn whiskey and toasted the world's first self-rising pancake.

The founders immediately began to package the mix for sale to the public. The first commercial batch was packaged in paper bags with a generic label, "Self-Rising Pancake Flour," since the Aunt Jemima name had not yet been conceived.

After the first ready-mix pancake was perfected in 1889 an immediate search began for a symbol that would make the product recognizable by all American housewives. Little did Chris L. Rutt know that his quest for a name and package design for his unprecedented product would be found in an unusual place.

While visiting a vaudeville house in St. Joseph, Missouri, one evening in the autumn of 1889, Rutt saw a team of blackface minstrel comedians known as Baker and Farrell. The high point of the act was a jazzy, rhythmic, New Orleans–style cakewalk performed to a tune called "Aunt Jemima" (Morgan, 1986, p. 55). The song was originally called "Old Aunt Jemima" and was one of the most popular songs of the day, performed by Billy Kersands, a well-known minstrel, from 1870 to 1900. By 1877 Kersands had performed the song more than 3,000 times and had developed three different improvisational texts for his audiences (Sacharow, 1982, p. 63). One of the most widely sung 1875 versions used these lyrics:

My old missus promise me
  Old Aunt Jemima, oh, oh, oh

When she died she'd set me free
  Old Aunt Jemima, oh, oh, oh

She lived so long her head got bald
  Old Aunt Jemima, oh, oh, oh

She swore she would not die at all
  Old Aunt Jemima, oh, oh, oh.[2]

Kersands has been labeled the highest paid black minstrel of his time, his remarkable popularity based partially on his theme song, "Old Aunt Jemima" (Sacharow, 1982, p. 64).

The team of Baker and Farrell, dressed in aprons and red bandannas, was reminiscent of the traditional Southern cook. The song was so captivating that it had the whole town rocking (Campbell, 1964, p. 40). Mesmerized, Rutt knew that the song and costume projected the image for which he had been searching. He decided to mimic it, using not only the name but the likeness of the Southern mammy emblazoned on the lithographed posters advertising the act of Baker and Farrell, thus beginning a new era in advertising. This would be the first time a living person would be used to personify a company's trademark (Kern-Foxworth, 1988, p. 18).

However, Rutt and Underwood could not raise the necessary capital to promote and market the product effectively. They soon ran out of money. After registering the trademark in 1890, they sold their interests to the R. T. Davis Mill and Manufacturing Company, also of St. Joseph, Missouri. Davis was more financially able to promote the product, having large manufacturing facilities, money, and an established reputation with wholesale and retail grocers throughout the Missouri Valley. A 50-year veteran of the milling business, he designed a promotional campaign that has been revered for years by many advertisers, promoters, and marketers.

The first miracle he performed was to improve the flavor and texture of the product by adding rice flour and corn sugar to the ingredients. The next step would be one of the most important to the success of the Aunt Jemima brand. "He simplified the ready-mix principle by adding powdered milk—an extremely significant simplification" (Kern-Foxworth, 1989a, p. 56). Cooks had only to add water to prepare the batter. With this change in the mixture, Aunt Jemima ushered in the beginning of the convenience foods era. Davis was a master at promotion, and the company flourished under his direction.

Subsequently, after his death in 1900, the company suffered one disaster after another. It declared bankruptcy and was reorganized in 1903 and re-named the Aunt Jemima Mills Company in 1914. A new, more accurate image of Aunt Jemima was adopted by the company in 1917 (Congdon-Martin, 1990, p. 57). In 1919 James Webb Young, manager in Chicago of the J. Walter Thompson advertising agency, revived the company with a series of advertisements. In each the campaign featured vignettes detailing the life of Aunt Jemima.

The market collapse of 1920 damaged the company severely, and it took decades to make a full recovery. The company was sold in January 1926 for $4.2 million to the Quaker Oats Company (Marquette, 1967, pp. 149–50, 152). After the sale the trademark experienced tremendous growth until the depression of the 1930s.

After recovering from the financial strains of the depression, Quaker Oats gained momentum and continued to rise economically. In the 1960s it be-came a nationally known leader in the frozen food business; among those foods were pancakes, waffles, corn sticks, and cinnamon twists. By the 1960s Quaker Oats was recovering more each year than its original investment. The company continued to be a leader in the breakfast food industry and later introduced the first reduced-calorie syrup and reduced-calorie, micro-wavable frozen pancakes.

WOMEN WHO HAVE PORTRAYED AUNT JEMIMA

The success experienced by the Aunt Jemima trademark for a century can be attributed in part to the remarkable women who brought the label to life.

Nancy Green

R. T. Davis sent requests to all his food broker friends to be on the lookout for a black woman who exemplified Southern hospitality and also had the personality necessary to make Aunt Jemima a household name throughout America (Sacharow, 1982, p. 64). His appeal was answered by Charles Jackson, a Chicago wholesaler, who knew of a black woman who worked for a friend of his, Judge Walker. She was well-known for making delicious pancakes. The woman was Nancy Green, who was born a slave in Montgomery County, Kentucky, in 1834 (McManus, 1991, p. 8). She later moved from Kentucky to Chicago, where she was a cook for Judge Walker and served as a nurse for his two sons.

Davis contacted Green and confirmed Jackson's appraisal. "She was a magnificent cook, an attractive woman of outgoing nature and friendly per-sonality, gregarious in the extreme" (Sacharow, 1982, p. 145). She was the perfect person to bring the Aunt Jemima trademark to life. Meeting with high approval from all of the company officials, Green was signed to an exclusive contract which would give her the right to impersonate Aunt Jemima for the rest of her life ("Did You Know. . . ?," 1989, p. 142).

On the brink of bankruptcy, the executives of the company decided to risk their entire fortune on a promotional exhibition featuring Nancy Green at the 1893 World's Columbian Exposition in Chicago (Sacharow, 1982, pp. 64, 65).

Davis Milling constructed the world's largest flour barrel, 24 feet high and 16 feet in diameter. Doors were mounted in the side, and the interior was fitted out as a reception parlor to entertain visitors. Outside the barrel, near the front, was Nancy Green in the persona of Aunt Jemima. She cooked pancakes, sang songs, and told stories of the Old South while greeting fair visitors. She had served more than a million pancakes by the time the fair ended, and more than 50,000 orders were placed for Aunt Jemima Pancake Mix from countries all over the world (Marquette, 1967, pp. 145, 146).

Nancy Green's dramatization of Aunt Jemima was such a huge success that special details of policemen were assigned to keep the crowds moving at the Davis exhibit. In recognition of her triumphant debut, Green was awarded a medal and certificate from fair organizers, who proclaimed her the Pancake Queen (Marquette, 1967, p. 146). She traveled around the country demonstrating Aunt Jemima pancake mix at fairs, food shows, and festivals. "She made a wide itinerary through the United States and Canada, and an aggressive advertising campaign of national proportions was undertaken." She was asked to attend the Paris Exposition in 1900, but refused to go on the ocean voyage. "I was born in this country," she said, "and here I'll die, not somewhere betwixt here and somewhere else" (Marquette, 1967, p. 146).

When not touring the United States and Canada as Aunt Jemima, Green lived on the south side of Chicago. She was one of the founders of Olivet Church, one of the largest Baptist congregations in the world. She remained a representative of the Davis Milling Company until her death on September 23, 1923, when she was fatally struck by a car in Chicago.

Anna Robinson

No one portrayed Aunt Jemima for ten years following the death of Nancy Green. In 1933 Anna Robinson made her debut as Aunt Jemima at the Chicago Century of Progress Exposition.

As Aunt Jemima, Robinson will forever be remembered in the annals of Quaker Oats history. "Never to be forgotten was the day they loaded 350 pounds of Anna Robinson on the Twentieth Century Limited and sent her to New York in the custody of the Lord and Thomas Advertising Agency to pose for pictures" (Kern-Foxworth, 1990, p. 59). An entire campaign was designed around her association with a parade of stars. She had personal appearances and posed with Hollywood celebrities at some of the most famous places, including El Morocco, "21", the Stork Club, and the Waldorf-Astoria. Everywhere Robinson went, she was photographed making pancakes for luminaries from motion pictures, radio, and Broadway. The advertisements derived from those photography sessions "ranked among the highest read of their time" (Marquette, 1967, p. 154).

The officials at Quaker Oats were so impressed with the advertisements using Robinson that they commissioned Haddon Sunblom, a nationally known commercial artist, to paint a portrait of her. The Aunt Jemima package was redesigned around the new likeness. Robinson stayed on the Quaker Oats Company payroll until her death in 1951.

Edith Wilson

Edith Wilson gained national notoriety as the motherly face on Aunt Jemima advertising materials. A classic blues singer from Chicago, she came from a well-educated family in Louisville (Harley and Terborg-Penn, 1978, p. 71). Her performances were not limited entirely to blues, though, as she also was a recorded vaudeville performer. She often noted that her family was very supportive of her career aspirations and appeared in concerts throughout the country. She further appeared on the "Amos 'n' Andy" and "Great Guildersleeve" radio serials during the 1940s. Her most famous movie was *To Have and Have Not,* starring Humphrey Bogart (Young, 1988, p. 10).

Quaker Oats capitalized on Wilson's outgoing personality and had her portray Aunt Jemima on radio, television, and in personal appearances all over the United States from 1948 to 1966. According to Derrick Stewart-Baxter (1970), she was the first Aunt Jemima featured on TV commercials, and although she received support from her family, "her appearance as Aunt Jemima on early commercials was criticized as demeaning" (p. 31).

Wilson died on March 30, 1981, after suffering a stroke. She lived in Chicago from the 1950s until her death.

Ethel Ernestine Harper

Ethel Ernestine Harper was featured as Aunt Jemima in advertising campaigns during the 1950s. She graduated from college at 17 and taught school for a while before portraying Aunt Jemima. Additionally, she starred in the theatrical productions *The Hot Macado* and the *Negro Follies* and sang with the Three Ginger Snaps while touring Europe. She died in Morristown, New Jersey, in April 1981.

Rosie Hall

For 17 years Rosie Lee Moore Hall captured the attention of the world in the persona of Aunt Jemima. Born in Robertson County, Texas, in 1900,

Hall was a native of the community of Pin Oak, located between Hearne and Wheelock. She married Ollie Chambers at age 17 and remained in Pin Oak (Kern-Foxworth, 1988, p. 17). She left Hearne in her late 20s when her marriage failed, losing contact with her family for 19 years. By then she had made Oklahoma City her home and was working for Quaker Oats (Bullock, 1987).

While working in the advertising department of Quaker Oats she learned of the search for a new Aunt Jemima. According to family and friends, she perfectly exemplified the trademark, which was why her round smiling face adorned Aunt Jemima products for almost two decades (Kern-Foxworth, 1991, p. 31).

From 1950 to 1967 Hall continued the tradition started by other Aunt Jemimas and traveled the country showing off her culinary talents by making melt-in-your-mouth pancakes. She was at her best when she was cooking pancakes. And cook pancakes she did: at world's fairs and annually at the Texas State Fair; everywhere she went, she jovially served her syrup and buckwheat cakes. During her last years at Quakers Oats, Hall told her family she was excited about a new syrup recipe she was creating.

Hall was the oldest girl of 14 children, and was always outgoing. After she began the role of Aunt Jemima, her family looked forward to her annual visit home during Christmas. They would gather at the family home and sing Christmas carols, while Hall would talk about her experiences as Aunt Jemima. Her sisters say she was perfect for the job because she liked people so much. Her family never saw any of her official demonstrations, but they were always delighted when she returned home, because she would cook her famous pancakes for them.

The last time she visited was Christmas 1966. Two months later she suffered a heart attack on her way to church and died on February 12, 1967. An elaborate funeral was held in Oklahoma City, and she was buried in the family plot in the Colony Cemetery near Wheelock, Texas.

Although she died over a quarter of a century ago, Hall had no grave marker until 1988. A special ceremony was held May 7, 1988, and her grave was declared a historical landmark.

Hall's reign as Aunt Jemima is significant because she was the last "living" Aunt Jemima.

Aylene Lewis

Aylene Lewis portrayed Aunt Jemima at the eponymous restaurant at Disneyland, which opened in 1955. Because it was such a popular eating place at the park, it was refurbished in June 1962. In the eight years prior to the remodeling the restaurant had served pancakes to 1.6 million guests (Marquette, 1967, p. 137). Lewis became well known for serving pancakes to dignitaries.

Clad in her bandanna and matching skirt and shawl, she posed for pictures with many visitors to Disneyland. She received souvenir pictures and letters "from all over the world, in all languages and from all races and creeds" (p. 157). Indian Prime Minister Nehru's normal calm turned to animation as he posed with Lewis's hand clasped in his. Quite a celebrity herself, she was also at ease in front of television cameras. She also developed a close relationship with Walt Disney. Lewis died in 1964, after posing as the Disneyland Aunt Jemima from 1957 to 1964.

From 1951 until the early 1960s, there were many Aunt Jemima's working simultaneously. They appeared at supermarkets, trade shows, and other promotional events and became recognized as the first organized sales promotion campaign, thus initiating an innovative strategy in advertising and serving as one of the first campaigns to create "an image."

Glenn Williams, Sr., chairman of the board and founder of First Federal Savings of Bryan, Texas, vividly remembers Aunt Jemima's demonstrations—an annual event sponsored by the Quaker Oats Company—in the family's grocery story, Williams IGA, in downtown Bryan. Anna Robinson would come to the store one Saturday a year. "Farmers came into town once a week on Saturdays back then [during the 40s], before there was a race issue," he says. "It was more like a social gathering. She had a good personality and was pretty good at getting people interested in the pancakes" (Williams, 1987).

His son, businessman Glenn Williams, Jr., echoes the sentiments of his father. One of the highlights of his childhood years was the appearance of Aunt Jemima at his father's store. People would stand around talking and laughing with her as the aroma of pancakes filled the air. The younger Williams laughed as he recalled that "the grown-ups usually sampled one pancake, but the children managed to get more." Grinning, he added that "those pancakes were the best I had ever eaten in my life" (Williams, 1987).

Some of the women who portrayed Aunt Jemima gained national stature, others did not, but all helped Americans learn to love Aunt Jemima pancakes. The women became so famous that several legends were created to document their success.

AUNT JEMIMA LEGENDS

Among the promotional tactics used by Quaker Oats was the marketing of legends about the miraculous power of Aunt Jemima's pancakes. One of the vehicles used to promote these myths was the napkins used at the Aunt Jemima Restaurant. According to one story printed on the napkins, Aunt Jemima was a mammy cook, famous throughout the South in those glorious days before the War. Her master, Colonel Higbee, was owner of a vast plantation at Higbee's Landing on the Mississippi River. The colonel was known for his extraordinary hospitality, which was enhanced because of pancakes served by his cook—Aunt Jemima. "Her pancakes, cooked from a secret recipe, made her the envy of many Southern cooks." As the tale goes, Aunt Jemima sold her recipe to the R. T. Davis Mill Company in St. Joseph, Missouri (Lambert, 1976, p. 57).

Another legend suggests that Aunt Jemima saved the life of Colonel Higbee. When Northern soldiers were about to pluck his mustache out by the roots, Aunt Jemima offered them some of her pancakes. Their attention was so diverted by the good taste that the troops forgot all about the colonel, and he escaped with every hair intact.

"A Southern officer and his adjutant," relates another story, "separated from their troops after a battle, reached Aunt Jemima's cabin door dejected and exhausted." She served them her pancakes, which rapidly returned them to a state of excellent health. They told others of their good fortune, and from that time on hundreds of soldiers came by to get samples of her pancakes. One of these soldiers returned after the war with some friends from the North to prove to them that Aunt Jemima cooked the most delicious pancakes in the world. They persuaded her to share her delicious recipe with the world.

> The story of Aunt Jemima, whom we know as Pancake Queen,
>   Starts on an Old Plantation, in a charming Southern scene.
>
> Here folks grow sweet magnolias and cotton in the sun,
>   And life was filled with happiness and old-time Southern fun.
>
> The owner, Colonel Higbee, a most kind and gracious host,
>   Served his guests fine dishes, though they liked his pancakes most.
>
> Of course, the cook who made them—or so the legend goes—
>   Was good old Aunt Jemima, as our pretty picture shows.
>
> Aunt Jemima's pancake fame
>   soon spread throughout the South.
>
> Folks loved that fluffy tenderness
>   that melted in yo' mouth.
>
> Girls crowded 'round Jemima,
>   in their dainty crinolines,
>
> And oh! Those Southern Colonels,
>   you should have seen their grins!

They begged our Aunt Jemima
    for her secret recipe

And, being nice and generous,
    she gave it to them free.

Those Southern belles and Colonels
    soon were serving piled-up plates

Of luscious Aunt Jemimas
    throughout the Southern states!

A Mississippi steamboat. . .
    Emily Dunstan was her name. . .

Then burned up on the river,
    in a mass of smoke and flame.

This terrible experience,
    which might have been so tragic,

Had a Happy Ending,
    thanks to Aunt Jemima's magic.

She served the cold, wet children
    and the husbands and their wives,

Steaming stacks of pancakes,
    so she helped to save their lives.

Then a Yankee in the party. . .
    a Northern Business man. . .

Took her recipe up North with him. . .
    and her world-wide fame began.

A series of these phony legends were used in an advertising campaign designed and implemented by James Webb Young, manager of the Chicago branch of J. Walter Thompson. Young used his memorable experiences of growing up in Covington, Kentucky, as the son of a Mississippi riverboat captain to structure a scenario in the minds of customers and position the Aunt Jemima product as the front runner in its class of breakfast foods.

Young's advertisements were illustrated by the eminent artist N. C. Wyeth in 1919. The series had a dominant theme centered around the Americana of the deep South and was representative of a new style of advertising. One carried the heading "The Night the Emily Burned," and showed an awe-struck Aunt Jemima watching a Mississippi riverboat burn to the water line. The text told how the grateful passengers found their way ashore to her cabin, where they were delighted by her pancakes. Another told of "The Visitors from the North," four enterprising gentlemen who threaded their way to Aunt Jemima's cabin door to negotiate with her for her famous recipe. Finally, another in the series told how Aunt Jemima became convinced and went North to begin a new career working for the Yankee millers, and thus came to belong to the whole United States.

The legends became a part of American folklore and helped create the Aunt Jemima mystique. They became an important part of the advertising campaigns and thus helped in the successful implementation of promotional strategy.

THE PROMOTIONAL STRATEGY

R. T. Davis masterminded the promotional strategy that set the Aunt Jemima trademark and products apart from all others in its category. Because of his ingenuity the Aunt Jemima name has maintained a first-place status for a century. Many premiums have been offered to customers in return for their loyalty and trust, but none received such acclaim as the Aunt Jemima rag doll, coveted by little girls throughout America. The company boasts that "literally every city child owned one" (Marquette, 1967, p. 148). The phenomenon can be equated to the craze of owning a Cabbage Patch doll several years ago.

Following the lead of other breakfast manufacturers, Davis offered box-top premiums, which became one the most famous in merchandising history. For one trademark (referred to today as a proof of purchase seal) and only five cents, customers received an Aunt Jemima rag doll. One advertisement in the *Ladies Home Journal* in October 1918 read as follows:

> Send for these jolly rag dolls
> Send one Aunt Jemima box top (Pancake or Buckwheat Flour) with only five cents in stamps and get one of the famous Aunt Jemima Rag Dolls. Or send four tops and only fifteen cents for Aunt Jemima and Uncle Mose, and two cunning pickaninnies. In bright colors, ready to cut out and stuff. Aunt Jemima Mills Company, St. Joseph, Missouri.

The rag doll concept was the renewal of a promotional strategy tried in 1895, when the pancake mix was sold in cartons rather than one-pound sacks. To bring notoriety to the product Davis printed cutout paper doll Aunt Jemimas on the cartons. The gimmick was very successful and was revived a decade later when the company was facing financial ruin. The Aunt Jemima rag doll saga continued, and employees of Quaker Oats reminisced:

The Aunt Jemima rag doll emerged, renewing itself year after year until an entire family of rag dolls had been created, featuring Uncle Mose and two moppets, Diana and Wade. Just before the Quaker Oats Company acquired Aunt Jemima, the rag doll was offered again in an advertisement in a women's magazine. The flood of requests almost swamped the sponsor. Almost every woman who answered the advertisement said that she had been raised on the Aunt Jemima dolls and now wanted them for her daughter. (Marquette, 1967, p. 148)

Other manufacturers decided to capitalize on the success of Aunt Jemima and introduced other dolls with similar characteristics: a round, smiling face exuding warmth and friendliness attired in domestic regalia. Johana Gast Anderson (1979, pp. 44–48) noted in *More Twentieth Century Dolls from Bisque to Vinyl* that at least five generations of black women were modeled after the original Aunt Jemima dolls.

According to Doris Wilkinson, who wrote in great detail about Aunt Jemima toys in *Images of Blacks in American Culture* (1988, p. 283), there were several dolls molded in the Aunt Jemima image. "Appearing in the 1890s, this doll was typically fat with a round, smiling face and was customarily attired in a domestic outfit" (Pantovic, 1974, p. 282). Most of the black dolls that were not depicted as Europeans were characterized in the traditional Aunt Jemima format; equipped with an apron, they were most often quite heavy-set with thick red lips and that ever-present broad-toothed smile. The "Cake Walker" mechanical toys and the "Mechanical Nurse" advertised in Marshall Field catalogs during the 1890s were cast in this mode as well. "Repeatedly, the images were rooted in stereotyped conceptions of women of African ancestry" (Wilkinson, 1988, p. 283).

The strategies used by the company's advertising and marketing departments were very effective and became one of the reasons the product became so well accepted by the public. Over the 100-year period the owners have issued many premiums in an attempt to promote the product. "The Aunt Jemima Pancake Flour Company used quite a few different objects in their promotion, all of which depicted the jolly black woman in her red turban. Salt and pepper shakers, cookie jars, plastic and cardboard items, even a pottery set of kitchen condiment holders made by the Weller Pottery Company were given away in their promotions" (Reno, 1986, p. 5).

The syrup pitcher was among the first items given to customers with the purchase of pancake mix. According to accounts by the F. and F. (Fielder and Fielder) Mold and Die Works Company of Dayton, Ohio (Reno, 1986,

p. 12), the idea for the pitcher was created over a luncheon date in Chicago when the F. and F. company manager met with a representative from Quaker Oats to discuss the promotional service F. and F. could provide. During the ensuing conversation, a sketch of an Aunt Jemima pitcher was drawn on the tablecloth and was used as the prototype for the original (Greenwood, 1988 p. 12). The success of the pitcher set the stage for the introduction of a long line of related items.[3]

The syrup pitcher was available during the early 1950s, and more than a million were distributed before they were discontinued (Marquette, 1967, p. 149). The rest of the series consisted of a cookie jar, salt and pepper shakers also featuring Uncle Mose, a six-piece Aunt Jemima spice set, an Uncle Mose creamer, and an Aunt Jemima sugar bowl with a lid. These items were favorites as premiums until the early 1960s (Greenwood, 1988, p. 12).

All the Aunt Jemima premiums were made of plastic, not celluloid as commonly believed. They were all painted with black faces and arms with the exception of the cookie jar, whose face and arms were painted brown in later years. Collectors have found the brown face to be much more scarce than the black. Today the premiums command high prices at auctions, flea markets, and antique shops across the country.[4]

Because of the popularity of the premiums, reproductions have been man-ufactured by F. and F. Mold and Die. But these products are not the "real McCoy," as all of the original premiums offered are stamped with the Aunt Jemima logo.

The Quaker Oats Company has not kept complete records of the variety of premiums offered by the company for the past 100 years. "There are no old catalogs that would list them; in fact no records exist for current pre-mium items. The company does, however, have records verifying the salt and pepper shakers, a cream and sugar set, a cookie jar and an antique bowl presumably offered in 1956" (Greenwood, 1988, p. 12).

During the civil rights movement the Aunt Jemima product line was discontinued because of objections from blacks who viewed the images as derogatory and denigrating. "These items of material culture gave a phys-ical reality to ideas of racial inferiority. They were the props that helped reinforce the racist ideology that emerged after Reconstruction" (Goings, 1990, p. B76). Before being discontinued, the premiums had become a part of the mystique that made the trademark one of the most popular of all time.

THE POPULARITY OF AUNT JEMIMA

A souvenir booklet published by the R. T. Davis Milling Company re-flected the popularity of Aunt Jemima after her appearance at the 1893

World's Fair. The pamphlet was titled *The Life of Aunt Jemima, the Most Famous Colored Woman in the World.*

An article in *The Poster,* a trade magazine for outdoor advertisers which existed around the turn of the century, reported that Aunt Jemima and the Armour meat chef were the two symbols most trusted by the American housewife (Sacharow, 1982, p. 62). In fact, few food trademarks rivaled them. Their familiarity was often extolled by the advertising industry, the general public, and the companies that represented them. But what exactly made her so popular? It certainly wasn't her good looks. Some writers have posited that Aunt Jemima's appeal centered around her inability to attract any attention from "Massa." Another writer sarcastically suggests that Aunt Jemima's "appeal as a product representative combined nostalgia for lifelong black servitude with modern convenience. Just add a Dixie cupful of water to the pancake mix and presto, access to soul food no longer required integration" (Campbell, 1989, p. 46).

Because of the advertising savvy and shrewd public relations campaigns masterminded by the owners of the Aunt Jemima trademark, the brand experienced extraordinary recognition and recall nationwide. By 1910 the Aunt Jemima trademark was known in every state (Campbell, 1964, p. 41). It was also estimated that by 1918 more than 120 million Aunt Jemima breakfasts were being served annually, according to a *Ladies Home Journal* ad of October 1918.

The trademark unquestionably has become a part of the fabric of America. In fact it could be argued that the phrase "as American as apple pie and baseball" should be expanded to "as American as apple pie, baseball, and Aunt Jemima." One writer comments that "of all the trademarks, Aunt Jemima is by far one of the most appealing and most expressive" (Sacharow, 1982, p. 63).

Despite the success of the Aunt Jemima trademark, the brand did not always have the Midas touch, and failed when "Quaker jumped into the field of packaged cake mixes" (Marquette, 1967, p. 155). After World War II the name was put on two flavors of cake mix distributed to limited areas. Officials at Quaker Oats are still baffled by their failure.

The company tested the cake market again ten years later with ultra-convenient preparations for corn bread and coffee cake. These met with more favorable response and are among the many products carrying the registered trademark today.[5]

Although the Aunt Jemima trademark was not registered until 1903 by Bert Underwood, brother of Charles, it has been used since 1889. Her popularity is so pervasive that others have sought to copy the Aunt Jemima name and image, but the company has been successful in upholding all rights. The last recorded court challenge was in 1917.

However, the trademark has been contested from an ethical standpoint by a different group—black consumers.

THE ANATOMY OF A STEREOTYPE

A historical perspective on the origination of stereotyping will show how it has been applied to blacks and how important it is that the effects of stereotyping be understood as they apply to Aunt Jemima.

The term stereotype was coined by a Frenchman named Didot in 1798. Stereotyping was associated with a printing mechanism that consisted of a plate upon which letters had been cast to create a permanent and unchangeable record (Gordon, 1961). Around 1824 the term was applied in a metaphorical sense because of its association with consistency and monotony.

It was introduced to the general public by Walter Lippmann in 1926. He described it as "an ordered more or less consistent picture of the world to which our habits, our capacities, our comforts and our hopes have adjusted themselves. . . , it is a form of perception which implies a certain character on the data of our senses before the data reach intelligence" (Lippmann, 1926).

F. H. Allport seems to take the concept of stereotype as an attitude a step further and suggests that stereotyping is synonymous with prejudice and can be described as "an oversimplified experience resulting in attitude." (Allport, 1924).

J. Bowes, in his study on "Stereotyping and Communication Accuracy," says stereotypes are images that are fixed and extreme despite changing events (Bowes, 1977).

In a report of the Ninety-fifth Congress on "Age Stereotyping and Television," stereotypes are defined as "simplified, inaccurate conceptions or images which have standardized and are commonly held" (House Select Committee on Aging, 1977).

A commonly accepted definition of stereotypes suggests that they are "the sets of traits that are used to explain and predict the behavior of members of socially defined groups" (Miller, 1982, p. 92). Joseph Boskin of Boston University, who has studied the stereotypical portrayals of black males as "Sambos," defines a stereotype as "a standardized mental picture, or series of pictures, representing an oversimplified opinion or an uncritical judgment that is staggeringly tenacious in its hold over rational thinking" (Martindale, 1986, p. 57).

Based on these definitions, stereotyping results in perception of an extreme consistent nature. It allows for little variation within the target it defines. For purposes of this analysis, a stereotype will be defined as a consistent representation of blacks in advertising via words, images, and situations that ultimately suggests that all members of the race are the same (Kern-Foxworth, 1982, p. 48).

Some researchers theorize that stereotypes may be favorable or pejorative, and thus they may be supported by facts or be false (Ogawa, 1971).

The stereotypes associated with Aunt Jemima are considered negative by most blacks. In fact, this designation has not been confined to blacks, and most social scientists agree that the traditional stereotypes associated with racial and ethnic groups are negative and normally portray those groups in an unfavorable light. "The chief problem with stereotypes of ethnic [and racial] groups is that one character (e.g., Uncle Tom or Fu Manchu) is allowed to stand for a whole diverse collection of human beings" (Farquhar and Doe, 1978). This is particularly true in the case of Aunt Jemima, who is nationally well-known.

Much research has been conducted with special emphasis on the stereotypes associated with blacks. Researchers feel that negative stereotypes hinder the upward mobility of blacks in many ways.

The International Association of Business Communicators published a book, *Without Bias: A Guidebook for Non-Discriminatory Communications,* which makes this comment on stereotyping: "When stereotypic words and images and culturally or racially biased standards appear, they actually perpetuate ethnic and racial bias and inadvertently work against affirmative action goals and policies forbidding discrimination" (Roberts, 1977, p. 6).

Researchers have also found that the mass media play a vital role in the perpetuation of stereotypes. Richard Carter, in his 1962 study on stereotyping, asserts that "the mass media can produce structural change directly by increasing homogeneity of attributes."

Needless to say, the stereotyping of minority groups by the mass media may have negative results. The portrayal of minorities in negative roles provides negative role models for both the minority and the majority and increases the distance between the two, making communication more difficult. Joseph Boskin extends the analysis by suggesting that once a stereotype of a group is solidly etched into American folklore, it becomes permanently "embedded in people's minds and profoundly affects thoughts and actions" (Martindale, 1986, p. 57).

Thus, the stereotypes associated with blacks, earlier versions of Aunt Jemima being among them, have been detrimental and have been influential in developing behavior patterns exhibited by dominant groups toward blacks. The impact of the insidious images presented of black women by the mass media was noted most recently by Audrey Edwards:

The medium is not only the message; it shapes the image, and four of the most powerful media in the last half of the 20th century—television, advertising, music videos and the press itself—have exerted the greatest impact on how black women not only are seen, but have come to view themselves. The message and the image haven't changed much during the black woman's history in America. Both perpetuate the stereotypes. (Edwards, 1993, p. 216)

American popular culture has contained blatant stereotypical depictions of the black woman for a long time. The impact of such images is succinctly explained by Kathleen Jamieson and Karlyn Campbell in *The Interplay of Influence* (1988), wherein they write:

Stereotypes are powerful means of reinforcing societal attitudes about groups of people because the process of stereotyping involves the receiver in creating the message. When the negative attitude that is reinforced . . . blacks, women or elders, and is recognized by spokespersons for that group as destructive, protest will follow because representatives of the stereotyped group fear that the stereotype will reinforce undesirable role models and will perpetuate discrimination against the group.

Lawrence Reddick (1944) specifies 19 basic stereotypical characteristics attributed to blacks:

1. The savage African
2. The happy slave
3. The devoted servant
4. The corrupt politician
5. The irresponsible citizen
6. The social delinquent
7. The petty thief
8. The vicious criminal
9. The sexual superman
10. The unhappy nonwhite
11. The superior athlete
12. The natural-born cook
13. The natural-born musician
14. The perfect entertainer
15. The superstitious churchgoer
16. The chicken and watermelon eater
17. The razor and knife toter
18. The uninhibited expressionist
19. The mental inferior

According to this list, Aunt Jemima meets the criteria for numbers 2, 3, and 12—or, the happy slave, devoted servant, and natural born cook.

Churchill Roberts (1970–71) lists guidelines to test for stereotypes of the black race:

1. happy-go-lucky, clowning, grinning, childlike, soulful, hostile, wary
2. powerful, tall, lithe, flashy, super-sexually endowed, shuffling, dirty
3. rhythmic, athletic, blue-collar
4. untrustworthy, aggressive, angry, violent, dangerous, militant
5. lazy, unmotivated, strong (women), irresponsible (men)
6. hustling, poor, deprived
7. ungrateful, swindling, dependent on society

According to Churchill, Aunt Jemima could be classified as primarily number 1.

Richard Maynard (1974, p. vii), editor of *The Black Man on Film*, contends that most of the stereotypes listed above have been portrayed in one form or another in the mass media. They are thus vividly reinforced in society, generation after generation. This perception was reinforced by Gordon W. Allport in *The Nature of Prejudice* when he wrote, "Stereotypes are socially supported, continually reviewed and hammered in, by our media of mass communication—by novels, short stories, newspaper items, movies, stage, radio and television" (1960, p. 200).

In his interpretive history of blacks in American films, Donald Bogle (1973) outlines five descriptive stereotypes that have been featured in American motion pictures: the Tom, the coon, the tragic mulatto, the mammy, and the brutal black buck. In explanation of the fourth he offers the following:

The fourth stereotype is the mammy, the female counterpart of the comic coon. She is usually big, fat, cantankerous, and fiercely independent. Much later in time she becomes the Aunt Jemima, less headstrong than the mammy—sweet, jolly, good-tempered.

The black mammy also is a central figure in Eugene Genovese's *Roll, Jordan, Roll* (1974). Genovese affords her a more superior position within the plantation household than most historians. He conjectures that the black mammy during slavery was not as much a servant as she is often depicted. "She was loyal to 'her' white family, but far from 'serving' it, she ran the Big House as the plantation mistress's executive officer or her 'de facto' superior. Her important roles and the white family's devotion to her made her a powerful woman" (Morton, 1991, p. 102).

Genovese's attempt to restore the credibility of the mammy runs throughout his book and is replete with themes suggesting that slavery was a paternalistic institution wherein all blacks and whites looked out and cared for each other fervently.

Mammies did not often have to worry about being sold or about having their husbands or children sold. The sacrifices they made for the white man earned them genuine affection in return, which provided a guarantee of protection, safety, and privilege for their own children. The relationship between the Mammies and their white folks exhibited that reciprocity so characteristic of paternalism. (p. 357)

James Anderson (1976) in a book review of *Roll, Jordan, Roll*, rebuked the assessment of the mammy given by Genovese and retorts that it "is Aunt Jemima sugar-coated in Marlian dialectics." Despite all of the negatives associated with stereotyping, it is functional within society. Present-day researchers theorize that

the major function of attaching labels to different racial and ethnic groups is to impose order on a chaotic social environment. The simplest and most widely used criteria are those that are immediately apprehended such as skin color, size, facial features, body shapes, nonverbal behavior and language. (Miller, 1982, p. 95)

The social world is divided into intelligible units by using categorical labels. Note the stereotypical labels that blacks and whites have assigned to each other (Miller, 1982, p. 95).

Blacks' View of

Blacks	*Whites*
Intelligent	Deceitful
Very religious	Sly
Sportsmanlike	Treacherous
Loud	Dirty
Pleasure-loving	Industrious
Athletic	Lazy
Sense of rhythm	Cruel
Lazy	Selfish
Superstitious	Nervous
	Conceited

Whites' View of

Blacks	*Whites*
Lazy	Industrious
Superstitious	Intelligent
Ignorant	Materialistic
Loud	Ambitious
Musical	Pleasure-loving
Poor	Efficient
Stupid	Individualistic
Dirty	Neat
Peace-loving	Clean
Happy-go-lucky	Good manners
Very religious	
Feel inferior	
Pleasure-loving	
Militant	
Proud	

The criteria for these divisions is either learned or created and is necessary for classifying people into groups and the maintenance of the status quo in reference to those groups. The one stereotype that has been the most prolific, the ultimate stereotype, has been that of Aunt Jemima. She was and is the stereotype of the black woman, multiplied a millionfold in advertising, cartoons, films, television, and books—for white Americans, an easygoing, non-threatening figure reminiscent of a distant past; for African Americans, a symbol of the denigration and domestication of black identity and of the way blacks have been reduced to functionaries in white fantasies (Pieterse, 1992, p. 155).

Dissension from the Black Race

Dissension from the black race relative to the portrayal of blacks in advertising can be documented as early as the 1920s and became more intense as blacks realized their power as consumers.

During the 1920s dissension relative to the Aunt Jemima trademark was revealed. To ascertain the reactions of blacks a study was conducted using two Aunt Jemima advertisements. Both were similar in mechanical arrangement and utilized the same fundamental selling appeals. The primary difference between them was that one had an illustration of Aunt Jemima prominently displayed, while in the other the pancakes were the center of attention. The test was conducted in Nashville and Richmond with 15 housewives and the heads of 15 families from four occupation classifications: (1) common and semi-skilled labor, (2) skilled labor, (3) business, and (4) professional. Each individual was instructed to pick out which advertisement caught his or her attention more quickly and thoroughly (Edwards, 1932). The results of the study revealed these responses to the ad with Aunt Jemima prominently featured:

A. Common and semi-skilled labor—males:
    1. Don't like reference in reading matter to Aunt Jemima's master.
    2. Because dislike pictures of Aunt Jemima with towel around head.
    3. Appearance of Aunt Jemima and log cabin sufficient to keep me from buying flour.
    4. This kind of advertisement always reminds me of slavery.
    5. Plays upon former slavery of Negroes.
    6. Picture of cook exaggerates color of Negro.
    7. Plays upon idea of Negro in slavery too much.
    8. Don't like Aunt Jemima with rag on head.
    9. Not lifelike.
    10. Would not look at it twice because of picture.

B. Common and semi-skilled labor—females:
    1. Don't like either the log cabin or picture of Aunt Jemima.
    2. Aunt Jemima dressed with rag on head and handkerchief on neck.
    3. Picture of Aunt Jemima actually keeps me from buying the flour.
    4. Picture reminds me of slavery.
    5. No. I have never bought Aunt Jemima flour, because it pertains to slavery type of Negro.
    6. Don't like slave idea of advertisement.
    7. Picture of Aunt Jemima not to my taste. We cooks do not look like that.
    8. Don't like idea of painting Negroes as they appeared fifty years ago.
    9. I dislike cabin, Aunt Jemima, and references to slavery.
    10. Not interested in picture of black mammy.
    11. Not interested. Don't like head rag and bandanna. Colored people don't wear them now. Don't see why they keep such pictures before the public.
C. Skilled labor—males:
    1. After seeing disgraceful picture of Aunt Jemima I am not interested.
    2. I dislike the colored cook's picture.
    3. Illustration of Aunt Jemima utterly disgusts me.
    4. I don't like slave picture of log cabin and "black mammy."
    5. Not necessary to portray colored woman so prominently.
    6. Slave-time picture arouses my distaste.
    7. After seeing the picture of slavery days I would not buy the product.
    8. This gives impression Aunt Jemima was a slave.
    9. Picture of old-time colored cook objectionable. Illiterate class.
    10. Because picture of colored cook is objectionable.
    11. Picture of Aunt Jemima would always be a detriment.
    12. Colored pictures arouse antagonism.
D. Skilled labor—females:
    1. I made my opinion about slave advertisements a long time ago and the picture of Aunt Jemima would make me pass it by.
    2. I don't like idea of playing upon subject of slavery.
    3. Picture so "old-time" and dressed for slavery—does not attract me.
    4. Dislike slave pictures in advertisements referring to white people.
    5. I dislike pictures which refer to the slavery of Negroes.
    6. Dislike "black mammy" type of picture of Aunt Jemima.
    7. Don't like colored characters in advertisements. Always shown as menials.
    8. Don't like Aunt Jemima in head rag.
E. Business—males:
    1. I have a prejudice against the picture of Aunt Jemima.
    2. Upon seeing crude picture of Aunt Jemima I would not look again to see what she is advertising.
    3. Having seen the slave advertisement I would not be interested in the flour.
    4. I am prejudiced intensely against any picture of former slave mammy.
    5. Don't like way colored woman is dressed.
    6. Wouldn't read it. Hate it.
    7. Don't like picture of Aunt Jemima. This type of picture is out of date.

F. Business—females:
   1. Log cabin and picture of Negro slave woman turns me against the flour.
   2. I am against the use of old-time Negro mammy.
   3. After seeing the disgraceful advertisement and reference to slavery I would not be interested in it.
   4. After seeing the picture of slave "mammy" I would not be interested.
   5. I dislike the slavery idea of this illustration.
   6. Picture of Negro "mammy" would keep me from reading advertisement.
   7. Don't like illustration. Would not look at it twice.
   8. Don't like exploitation of colored people. Whenever I see a picture such as this I am prejudiced against product.
   9. Don't care for colored picture at all.
  10. Don't care for illustration—old-time cook.
G. Professional—males:
   1. I would not be interested in it, as it seems to illustrate slavery.
   2. I am not accustomed to noticing pictures of this sort.
   3. I do not care for the picture of Negro woman dressed as this one is.
   4. I positively hate this illustration.
   5. The log cabin and colored woman cause me to lose interest in the brand of pancake flour.
   6. I don't like ignorant type shown in illustration.
   7. Attempt is made to exploit lowest type colored character.
   8. Would not look at advertisement when I saw colored picture.
H. Professional—females:
   1. I am deeply prejudiced against this type of advertisement.
   2. I hate the picture of Aunt Jemima, the log cabin, and the idea that all colored women are cooks.
   3. Aunt Jemima's picture makes me disregard it.
   4. I have always disliked this advertisement.
   5. I would not care to read advertisement after seeing illustration.
   6. The "mammy" picture prejudices me against this.
   7. Not interested in ignorant colored cook.
   8. Don't like colored woman—head rag and bandanna.
   9. Attracts attention, but arouses antagonism. Don't like head rag.
  10. Objectionable colored picture. Woman with head rag and bandanna.

The second advertisement received the larger number of votes, but by a scant 2.5 percent majority. In gaining this majority, however, the votes came only from the housewives in each city. Looking at the total responses received, support for this advertisement was greater from the laboring classes than from either the business or professional classes. Nevertheless, the advertisement where Aunt Jemima dominated the picture did capture the attention of the respondents more quickly than the one where her presence was miniscule. "Just the presence of the Negro woman in the illustration was sufficient in many cases to gain attention quickly and thoroughly; in other cases it was the 'historical' figure of Aunt Jemima" (Edwards, 1932, p. 229).

During the civil rights movement, in the era of black nationalism, Eldridge Cleaver (1968) vehemently voiced his opposition to Aunt Jemima, claiming that she, like so many other black women, was a traitor to black American racial pride, identity, values, and legacy. He accused the symbol of consorting with the enemy in the defeat of black America and asserted that "the black woman is an unconsenting ally and she may not even realize it—but the white man sure does" (p. 162). Cleaver's attack on Aunt Jemima was reinforced by another writer who surmised, "In the 1960s Aunt Jemima was the name the black-power movement used for what it called the female equivalent of Uncle Tom" (Berry, 1991, p. 9A).

Among the artifacts belonging to Alex Haley auctioned on October 1, 2, and 3, 1992, at the Conference Center of the University of Tennessee-Knoxville, was the original typescript of *The Autobiography of Malcolm X*. The edited manuscripts of *The Autobiography of Malcolm X* were procured by Detroit-based entertainment attorney, Gregory J. Reed. The manuscript, which commanded the highest price ever paid for an unpublished work of an African-American, contained a chapter titled "The Negro," which was mysteriously omitted from the published text (Patton, 1993, p. 82). The following is an excerpt of that chapter as it appeared in the *The New York Observer*, April 19, 1993 and conveys quite clearly the thoughts of Malcolm X on Aunt Jemima:

Instead of so much effort to escape being black, so much trying to be like the white man, he [the black man] might have the sense to wake up from his sleep and put to use for himself the image that the white man won't let him escape. Take the fact, consider the fact that three centuries of white people have loved black cooking so much that hardly any image is planted deeper in the American mind. Aunt Jemima, beaming and black—used by the white man—has sold billions of pancakes. Her counterpart, Uncle Ben, has sold shiploads of rice—for the white man. Where is the black money pooled into an industry hiring blacks in the total processing of frozen black Southern cooking that could share in the frozen food millions?

Where is this nation's black-owned chains of black-cooking restaurants? In the fall of 1963, Aunt Jemima moved from boxed pancake flour to a nation-spanning restaurant franchise. Among the features are 37 different kinds of pancakes and fried chicken that, according to the fill-page ad's copywriter, 'reduces a southern senator to tears.'

Guess who franchises the chain of Aunt Jemima restaurants?

The activism of the civil rights movement, the resistance to police brutality coupled with the assertiveness of the Black Power movement thus made it almost impossible to portray African-Americans as loyal, servile, but happy Aunt Jemimas and Uncle Moses [Aunt Jemima's husband]. Americans had only to turn on their television sets: It was obvious that Aunt Jemima and Uncle Mose were out marching, battling police dogs, and burning down Watts. . . . The militant Angela Davis traded places with

Aunt Jemima and Malcolm X attempted to put Uncle Mose to rest. (Goings, 1990, p. B76)

Cleaver and Malcolm X were not the only blacks to direct their attention toward advertising during this turbulent period in history. Black leaders sought equality for all in many areas, including housing, employment, voting, and advertising. One researcher assessed the dissatisfaction in reference to advertising in this manner:

Among their complaints were the facts that blacks were being used to advertise white men's products, thus making the white man rich, that the blacks used in ads were not made up well and did not show the Negro in complimentary ways, and that for some Americans, these ads, . . . constituted their first impression of the black race. Thus, it is true that when we speak of the black American in advertising, we speak of prejudice. (Reno, 1986, p. 2)

The Balch Institute for Ethnic Studies in Philadelphia and the Anti-Defamation League of B'nai B'rith cosponsored a 1984 exhibition of racial and ethnic images in advertising. Composed of more than 300 items, it displayed magazine advertisements, posters, storyboards for television commercials, and trade cards. In a publication designed to complement the show titled *Ethnic Images in Advertising*," Mark Stolarik, executive director of the institute, wrote:

In the early years they [advertisements] were usually crude and condescending images that appealed to largely Anglo-American audiences who found it difficult to reconcile their own vision of beauty, order and behavior with that of non-Anglo-Americans. Later, these images were softened because of complaints from the ethnic groups involved and the growing sophistication of the advertising industry. (Stern, 1984, p. 1)

Another exhibit centered around the portrayal of blacks in advertising is scheduled for 1994. Ruby Jackson, executive director of Black Archives of Mid-America in Kansas City, Missouri, indicated that the museum was planning an exhibit centered around black Americans in 1994. The exhibit titled, "Advertising and the Black American: 100 Years from Shame to Fame" will feature advertisements like Bull Durham, as well as more contemporary advertisements. In discussing the relevancy of the exposition she stated,

We were supposed to be funny. But it has undermined our quest for equality and assimilation. Today, advertisers recognize that we are an important market. Now advertising depicts doctors and engineers and wholesome family members. This transition from grotesque, Aunt Jemima and Uncle Ben, to today is a story we want to tell. (Sturgis, 1993, p. 22)

Physical Attributes of Aunt Jemima

The physical attributes of the original versions of Aunt Jemima were totally the opposite of how white America traditionally defined beauty. She was very dark-skinned, had extremely broad features, and was extremely overweight—a far cry from the thin, blond, blue-eyed, Barbie type heralded as the standard of beauty for decades. One writer described the original face of Aunt Jemima used in 1889 as a "frightening caricature of a black mammy" (Morgan, 1986, p. 55).

Karen Jewell examined the processes that evolved to create the mythical image of black females in her 1976 dissertation, "An Analysis of the Visual Development of a Stereotype: The Media's Portrayal of Mammy and Aunt Jemima as Symbols of Black Womanhood." Her assertion was that historically the mass media depicted black women as mammy and Aunt Jemima, and that these images perpetuated stereotypes that have ultimately been assigned to all black women, regardless of social class, financial stability, or age. Smith further argues that

these images of black women suggest that they are lacking in beauty, femininity, attractiveness, and other attributes generally associated with womanhood. In addition, the images suggest that black women are satisfied with their lives and want nothing better for themselves or their families. (Smith, 1988, p. 235)

A study by Juanita Sheperd (1980) suggested that black women are underrepresented in advertising in the popular press. According to her analysis, this is caused by (1) their physical characteristics, which are contrary to the definition of American beauty, and (2) their relatively limited buying power.

Having a very matronly appearance, Aunt Jemima was consciously portrayed as an asexual, unattractive being. Everyone pictured her as the motherly type—but not the type to marry. This stereotype has been perpetuated not only through advertising, but by television as well. Examples include Louise on "The Jeffersons," the mother on "What's Happening?", and Sapphire and her mother on "Amos 'n' Andy."

To conform to the mammy stereotype, the promoters purposely made the Aunt Jemima character obese. Historians and writers have been quite diplomatic in their discussions of Aunt Jemima, and have refrained from describing her as "fat." Instead, they have used other adjectives to camouflage her size:

". . . which featured a plump Aunt Jemima on the box" (Wilson and Gutierrez, 1985, p. 114)

". . . big-bottomed mammy" (Sacharow, 1982)

". . . her portly appearance remained essentially the same" (Stern, 1984, p. 18)

". . . the overweight, good-humored but unsophisticated Anna Robinson" (Marquette, 1967, p. 139)

"She was a massive woman with the face of an angel" (Marquette, 1967, p. 153)

"Never to be forgotten was the day they loaded 350 pounds of Anna Robinson on the Twentieth Century Limited" (Marquette, 1967, p. 154)

It is interesting that visual depictions offer more denigrating images than portrayals in prose. Janet Sims-Wood (1988), in the article "The Black Female: Mammy, Jemima, Sapphire, and Other Images," opines that these characterizations are often very harsh as presented by the mass media, and "are usually pictured as obese in unattractive or tattered clothing and bossy and stern while at the same time somewhat comical," yet she suggests that "literature generally depicts the mammy and Aunt Jemima as loving, caring, productive and vital in society" (p. 236).

The mammy image has enthralled Americans for decades. Since the time of slavery she has taken care of "massa" and "missus" and the kids as well. "The Black Mammy filled any gap that occurred in the southern household" (Hine, 1990, p. 1025). It has become one of the most common depictions of black women in American history. "One of the most persistent images of black women in media remains that of the nonthreatening desexualized mammy figure" (Edwards, 1993, p. 216). The portrayal has become so much a part of American culture that it has been representative of American womanhood from times of slavery to the present. And Aunt Jemima has been so skillfully advertised and marketed that she has prolonged "mammy's" influence on American history, culture, and folklore.

To understand the mystique and to get a grasp of her influence one need only visit the French Quarter in New Orleans. Even today it is easy to buy candy, Aunt Sally's in particular, with a mammy figure on the package. The list of additional items that can be purchased is quite extensive: dolls, banks, aprons, baskets, butter churns, bathroom plungers, refrigerator magnets—all emblazoned with the face of a heavy-set black woman clad in a red polka-dot bandanna and matching dress with apron, reminiscent of Aunt Jemima. Such items can also be purchased all over America in antique shops, flea markets, craft shops, and general stores.

Black and white consumers caught up in the myth continue to purchase the products, never consciously considering the ramifications of the image and its relevance to the status of contemporary black womanhood. "They were so familiar that few people had any notion that they degraded black Americans. Most people thought the caricatures were simply funny" (Lemmons, 1977, p. 103).

It is difficult to understand how fervently Southerners tried to hold on to the comforting allure of the mammy concept without mentioning the Black Mammy Memorial Movement. In 1911 *The Banner,* a white newspaper in

Athens, Georgia, reported a general Southern movement, with specific reference to Texas, to establish monuments and memorials to the "old Black Mammies of the South." According to *The Banner,* this movement had inspired a group of leading white citizens of Athens to form the Black Mammy Memorial Association in 1910. The association then spearheaded a project to charter and solicit funds in support of the Black Mammy Memorial Institute. The purpose of the institute was to train young blacks in domestic skills and "moral attitudes that were generally associated with 'old black mammy' in the south" (Patton, 1980, p. 150).

Samuel F. Harris, a founder of the black industrial evening school, was chosen as principal of the institute. He and four other blacks knowledgeable in industrial education comprised the primary members of the institute's board of colored directors, which served under the white board of trustees. On September 19, 1910, nine outstanding white citizens of Athens filed a petition for a charter with the clerk of the Superior Court of Clark County to establish the institute. In an attempt to raise funds, the Black Mammy Memorial Association published a 14-page pamphlet that gave details pertinent to the institute's history, purpose, and course curriculum. It stated that the institute was "a living monument where the sons and daughters of these distinctively Southern characters may be trained in the arts and industries that made the 'old Black Mammy' valuable and worthy of the tender memory of the South" (Patton, 1980, p. 153). Appealing to the nostalgic desires of Southerners, the writers asked the prospective donors:

Did you not have an "Old Black Mammy" who loved and cared for you in the days of your youth whose memory and spirit you want perpetuated? We would like to make this monument representative and worthy of the ideals and traditions of the "Great South." May we not ask your subscription to this great monument? The appeal is to Southerners. (Patton, 1980, p. 153)

The institute was chartered for twenty years, which would have necessitated a renewal in 1930. However, the racial climate during the 1930s and the view of most blacks toward slavery and any images associated with it probably undermined any attempt to renew the charter.

Enamored with the mystical image of mammy, in 1923 the Daughters of the Confederacy suggested that Congress set aside in the Capitol a site upon which they could erect a bronze monument in recognition of the "Black Mammy" ("Black Mammy," 1923, p. 4). Members of the black community became irate at the thought of honoring a concept that was denigrating to black womanhood and indicative of black servitude. Blacks suggested that a "better memorial would be to extend the full rights of American citizenship to the descendants of these Mammies" (*Washington Tribune,* 1923). The proposals made by the blacks included discontinuation of lynching, inequality in educational facilities, all discriminatory practices, and humiliation of blacks in public conveyances, and granting the right to vote. The pressure brought by various black leaders and groups was so fierce that the monument proposal was eventually killed in the House of Representatives (Parkhurst, 1938, pp. 349–350).

The petition was defeated "but in the 1930s, 1940s, and 1950s Hollywood film producers and New York advertising agencies built their own monuments to mammy. With their films, their pancake boxes, and their syrup bottles, they imprinted the image of mammy on the American pysche more indelibly than ever before" (White, 1985, p. 165).

Barbara Christian, author of *Black Women Novelists: The Development of a Tradition, 1892–1976* (1980), offers an even more vivid description of the black mammy and lists certain characteristics that can serve as a litmus test when trying to determine whether a caricature is a mammy image or not— black, fat with huge breasts, head covered with a kerchief to hide her nappy hair, strong, kind, loyal, sexless, religious, and superstitious.

In response to the objections raised by the black community, Aunt Jemima accomplished what millions of Americans have been trying to do unsuccessfully for years—she lost weight and reversed the aging process. "Unquestionably, there have been changes in the traditional images of mammy, Aunt Jemima. . . . The major changes that were made in the mammy image affected her physical characteristics more than her emotional makeup" (Jewell, 1993, p. 183).

The metamorphosis of Aunt Jemima did not go unnoticed. The dramatic change was recorded by several writers. The following analyses note the disparities in the role currently being played by Aunt Jemima:

She lost about 150 pounds, dropped 40 years, got herself a new headdress and moved from the plantation to New Orleans. It took more than 80 years, but the symbol on the label of the best selling pancake mix made the transformation from freed slave cook to Creole cooking teacher. (Scripps Howard, 1987, p. 1E)

The portrait on the current box is a younger, slimmer image of a black housewife. While the Quaker Oats Company, which has owned Aunt Jemima Mills since 1926, has transformed an outmoded representation of a black "mammy" to a younger, more upbeat stereotype, she is still recognizably Aunt Jemima. (Stern, 1984, p. 18)

Over the years Aunt Jemima has lost some weight, but the stereotyped face of the black servant continues to be featured on the box. (Wilson and Gutierrez, 1985, p. 114)

Aunt Jemima was redesigned from the familiar "mammy" character, making her slimmer and more youthful. (Hall, 1984, p. 30)

To make her image more appealing to blacks, she lost over 100 pounds, became 40 years younger, got a new headdress and moved from the Higbee Plantation to New Orleans. In essence, she was transformed from a caricature of a black mammy to a savvy creole cooking instructor. (Kern-Foxworth, 1988, p. 20)

Aunt Jemima no longer looks like Scarlett O'Hara's trusted Mammy. Gone is the head rag, apron and billowing housedress. Jemima is now a slimmed down house professional with a neatly coiffed hairstyle and attire that comes pretty close to looking like business dress. It may not be a revolution, but it's a start. (Edwards, 1993, p. 222)

James Anderson, in a 1976 review of Eugene Genovese's *Roll, Jordan, Roll* (1974), references the author's tendency to romanticize the role of the mammy during slavery. In his essay he posits this synopsis of the reformation of Aunt Jemima:

Many Americans, especially Afro-Americans, remember when Aunt Jemima appeared on pancake boxes in rather crude form. Then came the black power movement, espousing nationalistic ideology and black pride, and old Aunt Jemima was transfigured by bright and shining colors. . . . Underneath the bright colors Aunt Jemima stood for the same pillar of the black community, a durable black woman who took her cooking for the good white people as a matter of personal honor and pride, who sometimes swore and kicked, but never presented any serious challenge to the social system that oppressed her because of her dim political awareness. The changing of her form was meant to make her at once a spirit of accommodation in a symbol of black pride. Though her complexion had been presumably improved, her heart remained the same. The transformation, however, was enough to call for new resolutions of the tensions between dignity and oppression. While many could understand the embodiment of contradictions in a single process, questions were raised as to the predominant forces within Aunt Jemima. (p. 99)

The ghost of Aunt Jemima and mammy still haunt black women despite their success. In 1986 Oprah Winfrey became offended when "Saturday Night Live" producer Lorne Michaels wanted her to open the show with a sketch in which she played Aunt Jemima about to be laid off from Quaker Oats (Edwards, 1993, p. 215). At that time *People* magazine had reported that Winfrey had earned in excess of $11 million in that year. Although Winfrey refused to play the part and opted to open the show with a sketch that showed her getting into an argument with Michaels over the skit, it reinforced the notion that regardless of how much fame, how much money and prestige a black woman gets, in the end she is still but yet another Aunt Jemima. "The attempt by the white male producer of 'Saturday Night Live' to reduce the highest paid, most successful daytime talk show host to the role of mammy by casting her as Aunt Jemima not only reeked of racist, sexist stereotyping, but underscored a deeper, more primal insecurity" (Edwards, 1993, p. 217).

The author of the story reporting the incident regarding Oprah Winfrey further asserts that, "Even Oprah Winfrey's media success may be in large measure a reflection of America's love for the quintessential maid or mammy figure—the big, warm-hearted black woman is a natural in a medium as intimate as the television talk show format" (Edwards, 1993, p. 216).

Aunt Jemima's Headdress

The traditional headwear worn by Aunt Jemima may have been offensive to blacks because it reminded them of a demeaning period in their ancestry. The red bandanna worn by the original Aunt Jemima was symbolic of slavery. The formal name for the scarf is a *chignon*, a French word that actually refers to a different fashion, in which the hair is rolled to the back of the head.

To understand the resentment held by blacks for the headpiece, it is important to trace the origin of the practice of women wearing kerchiefs wrapped around the head. The practice began during slavery and was one of the devices used to put blacks in their place:

The clothes worn by the plantation slaves were simple. . . . Women wore full gathered skirts and tight bodice, sometimes adding spotless white neckerchiefs, aprons and tignons [chignons]. This headgear is said to have been brought to Louisiana from Martinique and San Domingo and evidence of this is borne out by the old family portraits of beautiful women with Madras kerchiefs bound about their heads. White women discontinued wearing the tignon in 1786, when a legal manifesto was issued, designating this headdress as the only one that might be worn by free women of color. These women, many of them beautiful and perfectly white in appearance, had caused so much disturbance in the colony by attracting the attention of white men that the law was issued, barring them from wearing hats or plumes or jewels, and designed to render them less attractive. It is said, however, that the tignons increased their beauty and made them more appealing than ever. (Saxon et al., 1987, p. 238)

Because the kerchief is such an important part of the Aunt Jemima persona, she has in some cases been dubbed "handkerchief head" (Warren, 1988, p. 56).

The Language of Aunt Jemima

During Reconstruction there was a dramatic increase in the publication of newspapers and magazines and thus an increase in advertising. Consequently, as blacks began to attain mobility and purchasing power, thousands of advertisements were designed to appeal to black and white Americans—

either drawings of blacks using and selling products or products designed for blacks only. Unfortunately, "the language of the ads was often 'bastardized' black English" (Brasch, 1981, p. 114).

Indeed the proliferation of the mass media spun a new era in the portrayal of blacks, and attention was focused not only on how they looked and what they said but also on how they said it. During this time, the nonstandard English patterns of blacks were accepted and expected.[6] Thus a stereotypical representation was perpetuated in language and verse, and "most literary representations of blacks were distortions of reality, butchered by incompetent writers" (Brasch, 1981 p. xiii).

With an increase in population growth, advertising expanded into more specialized forms. Flyers and advertising postcards with statements written in black English became widespread. These forms of advertising were less expensive than others, and the results were very effective. Along with sheet music covers of earlier black music and printed sermons in black dialect, these flyers have been lost in the annals of history. "Of the millions printed, only a few—now yellowed and torn, and usually secreted away in museums and attics—remain to help later generations understand the language and culture of an earlier different America" (Brasch, 1981, p. 115).

Was language an important element in analyzing the psychological effects of advertising during the period before and after Reconstruction? More specifically, did the bastardized language used by Aunt Jemima have any effect on the black psyche during that period? Roger D. Abrahams, a leading folklorist and black English scholar, observes:

In the controversy over the "legitimacy" of the speech of Afro-Americans in the United States we tend to forget that a person's image of himself is intimately bound up with the ways in which he chooses to talk. To criticize a way of speaking, or to denigrate it any way, is to attack the image a person has of himself. (Abrahams, 1977, p. 13)

During the 1960s America was rampant with civil unrest and despair. Blacks were being led in nonviolent protest by Dr. Martin Luther King, Jr. It was the time of rioting in Newark, Detroit, and Chicago. The overwhelming theme of the time was black pride, and blacks everywhere were chanting, "Say it out loud, I'm black and I'm proud" and "Black is beautiful." Blacks wore dashikis and afro hairstyles as symbols of their self-esteem. It was also during this time that blacks noted the symbolic power of language in their lives and sought the elimination of derogatory language from their history. Symbols have always been an integral part of black culture and have provided the fabric necessary to bridge the gap between self-defeat and self-esteem. Lance Morrow, a columnist for *Time*, wrote:

In the service of black morale, symbols are immensely important. . . . If they can only imagine themselves working as menials, then they will probably subside into that fate following that peasant logic by which son follows father into a genetic destiny. . . . Symbols can bring change. They have real power in the world. (Morrow, 1984, p. 84)

Even the name Aunt Jemima is highly symbolic and has negative connotations. The term "aunt" was used to refer to an elderly black woman during the early 1800s (Partridge, 1984). It was supposed to connote the closeness, affection, and trust in which black servants were held despite the lowly status to which they were relegated (Stern, 1984, p. 18). The practice of calling blacks "aunt" became popular because slaves were never called "Mr." or "Mrs."; "aunt" and "uncle" were used to address them. The use of such designations were continued "in all forms of popular culture well into the twentieth century" (Atwan et al., 1979, p. 92).

Jemima was a name that had different meanings during various times in history. Originally Jemima was a feminine name with historical beginnings in the Arabic and Hebrew languages. Only when it became Americanized was the trait of obesity added. The word also defined a chamber pot during the nineteenth and early part of the twentieth century, a servant girl during the nineteenth century, and a dressmaker's dummy from 1880 to 1930 (Chapman, 1986, p. 615).

The name Jemima has not always had a negative connotation. In *Black Women for Beginners* (1993), Saundra Sharp offers a glossary of terms germane to black women in which she notes the following:

AUNT JEMIMA: One of the most recognized symbols of the happy "mammy" used to market pancakes and other domestic products to whites since the 1880s. The name Jemimah once had esteem as the eldest of Job's (the Bible) daughters and as a city in ancient Arabia named after its queen. (p. 38)

From Aunt Jemima's inception, her language was clearly far from standard English. The slogan coined by the R. T. Davis Milling Company around the turn of the century for use in the advertising campaign was "I'se in town, Honey." In time "her audience took up the phrase and it became the catchline of the Fair [the Chicago World's Fair of 1893]" (Marquette, 1967, p. 146).

Advertising was one of the mechanisms used to enslave blacks. Although many have scorned the derogatory pictorials used in earlier advertising featuring blacks, researchers have seldom examined the words and their presentation by the graphic artists and copywriters.

Dawn Reno, an author and collector of black memorabilia, succinctly explained the effects of using distorted language in earlier advertisements when she wrote, "When the ads became more explicit and their 'characters' talked, it was always in a bastardized version of the English language. Such is the way prejudice is taught and maintained as a standard way of life" (1986).

In a book that scrutinizes the psychology of the "Sambo" image assigned to black males, Joseph Boskin alludes to the crude language used by Rastus (Cream of Wheat) and Aunt Jemima when advertising their products. He notes that they were "always clean, ready to serve with a crisp smile, . . . and distinctively southern in their spoken words" (1986, p. 139). Boskin's reference to a "southern" dialect suggests that the language was improper and poor.

Examples of the irregular dialect and broken speech patterns are illustrated in the advertising scenario below, from a 1918 issue of the *Ladies Home Journal*.

Aunt Jemima: "Seems like I'se needed 'roun' heah."

Young boy: "We don't get pancakes often enough," he shouts while holding a sign that reads, "We want Aunt Jemima pancakes."

Father: "And we want those delicious Aunt Jemimas," shouts the father while holding a sign that reads, "Vote for Aunt Jemima."

Aunt Jemima: "Dey say I'se helped mo' mothers win de lovin' votes dan any other cook in de world. Dat's cuz nothin' is happier eatin' dan my scrumptious tender pancakes."

Honey, it's easy to be de sweetheart o' yo' family. Yo' know how de men folks an' de young folks all loves my tasty pancakes. An' yo' can make dem fo' dem jiffy-quick, an' jus' right everytime, wid my magic ready-mix," she says as she smiles toward the mother and points to a box of Aunt Jemima pancakes.

The family sits around the table while Aunt Jemima serves her pancakes and sings "Pancakes Days Is Happy Days."

Ironically, Aunt Jemima's dialect, although ridiculed by whites, may have influenced white Southern speech. The linguist J. L. Dillard asserts that the Southern dialect has a strong African-American influence and that the black Southern mammy was the primary mode of transmission to whites. "During his travels in the United States in 1842 Charles Dickens observed that the women he met in the South 'speak more or less like Negroes, from having been constantly in their childhood with a black nurse" (Patton, 1993, p. 82). Today Aunt Jemima's speech patterns resemble those of a sophisticated English teacher.

The Stereotypical Situation: The Plantation

Most of the advertising copy created for Aunt Jemima revolved around a fictitious plantation, a setting that embodied all of the stereotypes associated with slavery. Such associations did not conjure up pleasant reminiscences for blacks. It is important to understand the rudimentary underpinnings of the role plantations have had in the development of black stereotypes. The correlation is explained by Walter Stephan and David Rosenfield in "Racial and Ethnic Stereotypes":

> Many aspects of the stereotypes of both groups [blacks and whites] can be traced to the role relationships involved in the plantation system and its successors in the South. The plantation evolved on the frontiers of America as a way of organizing agriculture for the production of a commercial staple resident labor force. Where land was plentiful but labor was scarce, the planters turned to indentured servants and later to slaves. . . . The concept of race and the stereotypes associated with it enabled the dominant group to view members of the subordinate group as inferior beings, and to treat them accordingly. Whites attempted to divest blacks of their traditions and language under the plantation system. This means that the stereotypes of blacks and whites were determined by the nature of the contact between the groups to a greater degree than was the case for ethnic groups in America that retained more of their traditions. The economic roles that blacks performed and the conditions under which they were forced to live became prime determinants of how they were viewed by the dominant group. It was inherent in a system of forced labor that slaves would be regarded as lazy, because there were few positive incentives for work. (1982, p. 98)

Because their maintenance was provided for in the most minimal manner, slaves were seen as unkempt and dirty. The education of slaves was actually illegal in nearly every state in the South. This fact, combined with the limited exposure blacks had to the wider white society, led to their being regarded as ignorant.

The almost total dependence of the subordinate group, together with the paternalistic attitude of the dominant group, led blacks to be viewed as if they were in a state of perpetual childhood. . . . The result was that blacks were characterized as pleasure loving and happy-go-lucky. The reluctance of blacks to display anger and resentment toward members of the dominant group, for fear of being punished, reinforced the view that they were happy with their situation.

Almost all of the references made by writers to the disposition of Aunt Jemima refer to her in this manner, suggesting that she was smiling and happy at all times—a state which blacks closely associate with slavery, an acquired disposition that was a must for survival during the era of plantations and masters. Nagueyalti Warren (1988), a noted author on black American culture, while acknowledging the strong similarities between Aunt Jemima and mammy, suggests, "Whereas the mammy is often irascible, Aunt Jemima is characterized as sweet, jolly, and even-tempered. Jemima is polite, never headstrong like mammy" (p. 56).

One researcher describes this "always laughing" disposition as an illusionary pre-encounter and suggests that the "illusionary pre-encounter ethnic expressions might also be thought of as operative compromise between pre-encounter and encounter ethnicity." He further asserts that "the motto of the expressive styles of illusionary pre-encounter seeks to be, 'You gotta do with what you got, and if you living in a white man's world, why, then you do everything you hafta to get the most you can . . . and you keep on laughing" (Guffy, 1971).

No one has captured the seemingly docile, yet cunning disposition of blacks during slavery better than Maya Angelou in the poem "Song for Old Ones" (1981). In the poem Angelou colorfully describes how the docile and submissive African forefathers in their "Uncle Tom" characters and "Aunt Jemima" smiles used their wit to live through over a quarter of a century of brutality (p. 53).

Despite the objections of the black community to the Aunt Jemima trademark, it has survived for more than 100 years. Aunt Jemima is reminiscent of a period in history that blacks and whites alike would rather forget, but the product still has stability. "Even in these post-plantation days, Aunt Jemima still appears on the package and suggests southern hospitality, making the southern black woman one of the best cooks in the land" (Sacharow, 1982, p. 63). The author further remarks that the product has been shown to be used by more blacks than whites. The author does not expand on this assertion, and there is no actual product mentioned. Another study did note that while 23 percent of white families purchased Aunt Jemima corn meal, only 3 percent of black families did so (Assael, 1987).

William Rasberry, a nationally known syndicated columnist, explained the stability of Aunt Jemima in an article originally written to note the objection of blacks to the opening of a Sambo restaurant. After the article ran there was an outcry from white observers claiming that blacks were too sensitive and looking for negatives where none existed. In another article Rasberry defended the longevity of Aunt Jemima in this manner:

On this basis, they would soon be taking offense at Aunt Jemima's Pancake Mix. If the pancake mix or Uncle Ben's Rice were to be launched today they would be offensive. There are a couple of reasons why those two brand names, both featuring black caricatures, are not offensive to blacks now. First, they have been around a long time, giving them the innocuousness that comes with familiarity. Second, they were never particularly obnoxious to begin with. Hardly any black youngster today will know that 'uncle' and 'aunt' were devices used by Old South whites to give a modicum of respect to older blacks without going to the unthinkable extreme of calling them 'Mr.' or 'Mrs.' Even so, the companies that package Uncle Ben and Aunt Jemima have been sensitive to changing times. Look at the face on the pancake box and, if you're over thirty, try to remember what Aunt Jemima used to look like. She always did wear a big smile, but in the earlier days she was a big coarse-featured woman in, say, the Hattie McDaniels mode—a black nanny. Today she is younger, slimmer, prettier, and her bandanna is closer to the headwraps you're likely to see at cocktail parties. (Hay, 1981, pp. 163–64)

The fortitude and ingenuity of the trademark owners have forged a permanent image of the symbol into the minds of most Americans. The ability of the trademark to sustain has not been an easy task, as evidenced by the closing of Sambo restaurants and the temporary discontinuation of Uncle Ben as Uncle Ben's trademark. Ben was not as fortunate as Jemima and was removed from the box amid objections from the black consumer market during the civil rights movement. It was later reinstated, but the trademark did not have the same prominence on the box as in earlier times.

Although Aunt Jemima has become a venerable character for print advertising, she has not achieved great success with television commercials. The Quaker Oats Company has been cautious. Fear of backlash from the black community has been an effective deterrent to the adoption of promotional strategies that would have worked in the past but would probably meet with staunch opposition today. The subservient, humble, "step-and-fetch-it," mammy stereotypes still haunt the memory of many blacks. For this reason, "television producers are very careful now about domestic employees—not to mention blacks—and progress is measured by the distance from the old offensive image" (Pinckney, 1983, p. 347). The unsuccessful transition of Aunt Jemima into the electronic age was characterized by one author when he wrote, "Video was never the home for Elsie the Cow, Aunt Jemima, or the Smith Brothers" (Hall, 1984, p. 14).

The "Old Auntie" offered white America warmth, devotion and love. She was an American counterpart to the European peasant, the Earth-mother. The romanticized plantation where Aunt Jemima served as a sanctuary where she could develop the family ties that were immune from the force of progress. In this mythic world she was "more than a mudder." To modern black leaders, she evidently does not represent slavery, degradation or servitude. Her long history and inclusion into American folklore has seemingly superseded these characteristics. (Sacharow, 1982, p. 65)

But in some invincible icon awoke subleties of pain more often than the warmth described time after time in the literature of days gone by.

As a child in the 1950s I could not look inside the image and see the African bones under those high cheeks. It was simply a bandana on her head not the American adaptation of the West African *gele* headwrap. The gleam of her teeth was only selfless accommodation—not the contrast of white against African skin, not survival. We were all children then, not so long ago, and didn't see what was behind the caricature. We felt only pain at what had been done to us in the name of white America. (Gomez, 1986, pp. 14–15)

THE 1989 METAMORPHOSIS OF AUNT JEMIMA

There are blacks today who are offended by the trademark and therefore refuse to purchase the product. As a symbol, Aunt Jemima has alienated some factions of black consumers because they fear that if they purchase the product, they are in essence perpetuating the stereotype and thus reinforcing all of the negative ramifications that accompany such portrayals. Nancy Hass (1989), in reporting the change that Aunt Jemima underwent in 1989, observed that "social groups call for the abolition of such logos as Aunt Jemima and the Cream of Wheat chef because they carry subservient connotations despite any changes" (p. 1E).

To make the symbol more acceptable to the black market, Quaker Oats introduced a new Aunt Jemima in April 1989, 100 years after the concept was begun, "because they became aware of people's lack of acceptance," notes Annette Carson, the founder of the National Black Memorabilia Collectors' Association (NBMCA) and publisher of *Black Ethnic Collectibles* magazine. "In my opinion, they fall into the same category of the mammy and the sambo" (Brown, 1990). The image had been altered 21 years earlier, but this time the change was quite dynamic. All that remained of the stereotypical Jemima was her effervescent, alluring smile. The headband was traded in for soft, gray-streaked hair, and to give her a more contemporary look she now wears pearl earrings and a dainty lace collar. The Aunt Jemima transformation was capsuled in this way by one writer: "When Aunt Jemima wore that head rag as she flipped those pancakes, we didn't like it much. (But that didn't stop us from buying the product.) Well, about two years ago Quaker Oats gave Auntie a makeover. They advised Girlfriend against the head rag, gave her a soft do, and did her colors" (DeLeon, 1992, p. 25). In fact, she looks more like a black Betty Crocker than the Aunt Jemima who has graced our breakfast tables for over a century. By the end of the summer of 1989 the new image adorned all forty Aunt Jemima products.[7]

In 1991 the Quaker Oats Company introduced the newest product to the line—pancakes in a bottle. In the fast-paced world where convenience is of the utmost importance to homemakers, Quaker Oats, in an attempt to prepare for the 21st-century consumer, introduced Aunt Jemima Pancake Express. The product consists of small plastic bottles partially filled with mix. Cooks need only add water, shake, then pour the batter onto the griddle.

To gear up for the 1990s the company conducted market research studies in 12 American cities. Naomi Henderson, principal of RIVA Marketing and Research, conducted a target focus-group study. She said that most of the women interviewed "did not like the bandanna. They viewed it as a symbol of slavery" (Brown, 1990, p. 5). Based on the results of those studies the company revamped the image "in a more contemporary light, while preserving the important attributes of warmth, quality, good taste, heritage and reliability," said Barbara R. Allen, vice president of marketing for the Quaker Oats Company's convenience foods division ("Aunt Jemima Trademark," 1989, p. 2).

Aunt Jemima dominates the pancake batter mix with a greater than 40 percent market share. The Aunt Jemima product line represents $300 million of Quaker Oats' $5.3 billion in annual sales, and this marketing strategy is indicative of the promotional savvy employed in the present and past. It has been used to keep Aunt Jemima the most popular pancake mix in America.

One year to the date of the release of the latest cosmetic change for Aunt Jemima, a study was conducted by the author and Susanna Hornig (1992) to see what impact the change had had on consumers' perception of Aunt Jemima. The researchers were interested in doing this study because the 1989 makeover was the most radical Aunt Jemima had ever undergone. It would be the first Aunt Jemima logo to distance itself totally from domestic work and the first not to have any kind of headwear.

The purpose of the study was to provide information on how the Aunt Jemima and Betty Crocker trademarks have been infused into American popular culture. The authors also were interested in finding out what characteristics made the two cooks so well liked by the general public, and in determining which of the two trademarks is more popular or recognizable. To conduct the analysis students at a large Southern university were surveyed in three different journalism classes to determine their impressions of both trademarks. Along with the 20-item questionnaire students were given three photocopies of each trademark depicting various makeovers at strategic times in the characters' existence. The pictures of Aunt Jemima showed her appearance for the years 1936, 1968, and 1989; the years selected for Betty Crocker were 1936, 1965, and 1986. Students were asked to rank each character on her attractiveness, intelligence, and warmth. In addition, the respondents were asked to estimate the trademarks' income level and profession. The researchers also wanted to determine if the students knew what products the trademarks represented.

The early Aunt Jemima was correctly identified by all respondents; 80 percent identified the second image used. Both images were generally classified as "food company representatives." The more contemporary Aunt Jemima was correctly identified by only 42 percent of the respondents and classified as a food company representative by only 63 percent. The new Aunt Jemima is thus less recognizable than the older ones, but still substantially more recognizable than any of the Betty Crocker images. The new Aunt Jemima also has a sharply different socioeconomic image, evidenced by the fact that she was classified as professional or managerial by 68 percent of the respondents. Earlier images were classified as household worker by 78 percent (earliest photo) and 64 percent (second photo) of the respondents. She has almost caught up to Betty Crocker on income level, with the mean assigned by respondents falling in the $40,000 to $45,000 range. On the semantic differential scales the new Aunt Jemima is seen as nearly as attractive as, and not much different in intelligence from, the newest Betty Crocker. She remains very motherly—unlike Betty, whose newest image is even less motherly than the old.

ARTISTIC REACTIONS TO THE CONCEPT OF AUNT JEMIMA

Despite the changes made in 1968 and 1989 the image of the bandanna-wearing, unsophisticated, plantation mammy will linger in the minds of some black consumers because the original trademark perpetuated a stereotype that enslaved not only the race being portrayed but those who sought to enslave. Reaction to the symbol has surfaced in different forms from the black community.

During the 1960s blacks used various forms of artistic expression to illustrate their discontent with racial and cultural alienation reinforced by racism and segregation. One author summarized the plight of these artists by writing:

In an attempt to dislodge the cultural hegemony of mainstream American society over the lives of Afro-American, the art of black nationalism affirms its militancy. The major expressive intent of protest artists is political activism. Like the work of their musical counterparts, their contributions are primarily 'message art,' or symbolic images and statements about the living conditions of blacks and their political goal of redress. For them art becomes political, and politics becomes artistic. They use their art to inspire black unity and dignity; to articulate the needs of their people's experience and potential. (Fine, 1973, p. 195)

Betye Saar's painting *The Liberation of Aunt Jemima* cries out for political and psychological freedom for all black people. It silently speaks against the subjugation of black womanhood and black women's self-esteem. Using a backdrop of smiling Aunt Jemima faces, she subliminally suggests the servitude that has enslaved Aunt Jemima and those whom she represented. The foreground of the painting is empowered by a massive Aunt Jemima figure, grotesque and scary, clothed in the traditional Aunt Jemima costume, bandanna included.

In one hand she holds a broom, which symbolizes the subservient position to which American black women were relegated for such a long time. In the other she brandishes a rifle, symbolizing militant protest. Immediately in front of the gun-toting Jemima is a framed picture of her as a loving, caring nanny, holding a crying white child. The smile, although quite broad, is also quite deceiving. It appears that she is not smiling because she is happy, and not to appease her white master, but at the prospect of one day gaining her freedom. By superimposing several different images of Aunt Jemima in a single composition Saar is seemingly able to reflect Aunt Jemima's past, present, and future. In particular, she uses different media to convey the plurality of the black existence in America. As one author wrote, "The message of the painting is without a doubt, that 'a change gon' come" (Lewis,

1978). The writer further asserts that "Saar's seemingly contradictory image suggests that for Afro-Americans, laughter and anger, docility and hostility are merely different means for achieving the same outcome" (p. 173).

Betye Saar describes this work on Aunt Jemima as one of the pieces in a collection titled, "Exploding the Myth" in which she used derogatory images such as Aunt Jemima and Uncle Tom and related them to the black liberation movement in America. The nucleus of "The Liberation of Aunt Jemima Series" was represented by a black woman—an Aunt Jemima type— holding a gun instead of a rolling pin (Andrews, 1975). For those curious about why Saar frames all her work in boxes or windows she offers the following explanation:

The window is a way of traveling from one conscious level to another, like the physical looking to the mental or the spiritual. The boxes represent a 'contained' kind of secret that one can open and look into, then close if he wishes to leave that particular idea. (Andrews, 1975, p. 30)

A pen-and-ink drawing by Murray N. DePillars depicts an androgynous-looking Aunt Jemima exploding from a pancake-box bed with unparalleled defiance while holding high a large spatula. In the left-hand corner of the box the traditional mammy trademark has been strategically replaced with an ultra-slim black female sporting a short afro haircut. Another DePillars drawing depicted Aunt Jemima against a background of the American flag (the stars are Chicago police badges). She is bursting from her pancake box, ready to do some damage with her raised flyswatter, under the gaze of an angry contemporary African-American female. The boxes arranged like a series of books at the right are each topped by a clenched fist, and texts about African-American history are found under the "Ingredients" of "The Original Aunt Jemima Pancake and Waffle Mix" (Lippard, 1990, p. 235). The "Ingredients" on the side of the first box explain the protest by black athletes seated in Section 22 at the 1968 Summer Olympics. The other boxes list 21 places where racial conflict had occurred. The symbolic 22nd location is yet to be named—DePillars leaves it as a question mark.

The symbol of the clenched fist first gained prominence during the 1968 Summer Olympics when sprinters Tommie Smith and John Carlos wore black leather gloves raised in defiance during the playing of the American national anthem. The clenched fist signifies racial unity and "black power." The picture of the two holding their fists high in the air as they stood on the Olympic victory platform to receive their medals became one of the most visible signs of the 1968 Olympics (Granda, 1992, p. 57).

DePillars, who during the 1960s was a member of AFRI-COBRA (African Commune of Bad and Relevant Artists), had 4000 copies of the drawing made (originally done in conte crayon), and sold them to black businesses in inner city neighborhoods in Chicago to refute the idea that poor blacks would not buy art (Granda, 1992, p. 71).

The obvious point of the drawings is Aunt Jemima's reluctance to remain caged in the stereotypical format she occupied during her lengthy existence. The artist was trying desperately to depict Aunt Jemima in a representation totally opposite to "the dependable, benign, usually fat, grinning great black mammy in white kitchens and nurseries." Instead, DePillars chose a concept more reflective "of a very angry woman who may still be in the white lady's kitchen, but on very different terms—shorter, more reasonable working hours, familiarity is allowed, and social security" (Klotman, 1977, p. 172).

Indifference to the Aunt Jemima trademark also was the focus of a poster designed by another black artist, John Onye Lockard. The work shows a very coarse-looking Aunt Jemima with the liberation colors of red, black, and green wrapped around her head. With a stern look on her face, the character forcefully puts her fist through the box, and the caption at the bottom reads, "No More." The implication is that she is saying no more to being portrayed as the obese, subservient, domestic standard by which all black womanhood was measured.

Note the resentment for the trademark in the poems "Aunt Jemima" and "In Search of Aunt Jemima," written by blacks in 1983 and 1978 respectively.

Aunt Jemima

Does anybody know what ever happened to
    Aunt Jemima on the pancake box?
Rumor has it that she just up and disappeared.
    Well, I know the real story
You see I ran into Aunt Jemima one day.
    She told me she got tired of wearing that rag wrapped around her
    head.
And she got tired of making pancakes and waffles for other people to
    eat while she couldn't sit down at the table.
    She told me that Lincoln emancipated the slaves
But she freed her own damn self.
    You know
The last time I saw Aunt Jemima
    She was driving a Mercedes-Benz
    with a bumper sticker on back that said
"Free at last, free at last,
    Thank God all mighty
    I am free at last."

                              Sylvia Dunnavant

In Search of Aunt Jemima
(Alias Big Mama)

Everbody's looking for Big Mama,
spatula in hand and ample
table set for all of master's children
serving generous portions
of forgiving love with open
gold-tooth smile.

Everybody needs to nestle in
her warm, full bosom, hear again
that throaty voice belt out
deep-valleyed lullabies of blackness
(shouting hosannas or moaning
blues for good man gone).

Where did Aunt Jemima go? And when
will she return to reassure us
that her delicious laughter
was innocent and wholesome to partake of
and no more subtle
and no more dangerous
than her pancakes?

                                                        Naomi Long Madgett

AUNT JEMIMA AND THE NATIONAL COUNCIL OF NEGRO WOMEN

The indifference and resentment to the Aunt Jemima logo was confronted head on when Quaker Oats entered into a venture that the company hoped would make the trademark a more positive symbol within the African-American community. "For decades the image of Aunt Jemima, who originally wore a head rag while she flipped her pancakes, was associated with denigration of black women" (Brace, 1991, p. 3). That venture was a community partnership program with the National Council of Negro Women (NCNW) titled "A Tribute to Black Women Community Leaders." Founded by human rights activist Mary McLeod Bethune in 1935, NCNW has an outreach to more than four million women and is recognized as the principal advocacy group for African-American women and their families.

The program included a contest in seven cities with NCNW community-based sections that encouraged individuals to nominate the black, female leader who best exemplified community service, church activism, family ideals, and career development. A breakfast fund-raiser that benefitted the local

NCNW section was the platform for announcing winners in each city. Cash awards and gift baskets were provided.

Also included in the program was a recognition of the leadership skills and talents of local, female college students. Each of the participating sections selected a student who had exhibited unique leadership qualities and had served her community selflessly.

The year-long program was launched in Washington, D.C., with a breakfast at which five of Washington's most prominent female leaders were honored on October 31, 1991. "We are proud to join NCNW in announcing the launch of this exciting seven-city program that will pay tribute to local leaders who serve as role models in their respective communities," said Barbara Allen, president of the Frozen Division at the Quaker Oats Company (p. 2).

The women honored included Monica Dancy, Pre-Trial Services Officer, D. C. Superior Court; Brita Kemp, NCNW Volunteer, Operation Sisters United; Carol Lowe, Executive Director, D. C. Commission for Women; Ella McCall, Social Worker, Voices From the Street; Lorraine Miller, Floor Assistant, U. S. House of Representatives. "The nominees and winners in each city will symbolize community involvement and strong family values—those traditional qualities that Aunt Jemima brands continue to represent and support," commented Allen (p. 2).

"There are many women across the country whose hard work and dedication deserve recognition and appreciation. We want to lift up examples of women in different fields who inspire us all to greater community service," stated Dr. Dorothy I. Height, president and CEO of the National Council of Negro Women (p. 2).

The program included leadership contests and fundraising breakfasts for the local Sections of NCNW in the following cities: Charleston, Chicago, Cleveland, Detroit, Houston, New Orleans, and Philadelphia. The program culminated with a national winner being selected by a panel of judges from NCNW. The winner was named the "Black Woman Community Leader of the Year" during an awards breakfast in Chicago, headquarters of the Quaker Oats Company. The program did receive some objection from the black community, however.

AUNT JEMIMA'S LEGACY

Trademark designs form a panoramic image of American popular culture, and Aunt Jemima has carved herself an indelible place by being nationally known for over a century. Regardless of their original purpose, trademarks are an important entity in society. They are responsible for documenting the socialization and acculturation processes of people. By carefully scrutinizing the transformation of the Aunt Jemima trademark it is easy to note changing attitudes toward black Americans. By examining the physical attributes, language, and situation it is easy to see the changes that have occurred.

"Trademarks and package designs form an important part of our experience of being Americans. These are the symbols—the personalities—of the products we have bought, of the food we have eaten, and of the companies that we have relied on throughout our lives." (Morgan, 1986, p. 13)

Because Aunt Jemima's manufacturers were so skillful in integrating the symbol into American culture, it has had a profound impact on the image that blacks have had of themselves and of the image whites have had of blacks. Going beyond that point, black women saw themselves confined to a low economic status in life; even though free, they were slaves to a stereotypical symbol. Despite their fortitude the mammy phenomenon always put them back into the plantation kitchen. This concept was artfully outlined by Deborah Gray White, author of *Ar'n't I a Woman?* (1985):

In the pictures painted by Americans, Mammy towered behind every orange blossom, mint julep, erring white child, and gracious Southern lady. . . . In the 1930s, 1940s, 1950s Hollywood film producers and New York advertising agencies built their own monuments to Mammy. With their films, their pancake boxes, and their syrup bottles, they imprinted the image of Mammy on the American psyche more indelibly perhaps than ever before. We probably can not measure the effect of the mass packaging of Mammy with precision, but the fact is that Mammy became a national symbol of perfect domesticity at the very time that millions of black women were leaving the cotton fields of the South in search of employment in Northern urban areas. Surely there is some connection between the idea of Mammy, the service and domestic jobs readily offered to black women, and their near-exclusion from other kinds of work. (p. 165)

Were Chris Rutt, Charles Underwood, or any of the other manufacturers aware of the deeper implications of the pervasiveness of Aunt Jemima on American society and culture? Did they foresee the intrinsic values of the symbolism that they so meticulously promoted? Was it perchance that they wanted just to sell pancakes but instead circumscribed the aspirations and dreams of a whole race? Because of their concerted abilities to create a trademark with a personality that transcended all usual marketing expectations, they moved Aunt Jemima beyond the breakfast table into the American culture and psyche.

Aunt Jemima slipped into the consciousness of black Americans like old age sneaks into our existence and surfaced in some very unconventional ways. In a game called "playing the dozens" young blacks would exhibit their communication prowess by stating, "Hey man, ain't ya' momma on the pancake box?" Stated as fast as one could, this would ultimately sound like, "Aunt Jemima on the pancake box." It was often used as a method of verbal defense during a friendly exchange of insults that "transcended all socioeconomic levels within the African American community" (Jewell, 1993, p. 62).

Again, Aunt Jemima makes history by becoming one of the few trademarks that have remained a part of consumer-oriented products for more than 100 years. The promotional and marketing savvy of the trademark's owners has been unquestionably ingenious. They have been pioneers in American advertising, and in so doing have made a permanent mark in its history. By creating the first living trademark, the owners indirectly gave birth to Mr. Whipple (Charmin toilet tissue) and Madge (Palmolive dishwashing liquid) and made Aunt Jemima a household word.

It should be noted, however, that the insight to modify Aunt Jemima's image was not solely the idea of her owners. Quaker Oats, like so many other companies, was given the impetus to change because of the concerted efforts of organizations concerned about the concepts such stereotypical portrayals were forging in young, impressionable minds.

Appendix: Chronology of Important Dates in the History of Aunt Jemima

1889	Pearl Milling Company founded by Charles Rutt and Chris Underwood.
	Creation of the first ready-mixed pancake flour.
	Aunt Jemima chosen by Charles Rutt as advertising's first living trademark.
	Aunt Jemima Manufacturing Company replaces Pearl Milling Company.
1890	Aunt Jemima trademark registered by Bert Underwood, brother of Chris.
	Aunt Jemima Manufacturing Company sold to R. T. Davis Milling Company.
1893	Nancy Green debuts as Aunt Jemima at World's Columbian Exhibition, Chicago, 1893.
1895	Aunt Jemima paper dolls introduced.
1900	Master of promotional strategies for Aunt Jemima trademark, R. T. Davis, dies.
1903	Reorganization of R. T. Davis Milling Company.
1905	Aunt Jemima rag dolls introduced.
1914	R. T. Davis Milling Company reincorporated as Aunt Jemima Mills Company.
1926	Aunt Jemima Mills Company sold to Quaker Oats Company for $4,202,077.28.

1940s	Painted package illustration of Aunt Jemima becomes a realistic photograph.
1955	Aunt Jemima Restaurant opens at Disneyland.
1960s	Aunt Jemima image featured on packages and in advertising campaigns becomes a composite.
	Introduction of Aunt Jemima frozen foods.
1989	Aunt Jemima trademark is 100 years old.
1989	Trademark modified and reintroduced on May 27.
1991	Quaker Oats/Aunt Jemima forms an alliance with the National Council of Negro Women.

NOTES

1. During the Middle Ages, pancakes became associated with the celebration preceding Lent. It became the custom to eat pancakes on Shrove Tuesday as a means of using up fats before the Lenten fast began. Shrove Tuesday may have been patterned after an ancient Roman feast held in the early spring.

2. The full verses of "Old Aunt Jemima" appear in *J. H. Haverly's Genuine Colored Minstrels Songster* (Chicago, 1880).

3. Fielder and Fielder Mold and Die Works was a favorite for the production of premium giveaways: Salt and pepper shakers for several well-known companies in the guise of the Campbell Kids, a pair of penguins, "Willie" and "Millie," for Kool cigarettes, and a dog and cat set representing Ken-L-Ration pet food were all used as gimmicks to increase name recognition.

4. The price of the cookie jars ranges from $100 to $500, and they are quite rare. The syrup pitchers are valued at $30, and the salt and pepper shaker sets (in mint condition) sell for $50. It is unusual to find the complete family of items, although some do exist.

5. Today Aunt Jemima is primarily associated with pancakes, flour, syrup, corn meal, and grits.

6. Here are ten of the most common syntactic features of black dialect found in many earlier writings, as cited in Marlene G. Fine, Carolyn Anderson, and Gary Eckles, "Black English on Black Situation Comedies," *Journal of Communication,* Summer 1979, pp. 21–29:

1. Deletion of the past tense marker of the verb, e.g., "passed" = "pass."

2. Deletion of the *s* suffix for the third person present tense, e.g., "he run home" = "he runs home."

3. Deletion of the auxiliary verb, e.g., "you hear" = "do you hear."

4. Deletion of the copula, e.g., "you tired" = "you are tired."

5. Use of "be" to mean habitation, e.g., "he be workin'."

6. Negative concord, e.g., "don't nobody know" = "nobody knows."

7. Plural subject with singular form of "be," e.g., "they is."

8. Deletion of the *s* suffix marking the possessive, e.g., "John book" = "John's book."

9. Deletion of the *s* suffix marking the plural, e.g., "whole lotta song" = "a lot of songs."

10. Use of a pleonastic noun, e.g., "John, he live in New York" = "John lives in New York."

7. For more about the makeover, see: Julie Liesse Erickson, "Aunt Jemima Makeover," *Advertising*, May 1, 1989, p. 8; "Aunt Jemima Gets New Hairdo, Keeps Same Smile," *Bryan-College Station Eagle*, April 28, 1989, p. 9; "Aunt Jemima Grays," *Houston Post*, April 28, 1989, p. A2; "Quaker Oats Is Shedding New Light on Aunt Jemima," *Wall Street Journal*, April 28, 1989, p. A4; "You've Come a Long Way, Jemima," *Emerge*, January 1990, p. 31; "Aunt Jemima Updated," *Houston Chronicle*, April 30, 1989, p. 2A; "Aunt Jemima Trademark to Get 1990s Makeover," *Jet*, May 15, 1989.

REFERENCES

Abrahams, Roger D. 1977. *Talking Black*. Rowley, Mass.: Newbury House.

Allport, F. H. 1924. *Social Psychology*. Boston: Houghton Mifflin.

Allport, Gordon. 1954. *The Nature of Prejudice*. Reading, Mass.: Addison-Wesley.

Anderson, James. 1976. "Aunt Jemima in Dialectics: Genovese on Slave Culture." *Journal of Negro History* 61: 99.

Anderson, Johana Gast. 1979. *More Twentieth Century Dolls from Bisque to Vinyl*. Des Moines: Wallace Homestead Book Company.

Andrews, Benny. 1975. "Jemimas, Mysticism, and Mojos: The Art of Betye Saar." *Encore American and Worldwide*, March 17, p. 30.

Angelou, Maya. 1981. "Song for the Old Ones." In *Maya Angelou: Poems*. New York: Bantam Books.

Assael, Henry. 1987. *Consumer Behavior and Marketing Action*. Boston: Kent Publishing Company.

Atwan, Robert, Donald McQuade, and John W. Wright. 1979. *Edsels, Luckies and Frigidaires: Advertising the American Way*. New York: Dell Publishing Company.

"Aunt Jemima of Pancake Box Fame Dies at 76." 1981. *Knoxville* (Tenn.) *News-Sentinel*, April 2, p. 9.

"Aunt Jemima Trademark to Be Updated." 1989. Press release issued by the Quaker Oats Company, Chicago, April 27.

Barnett, Marguerite Ross. 1982. "Nostalgia as Nightmare: Blacks and American Popular Culture." *The Crisis*, (February): 42.

Berry, Jon. "Marketers Reach Out to Blacks." *Chicago Tribune*, May 12, 1991, p. 9A.

The Black Mammy Monument. 1923. *New York Age*, January 6, p. 4.

Bogle, Donald. 1973. *Coons, Mulattoes, Mammies and Bucks*. New York: Viking.

Boskin, Joseph. 1986. *Sambo: The Rise and Demise of an American Jester.* New York: Oxford University Press.

Bottrell, Ron. 1988. Personal interview, December 18.

Bowes, J. 1977. "Stereotyping and Communication Accuracy." *Journalism Quarterly* 54 (Spring): 70–76.

Brace, Eric. 1991. "Personalities." *Washington Post,* October 29, p. 3.

Brasch, Walter M. 1981. *Black English and the Mass Media.* Amherst: University of Massachusetts.

Brown, Fred. 1990. "Collecting African-American Images." *Washington Post,* February 6, p. 5.

Bullock, Algie. 1987. Personal interview, December 12.

Campbell, Cathy. 1989. "A Battered Woman Rises: Aunt Jemima's Corporate Makeover." *Village Voice,* November 7, pp. 45–46.

Campbell, Hannah. 1964. *Why Did They Name It. . .?* New York: Fleet Publishing.

Carter, Richard. 1962. "Stereotyping as a Process." *Public Opinion Quarterly* 26 (Fall):77–91.

Chapman, Robert L. 1986. *New Dictionary of American Slang.* New York: Harper and Row.

Christian, Barbara. 1980. *Black Women Novelists: The Development of a Tradition, 1892–1976.* Westport, Conn: Greenwood Press.

Cleaver, Eldridge. 1968. *Soul on Ice.* New York: Delta/Dell.

Congdon-Martin, Douglas. 1990. *Images in Black: 150 Years of Black Collectibles.* West Chester, Pa.: Schiffer Publishing.

Davis, Alec. 1967. *Package and Print: The Development of Containers and Label Design.* New York: Faber and Faber.

DeLeon, Lauren Adama. 1992. "Friendly Fire." *Emerge* (March): 25.

"Did You Know. . .?" 1989. *Essence.* (February): 142.

Dunnavant, Sylvia. 1983. "Aunt Jemima." In *An Affair of the Heart.* Madison, Wis.: National Minority Campus Chronicle.

Edwards, Audrey. 1993. "From Aunt Jemima to Anita Hill: Media's Split Image of Black Women." *Media Studies Journal,* 7 (Winter/Spring):215–22.

Edwards, Paul Kenneth. 1932. *The Southern Urban Negro as a Consumer.* New York: Prentice-Hall.

Farquhar, J., and M. L. Doe. 1978. "Bruce Lee vs. Fu Manchu: Kung Fu Films and Asian American Stereotypes in America." *Bridge* 6:13–50.

Fine, E. H. 1973. *The Afro-American Artist: A Search for Identity.* New York: Holt, Rhinehart and Winston.

Genovese, Eugene. 1974. *Roll, Jordan, Roll: The World the Slaves Made.* New York: Pantheon.

Goings, Kenneth W. 1990. "Memorabilia That Have Perpetuated Stereotypes about African Americans." *Chronicle of Higher Education* (February 14): B76.

Gomez, J. 1986. Showing Our Faces: A Century of Black Women Photographed. Ten.

Gordon, Rosemary. 1961. "Stereotyping of Imagery and Belief as an Ego Defense." *British Journal of Psychology* 34 (September): 1–96.

Granda, Megan. 1992. Aunt Jemima in Black and White: America Advertises in Color. Master's thesis, University of Texas.

Greenwood, Jacquie. 1988. "Black Promotional Products." *Black Ethnic Collectibles* (July/August):12.

Guffy, O. 1971. *The Autobiography of a Black Woman*. New York: W. W. Norton.

Hall, Jim. 1984. *Mighty Minutes: An Illustrated History of Television's Best Commercials*. New York: Harmony Books.

Harley, Sharon, and Rosalyn Terborg-Penn. 1978. *The Afro-American Woman: Struggles and Images*. Port Washington, N.Y.: Kennikat Press.

Harrison, John Thornton. 1933. *The History of the Quaker Oats Company*. Chicago: University of Chicago Press.

Hass, Nancy. 1989. "Logos: Brands Trying to Lose Stereotypes, Not Sales." *Bryan-College Station* (Texas) *Eagle*, May 7, p. 1E.

Hay, Elizabeth. 1981. *Sambo Sahib*. New York: Barnes and Noble.

Heller, Steven. 1982. *Racist Ephemera: The Melting Pot Reconsidered*. American Book Collector.

Henderson, Robbin, Pamela Fabry, and Adam David Miller, eds. 1982. *Ethnic Notions: Black Image in the White Mind*. Berkeley, Calif.: Art Center Association.

Hine, Darlene Clark, ed. 1990. *Black Women in United States History*. Brooklyn: Carlson Publishing.

House Select Committee on Aging. 1977. Age Stereotyping and Television. U.S. Government Printing Office, Communications Publications Number 95–109, September.

Jamieson, Kathleen Hall, and Karlyn Kohrs Campbell. 1988. *The Interplay of Influence: Mass Media and Their Publics in News, Advertising, Politics*. Belmont, Calif.: Wadsworth.

Jewell, Karen Sue Warren. 1976. An Analysis of the Visual Development of a Stereotype: The Media's Portrayal of Mammy and Aunt Jemima as Symbols of Black Womanhood. Ph.D. diss., Ohio State University.

Kern, Marilyn L. 1982. A Comparative Analysis of the Portrayal of Blacks and Whites in White-Oriented Mass Circulation Advertisements during, 1959, 1969, and 1979. Ph.D. diss., University of Wisconsin, Madison.

Kern-Foxworth, Marilyn. 1988. "Aunt Jemima." *Insite* (June):17–20.

———. 1989a. "Aunt Jemima Is 100, but Looking Good." *Media History Digest* 9 (Fall-Winter): 54–58.

———. 1989b. "Aunt Jemima: Part I." *Black Ethnic Collectibles* (January/February): 18–19.

———. 1990. "From Plantation Kitchen to American Icon: Aunt Jemima." *Public Relations Review* 16 (Fall):55–67.

———. 1991. "Aunt Jemima." *Black Ethnic Collectibles* 4 (August):31–32.

Kern-Foxworth, Marilyn, and Susanna Hornig. 1992. Aunt Jemima and Betty Crocker: The Infusion of Two American Icons into American Culture. Paper presented to the International Communication Association, Miami, May 23.

Klotman, Phyllis Rauch. 1977. *Humanities through the Black Experience*. Dubuque, Iowa: Kendall/Hunt.

Lambert, Isaac E. 1976. *The Public Accepts: Stories behind Famous Trade-Marks, Names and Slogans*. New York: Arno Press.

Lemmons, J. Stanley. 1977. "Black Stereotypes as Reflected in Popular Culture." *American Quarterly* 21 (Spring):103–16.

Lewis, S. S. 1978. *Art: African American*. New York: Harcourt Brace Jovanovich.

Lippard, Lucy R. 1990. *Mixed Blessings: New Art in a Multicultural America*. New York: Pantheon Books.

Lippmann, Walter. 1926. *Public Opinion*. London: Allen and Unwin.

Mabry, Marcus. 1989. "A Long Way from 'Aunt Jemima.' " *Newsweek* (August 14): 34–35.

Madgett, Naomi Long. 1978. *Exits and Entrances*. Detroit: Lotus Press.

Mae, Verta. 1972. *Thursdays and Every Other Sunday Off: A Domestic Rap*. New York: Doubleday.

Map, Edward. 1973. "Black Women in Films." *The Black Scholar* 4:42.

Marquette, Arthur F. 1967. *Brands, Trademarks and Goodwill: The Story of the Quaker Oats Company*. New York: McGraw-Hill.

Martindale, Carolyn. 1986. *The White Press and Black America*. Westport, Conn.: Greenwood Press.

Maynard, Richard, ed. 1974. *The Black Man on Film: Racial Stereotyping*. Rochelle Park, N.J.: Hayden Book Company.

McManus, Kevin. 1991. "Collections from a Painful Past." *Washington Post*, February 1, p. 8.

Miller, Arthur G., ed. 1982. *In the Eye of the Beholder: Contemporary Issues in Stereotyping*. New York: Praeger.

Morgan, Hal. 1986. *Symbols of America*. New York: Viking Penguin.

Morrow, Lance. 1984. "The Power of Racial Example." *Time* (April 16): 84.

Morton, Patricia. 1991. *Disfigured Images: The Historical Assault on Afro-American Women*. Westport, Conn.: Greenwood Press.

Ogawa, D. M. 1971. *From Japs to Japanese: An Evolution of Japanese American Stereotypes*. Berkeley, Calif.: McCutchen.

Pantovic, Stan. 1974. "Black Antiques Reveal History of Stereotypes." *Sepia* (July 23): 44–48.

Parkhurst, Jessie W. 1938. "The Role of the Black Mammy in the Plantation Household." *Journal of Negro History* 23 (July):349–69.

Partridge, Eric. 1984. *A Dictionary of Slang and Unconventional English*. New York: Macmillan.

Patton, June O. 1980. "Moonlight and Magnolias in Southern Education: The Black Mammy Memorial Institute." *Journal of Negro History* 65 (Spring): 149–55.

Patton, Phil. 1993. "Mammy: Her Life and Times." *American Heritage* (September): 79–87.

Pieterse, Jan Nederveen. 1992. *White on Black: Images of Africa and Blacks in Western Popular Culture*. New Haven, Conn.: Yale University Press.

Pinckney, Darryl. 1983. "Step and Fetch It: The Darker Side of the Sitcoms." *Vanity Fair* (March).

Reddick, Lawrence. 1944. "Educational Programs for the Improvement of Race Relations: Motion Pictures, Radio, the Press and Libraries." *Journal of Negro Education* 13 (Summer): 369.

Reno, Dawn E. 1986. *Collecting Black Americana*. New York: Crown.

———. 1992. "Familiar Faces in Advertising: Aunt Jemima and Rastus, the Cream of Wheat Man." *The Antique Trader* 36 (July): 68–69.

Roberts, Churchill. 1970–71. "The Portrayal of Blacks on Network Television." *Journal of Broadcasting* 15 (Winter): 45–53.

Roberts, Linda. 1977. *Without Bias: A Guidebook for Non-Discriminatory Commu-

nication. San Francisco: International Association of Business Communicators.

Rogers, J. A. 1952. *Nature Knows No Color-Line*. New York: Helga M. Rogers.

Sacharow, Stanley. 1982. *Symbols of Trade: Your Favorite Trademarks and the Companies They Represent*. New York: Art Direction Book Company.

Saxon, Lyle, Edward Dreyer, and Robert Tallant. 1987. *Gumbo Ya-Ya: A Collection of Louisiana Folk Tales*. Gretna, La.: Pelican Publishing.

Scripps Howard News Service. 1987. "Blacks' Image in Advertising Has Improved over the Years." *Bryan-College Station Eagle,* March 1, p. 1E.

Sharp, Saundra. 1993. *Black Women for Beginners*. New York: Writers and Readers Publishing, Inc.

Sheperd, Juanita M. 1980. "The Portrayal of Black Women in the Ads of Popular Magazines." *Western Journal of Black Studies* 4 (Fall): 179–82.

Sims-Wood, Janet. 1988. "The Black Female: Mammy, Jemima, Sapphire, and Other Images." In Jessie Carney Smith, ed., *Images of Blacks in American Culture*. Westport, Conn.: Greenwood Press.

Smith, Jessie Carney, ed. 1988. *Images of Blacks in American Culture*. Westport, Conn.: Greenwood Press.

Stephan, Walter, and David Rosenfield. 1982. "Racial and Ethnic Stereotypes." In Arthur G. Miller, ed., *In the Eye of the Beholder: Contemporary Issues in Stereotyping*. New York: Praeger.

Stern, Gail. 1984. *Ethnic Images in Advertising*. New York and Philadelphia: Balch Institute for Ethnic Studies and the Anti-Defamation League of B'nai B'rith.

Stewart-Baxter, Derrick. 1970. *Ma Rainey and the Classic Blues Singers*. New York: Stein and Day.

Sturgis, Ingrid. 1993. "Black Images in Advertising: A Revolution Is Being Televised in 30-Second Commercials." *Emerge* (September): 21–23.

Unger, Gracia. 1985. "Aunt Jemima." *Calvert Tribune,* May 8, p. 12.

———. 1987. "Aunt Jemima Buried near Wheelock. *Hearne* (Texas) *Democrat,* April 9, p. 4A.

Warren, Nagueyalti. 1988. "From Uncle Tom to Cliff Huxtable, Aunt Jemima to Aunt Nell: Images of Blacks in Film and the Television Industry." In Jessie Carney Smith, ed., *Images of Blacks in American Culture*. Westport, Conn.: Greenwood Press.

Washington Tribune, Washington, D. C., February 3, 1923; *National Baptist Union Review,* Nashville, Tennessee, May 4, 1923; *Christian Index,* Jackson, Tennessee, February 22, 1923; *Birmingham Reporter,* Birmingham, Alabama, March 17, 1923; *New York Age,* New York City, January 6, 1923.

White, Deborah Gray. 1985. *Ar'n't I a Woman? Female Slaves in the Plantation South*. New York: W. W. Norton.

Wilkinson, Doris Y. 1988. "The Toy Menagerie: Early Images of Blacks in Toys, Games and Dolls." In Jessie Carney Smith, ed., *Images of Blacks in American Culture*. Westport, Conn.: Greenwood Press.

Williams, Glenn, Sr., and Jr. 1987. Personal interview, December 28.

Wilson, Clint, and Felix Gutierrez. 1985. *Minorities and Media: The End of Diversity*. New York: Sage Publications.

Young, Jackie. 1988. *Black Collectibles: Mammy and Her Friends*. West Chester, Pa.: Schiffer Publishing.

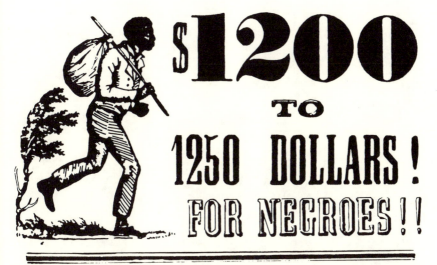

$1200 TO 1250 DOLLARS! FOR NEGROES!!

THE undersigned wishes to purchase a large lot of NEGROES for the New Orleans market. I will pay $1200 to $1250 for No. 1 young men, and $850 to $1000 for No. 1 young women. In fact I will pay more for likely

NEGROES,

Than any other trader in Kentucky. My office is adjoining the Broadway Hotel, on Broadway, Lexington, Ky., where I or my Agent can always be found.

WM. F. TALBOTT.

LEXINGTON, JULY 2, 1853.

Advertisement of Kentucky slave trader buying for the New Orleans market. From J. Winston Coleman, Jr., *Slavery Times in Kentucky* (copyright 1940, 1968). Reproduced courtesy of The University of North Carolina Press.

Slave advertisement. This advertisement is typical of advertisements placed by slave traders who were skilled at purchasing slaves and selling them for a profit.

Beech-Nut Gum. This Beech-Nut Gum advertisement appeared in 1933 and reinforced the stereotype of blacks as cannibals.

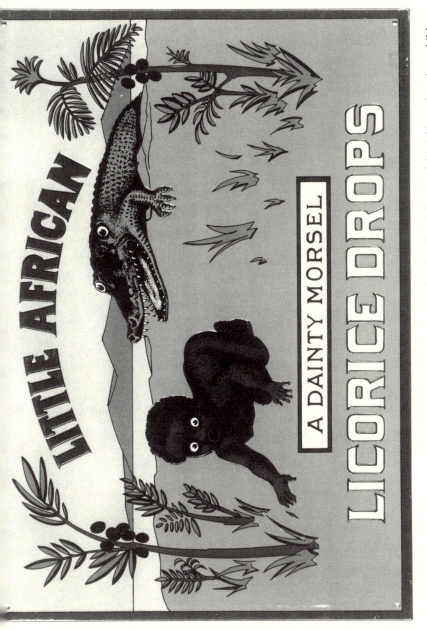

Licorice Gator Bait. This advertisement for Licorice illustrates early advertisers' disregard for African-American children and their blatant attempts to reinforce the notion that black children were only good for "gator bait."

Drawn for THE CENTURY CO.

Ivory Soap   It Floats

FIRST FEATURING OF THE SLOGAN "IT FLOATS"

Ivory—little girl. "Ivory Soap . . . . . It Floats!" First appearance of the slogan in the *Century Magazine*, July, 1891.

VOL. LVIII. No. 1496   PUCK BUILDING, New York, November 1, 1905.   PRICE TEN CENTS.

"What Fools these Mortals be!"

Copyright 1905, by Keppler & Schwarzmann   Entered at N. Y. P. O. as Second-class Mail Matter.

"LET THE GOLD DUST TWINS DO YOUR WORK.'

(You might as well, Uncle. They 'll do it, anyway.)

Around the turn of the century, the Gold Dust Twins, Goldie and Dustie, could be seen almost everywhere telling American housewives to let them do the work.

Buttons. Examples of buttons used in early advertising which featured blacks.

A man of action knows—
you get *action* when you telephone

Whenever you see a phone booth, ask yourself, "Isn't there a call I should make right now?" Call to change an appointment. Call the office to keep in touch with developments. Call home to let them know you'll be late for dinner. Why not let the telephone help you get things done, wherever you are!

 **New York Telephone**
Part of the nationwide Bell Telephone System

New York Telephone. This advertisement for New York Telephone Company appeared on May 7, 1963 and represented the first time an African-American was used in a general circulation publication.

Cream of Wheat child with blocks. 1909 version.

Standing back of
UNCLE SAM

CREAM OF WHEAT
is Economical – One
package will make ten
quarts of cooked food

E PLVRIBVS VNVM

Cream of Wheat Uncle Sam. Cream of Wheat played its part to galvanize American patriotism by using two of the most well known faces in America: Rastus and Uncle Sam.

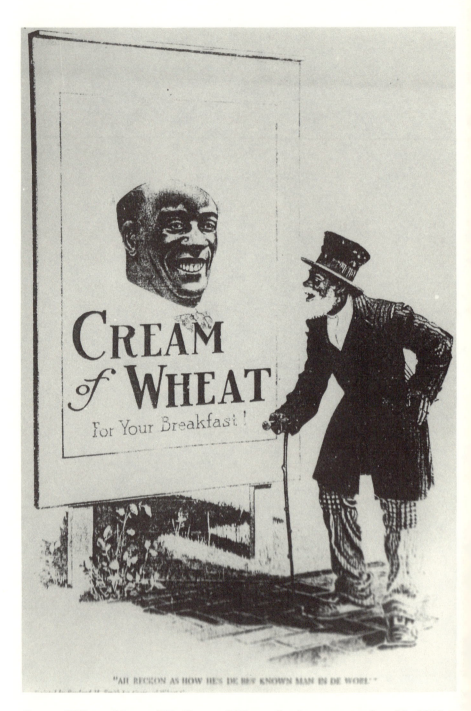

Cream of Wheat old man. This Cream of Wheat advertisement was selected in 1949 as one of *The 100 Greatest Advertisements* written by Julian Lewis Watkins.

Michael Jackson—Pepsi. In 1988 Michael Jackson received $10 million to advertise Pepsi Cola. This was the largest advertising contract given to any performer at that time.

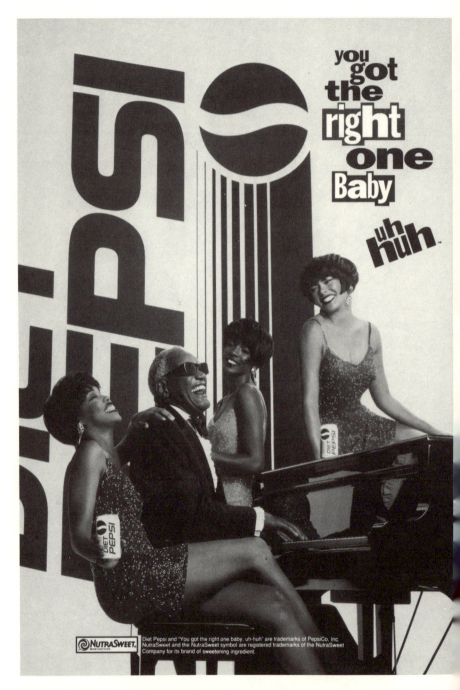

Ray Charles—Pepsi. Ray Charles and the "Uh-Huh" girls boosted awareness of Diet Pepsi during the early 1990s with their rhythmic affirmation of "You've Got the Right One Baby, Uh-Huh."

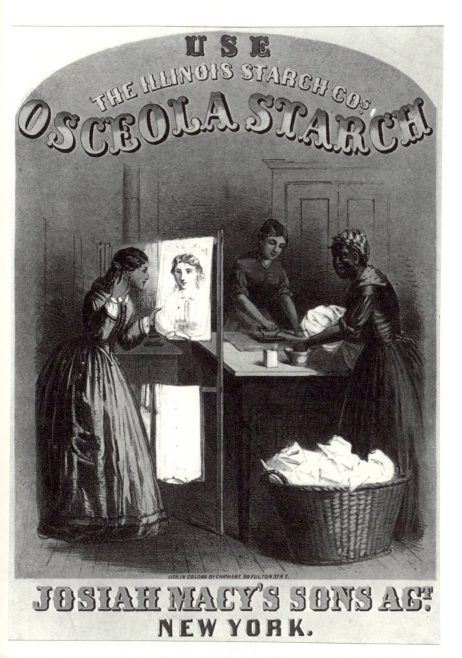

Oceola Starch. This 1862 advertisement is indicative of the stereotypical advertisments fea-
uring black women during that period.

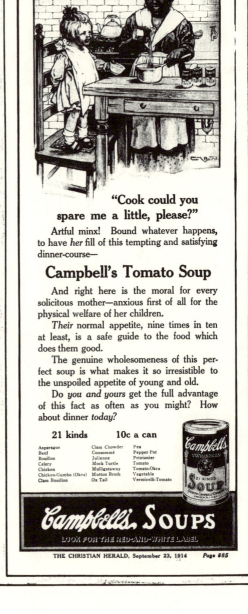

Campbell Soup. The relationship between black "mam-
mies" and the white children
they nurtured is exemplified in
this 1914 Campbell Soup
advertisment.

Aunt Jemima legend   Coax as long as they might, guests at Colonel Higbee's plantation never could get from Aunt Jemima the flavor secret of those wonderful pancakes.

What Aunt Jemima would <u>never</u> tell them...she got her matchless flavor with a blend of <u>four</u> flours

Wheat, corn, rye and rice flours were blended in the treasured Aunt Jemima recipe to give the tenderest, best-tasting pancakes anyone ever had.

Today, Aunt Jemima Pancake Mix is faithful to that recipe. It's produced now, of course, with all the advantages of modern milling methods.

Over the years as other pancake mixes have come and gone, none ever made pancakes with such *flavor* as the Aunt Jemima brand. Really, it's true: You can't duplicate in a homemade batter or get with any other mix the matchless flavor of Aunt Jemima pancakes. For a special treat team up that flavor with fresh asparagus in the delightful springtime way shown here.

ASPARAGUS ROLL-UPS. Prepare pancakes according to Deluxe recipe on the Aunt Jemima package. Roll each hot pancake around several spears of cooked asparagus. Serve with cheese sauce. Garnish each roll-up with a strip of pimiento or sprinkle with paprika.

Aunt Jemima and Colonel Higbee. As legend has it, Aunt Jemima's pancakes made Colonel Higbee one of the most popular plantation owners of his time.

Aunt Jemima. Aunt Jemima Pancake Advertisement *G* Used in Test with Negro Houswives and Family Heads (*printed on ad*).

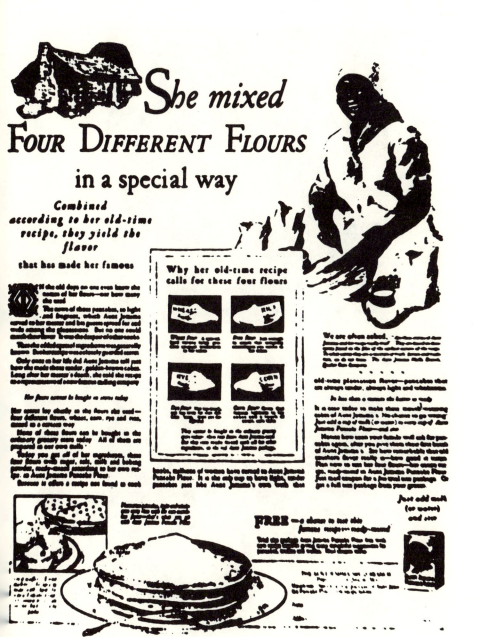

Aunt Jemima. Aunt Jemima Pancake Flour Advertisement *H* Used in Test with Negro Housewives and Family Heads (*printed on ad*).

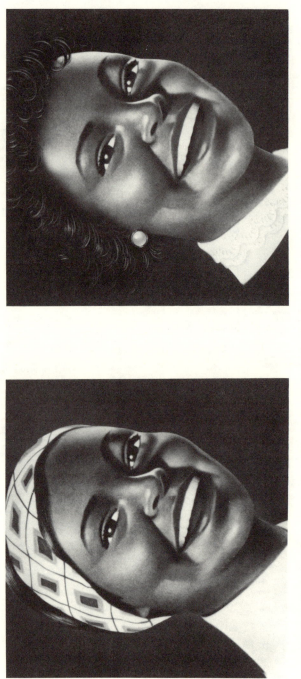

Aunt Jemima. The advertisement on the left is the 1968 Aunt Jemima logo that was not a picture of a real person with the composite of an artist. On April 27, 1989 the logo was given a more contemporary look to conform to the trends of the 1990s as exemplified in the picture on the right.

Aunt Jemima with spatula. Murray DePillar's spoof on the Aunt Jemima trademark symbolizes African-American resentment toward the product during the Civil Rights Movement.

An angry Aunt Jemima with clenched fist. This advertisement by Jon Onye Lockard represents the reluctance of some African-Americans to accept the stereotypical portrayal of Aunt Jemima during the 1970s.

Chapter 5

INVISIBLE CONSUMERS: GAINING EQUAL REPRESENTATION FOR BLACKS IN ADVERTISING

> I am an invisible man. No, I am not a spook like those who haunted Edgar Allen Poe; nor am I one of your Hollywood movie ectoplasms. I am a man of substance, of flesh and bone, fiber and liquids—and I might even be said to possess a mind. Like the bodiless heads you see sometimes in circus sideshows, it is as though I have been surrounded by mirrors of hard, distorting glass. When they approach me they see only my surroundings, themselves, or figments of their imagination—indeed, everything and anything except me.
>
> Ralph Ellison, *Invisible Man*, 1952

In Ralph Ellison's much acclaimed, *Invisible Man,* the character, a black male known as the "Invisible Man," comes across a piece of "early African-American Americana"—a "jolly nigger bank"—and sees this grotesque caricature with its coal black skin, ruby red lips, and milky white eyes staring up at him from the floor. He holds much contempt for the object and even more for his landlady for keeping such an image around. The "Invisible Man" breaks the bank into small pieces and attempts to dispose of it in his neighbor's trash can, but is circumvented from doing so by his neighbor. He then tries to leave the pieces very casually along the street, but a good samaritan returns the bundle to him. In the end, he is unable to discard the broken bank and resorts to carrying the pieces with him into his underground hiding place.

The "Invisible Man's" attempt to rid himself of this nuisance is symbolic of the attempt of Negroes, Blacks, Afro-Americans, and African-Americans to eradicate themselves of the stereotypes that have permeated and prolif-erated about them for centuries. Because many organizations felt that the representation of blacks in advertising was distorted and stereotypical, they designed programs to help ameliorate the images presented.

During the fall of 1962 several groups requested advertisers and advertis-ing agencies to incorporate blacks into their campaigns (Boyenton, 1965, pp. 228–230). For many years executives in the industry had not considered the black consumer when planning promotional strategy. They basically as-sumed that the advertising messages disseminated nationally for the white consumer would also reach the black consumer. Kevin Wall, former vice president and manager of marketing development for Coca-Cola, asserts that "for every $1 million put into television in top markets by major ad-vertisers, about $250,000 goes toward reaching an audience of black Amer-icans. Because most television campaigns today are not geared to that fact, the waste is appalling" (Wall, 1970, p. 42).

The exclusion of blacks by the advertising industry was brought to the attention of advertisers and advertising agencies by the Congress of Racial Equality and the National Association for the Advancement of Colored Peo-ple. Requests were made to implement blacks totally into their advertising. Nevertheless, the requests were not enough, so the organizations threatened to boycott if advertisers and advertising agencies did not comply (Block, 1967; Vogl, 1963; "Boycott by Negroes," 1963).

Although black leaders decided to take this course of action, they were skeptical about the support of the black community. Edward Wallerstein, executive director of the Center for Research in Marketing, conducted a study to determine how supportive the black community would be if boy-cotts were staged. The study concluded that of the 1,164 blacks interviewed from various sections of the country, 89 percent would participate if boy-cotts were called ("Negroes Respond Negatively," 1963, p. 22).

Members of the NAACP promised to petition the California State Fair Employment Commission if their complaints of unfair treatment of blacks were not heeded (Colle, 1968, p. 58). After the NAACP held several meet-ings with advertisers and advertising agencies, the *Saturday Review* reported, "No question the color line has been irrevocably splintered in national ad-vertising as of the fall of 1963" (Boyenton, 1965, p. 229).

In 1964 the NAACP sent letters to the top 100 advertising agencies, requesting they scrutinize the media used by clients in Mississippi. The let-ters asked the agencies to support "fundamental American principles by withholding accounts from media that do not uphold these principles" ("NAACP Bids Agencies," 1964, p. 19).

After reviewing the number of blacks in commercials for a special selection of sports telecasts, the NAACP appealed to the Federal Communications Commission to use its legal powers to combat discriminatory advertising (NAACP Asks FCC, 1970, p. 29).

In 1962 New York Mayor Robert Wagner's Committee on Job Advancement approached some 500 advertisers and advertising agencies, requesting them to integrate their advertising (Colle, 1968, p. 58). The committee made the following charge:

The portrait of America painted in our advertisements—in television, mass-circulation magazines, and other media—is a distorted one and has through systematic exclusion from advertising layouts of Negroes . . . created a serious impediment to job advancement and better race relations. (Boycott by Negroes, 1963).

The New York State Commission on Human Rights held hearings in 1966 and 1967 regarding the employment status of blacks in advertising (Powers, 1974, p. 5; Cohen, 1970). As a result, about 500 more blacks were working for the top 12 agencies in 1967 ("Black Image Makers," 1971, p. 15). Emphasis was placed on getting blacks into agencies, because in these capacities they could have an influence on the number of black models used in advertising as well as the manner in which they were portrayed.

In 1968 the Group for Advertising Progress was formed, an organization composed of blacks working in the advertising industry. It was headed by Douglass Alligood, a black account executive at Batten, Barton, Durstine and Osborn. The primary objective of the organization was "to advance the social and economic status of minority group persons in the fields of advertising, radio, television and the communicative arts" (Stein, 1972). The number of black-owned agencies increased to 24 as a result of the group's efforts ("Black Image Makers," 1971, p. 16).

The success of the group can be attributed to the fact that many of the members were directly involved with advertising, and some had influence in policy-making decisions. Their affiliation with advertisers and agencies made them more accessible to the problems occurring within the industry regarding blacks. These factors were important in bridging communication gaps between advertising and the black community.

The absence of blacks in advertising was also noted in the Kerner Report published in 1968. The Kerner Commission concluded that a mass medium dominated by whites would be unable to communicate with an audience that also included blacks (Report of the United States Commission on Civil Rights, 1977; Hartmann and Husband, 1974; Baker and Ball, 1969; Report of the National Advisory Commission on Civil Disorders, 1968; Fisher and Lowenstein, 1967). The report, therefore, recommended that black performers appear more frequently in advertising. The commission further stated that "any initial surprise at seeing a Negro selling a sponsor's product will essentially fade into routine acceptance, an attitude that white society must ultimately develop toward all Negroes" (Report of the National Advisory Commission on Civil Disorders, 1968).

Four years following these recommendations by the Kerner Commission, the Congressional Black Caucus issued these statements:

1. The social and occupational progress of blacks is being hindered by the negative stereotypes appearing on television.
2. Negative stereotypes teach self-hate and consequently destructive self-images to blacks, and
3. Negative stereotypes create and reinforce the myth of white superiority (Congressional Black Caucus, 1972).

In March 1975 Vernon Jordan, executive director of the National Urban League, made a charge of discriminatory practice regarding the employment of blacks in advertising agencies. He defended his position by demonstrating that 25 million black people spent $60 billion annually in America (Jordan, 1975; "Urban League Exec," 1975 p. 29). In summarizing the allegations he stated, "The advertising industry is one that deals in image selling, ideas and new concepts, but it badly needs to sell itself the idea of affirmative action" (Jordan, 1975).

Apparently, the industry still has not sold itself on affirmative action. According to the U.S. Bureau of Labor Statistics, African-Americans comprise 10.1 percent of the nation's total work force yet account for only 5.2 percent of advertising agency employees. More specifically, African-Americans account for just 2.1 percent of all marketing, advertising and public relations managers, which ranks these industries as 336 out of 351 monitored by the Bureau. Additionally, *Advertising Age* estimates the percentage of African-American managers in mainstream agencies as low as 1 percent (Holman, 1993, p. 10).

Black Enterprise characterized the disparingly low numbers of African-Americans working in advertising in this way: "The boardrooms and executive suites of general-market advertising agencies nationwide resemble percale sheets washed by the latest detergent—whiter than white" (Holman, 1993, p. 10). This sentiment was echoed again during a speech before the New Orleans Chapter of the American Advertising Federation, "The only thing that I have seen lately that is whiter than the advertising industry is snow" (Kern-Foxworth, 1992).

The necessity of having more African-Americans employed in advertising cannot be swept under the rug and treated cavalierly. Wally Snyder, 1993 president and CEO of the American Advertising Federation, states the directive:

Advertising that effectively addresses the realities of America's multicultural population must be created by qualified professionals who understand the nuances of the disparate cultures. Otherwise, agencies and marketers risk losing or worse, alienating, millions of consumers eager to buy their products or services. Building a business that "looks like" the nation's increasingly multicultural population is no longer simply a moral choice; it is a business imperative. (Snyder, 1993, p. 28)

Appalled and dismayed by the decreasing number of black advertising agencies, the Society of Black Communicators was formed in 1978. Headed by Prentice Weaver, the group's objective was "to call attention to the skilled blacks in advertising and communication" (Revett, 1978, p. 32).

In December 1982 the Black Media Association (BMA) located in Charlotte, North Carolina, became dissatisfied with some of the commercials that featured blacks. The group, made up of black professionals working in television, radio, newspapers, and public relations, confronted the advertising industry about the portrayal of blacks in print and broadcast advertisements ("Black Media Group," 1982, p. 17). This was accomplished with a letter-writing campaign.

Two letters, one complimentary and one critical, were sent each month. "We're fighting against stereotypes," said Rosalyn Gist Porter, chairperson of the Ad Watch Committee that spearheaded the letter-writing campaign (Fulwood, 1983, p. 3c). With this course of action, the group had two goals. First, the association wanted advertisers to know that blacks don't appreciate negative images of themselves in advertisements. Second, they wanted blacks to become more sensitized to images of them presented in advertising and do something to get the negative portrayals changed. The Ad Watch Committee criteria for sending letters of praise included the following (Gist, 1992, p. 3):

1. A black person is the sole spokesperson for a product or service. He or she is discussing the product's attributes intelligently without singing, dancing, or clowning.

2. The black(s) is portrayed as a serious person, a decision maker, and a responsible citizen.

3. Black youth are portrayed as honest, intelligent, and studious.

4. Ads that show a slice of black life (weddings, births). Ads that show being black in America is not always synonymous with poverty and frustration. Ads that show that blacks, like other Americans, have joys and triumphs.

5. Ads that show a dual-parent black family.

6. Ads that show black adults in caring relationships with their children. Ads that show parents concerned about their children's health, education, and safety.

The criteria for sending critical letters included the following (Gist, 1992, p. 3):

1. Blacks using slang or talking jive.

2. The fat black mother, single parent.

3. Ads that portray blacks as living in only low-income communities.

4. Ads that portray all blacks as criminals, unemployed, and/or welfare freeloaders.

5. Everyone in ad has lines to say except black persons.

6. Blacks absent from situations in which they are present in reality. Example: an ad featuring an all-white professional basketball team.

7. Ads that resort to the following stereotypes: irresponsible black man, overbearing black woman, hustler, savage African, happy slave, petty thief, vicious criminal, sexual superman, natural-born athlete, chicken and watermelon eaters, intellectually inferior to whites.

The first letter criticized the makers of Ac'cent food seasoning and their Boston-based agency, Kenyon and Eckhardt. The commercial in question featured black actress Sarah Rawls cooking fried chicken and hollering about the flavor that Ac'cent adds: "Ohhhh, honeyyyyy, Ac'cent reaaaly wakes up my chi'keen and my poke [she was trying to say pork]" (Simmons, 1983, p. 7B). The group objected to the comedic performance and noted that the advertisement depicted black women as inarticulate, gruff, and able to cook chicken (Stroud, 1983). As a result of the letter written by the BMA, the advertising agency apologized for offending them and said it would take their comments into consideration when developing future Ac'cent commercials (Simmons, 1983, p. 7B). Richard A. King, account supervisor for the agency, did defend the use of Rawls, however, describing her as "lively and at home in the kitchen" (Fulwood, April 4, 1983, 6D). He went on by stating, "Sarah's own style and personality is an important element in our commercials."

A letter sent to the Scott Paper Company and its advertising agency, J. Walter Thompson, was complimentary of a toilet tissue commercial featuring a young black couple moving into a new house. Another letter complimented Secret deodorant for featuring a black father and his daughter on her wedding day.

Among others responding to the letters were the Knight Publishing Company, publisher of the *Charlotte Observer* and *Charlotte News,* and Central Piedmont Community College. The two advertisers admitted that they had "erred in failing to include blacks in advertisements even though 31% of Charlotte's population and 24% of CPCC's student body is black" (Fulwood, August 1983, 1C).

The BMA was organized in 1977 and took up the struggle for equality in advertising five years later. In defense of the time and energy she devoted to this cause, Porter remarked, "If people never see a black person in ads, or if all the black people they show are speaking nonstandard English and singing and dancing, what kind of image does that leave with a black child?" ("Group Tracks Blacks in Ads," 1983).

In the mid-eighties there were still civil rights organizations interested in the roles and portrayals of blacks in advertising of which the National Black Network and the Black Media Coalition were the most vocal (Pratt, Pratt, and Rumptz, 1993, p. 3; Stearns, Unger, and Luebkeman, 1987).

On another front, the Black Media Coalition, under the leadership of Pluria Marshall, directed its attention from broadcasting to advertising in 1984. At that time it formed an advertising committee and vowed to survey major advertisers to learn how they use black-owned media, black-owned agencies, and to determine how blacks are used in advertising directed to a general audience ("Blacks in Advertising," 1984, p. 16).

All of the criticism lodged against advertisers was not mounted by traditional organizations. In some instances small factions of people banded together for the sole purpose of changing situations where blacks were either ignored or portrayed unfavorably by the advertising industry. Such was the case when a group of Washington-based civil rights attorneys noticed that black faces were absent from most of the real-estate advertisements in the Washington, D.C., metropolitan area. Their reaction to the blatant omissions was vividly expressed in this way:

From newspaper to newspaper, the real-estate advertisements share much in common—well-dressed, smiling young people, a swimming pool, perhaps, or a tennis court, a plug for cut-rate financing. Something else too: nationally, in advertising for houses, condominiums and apartment buildings, the models are almost all white. (Lauter, 1987, p. 10)

Noting that the single-race advertisements were a violation of federal antidiscrimination laws, the Washington Lawyers' Committee for Civil Rights Under Law conducted a survey of the *Washington Post* for a 16-month period. The group discovered that only 2 percent of the 5,300 models featured in the real-estate advertisements were nonwhite. The 1968 Fair Housing Act prohibits any "practice that indicates a preference in selling or renting homes," and thus the all-white advertisements in the *Post* were in noncompliance and illegal. The rationale surrounding the law is based on the argument that advertisements picturing only one race suggest a preference, and such procedures could possibly make both the advertiser and the publisher liable under the law (Lauter, 1987, p. 12).

In August 1986 the committee had one of its most celebrated successes when the *Washington Post* voluntarily became the first newspaper in the country to require real-estate advertisers using models to provide pictures that are racially and ethnically diverse. More specifically, policy directed the paper's advertisers "to picture an array of people that reflects the population of the newspaper's circulation area." One of the reasons that the committee became involved in this problem was the fact that the omission of blacks from advertising was so obvious in a city whose population was overwhelmingly black. In other words, it would be reasonable to assume that a city composed of 75 percent African-Americans would have African-Americans purchasing or renting homes, tenements, condominiums, townhouses, and apartments on a regular basis. Based on this rationalization, the *Washington Post* decided that one-fourth of all real-estate advertising should contain African-American models (Lauter, 1987, p. 10).

In a similar action, a voluntary plan proposed by the New York State Division of Human Rights and other civil rights groups called for at least one-third of all models in real-estate advertising to be black. This plan was initiated in response to complaints filed with the Open Housing Center, a private advocacy group, by the state and the NAACP. The complaints charged that newspaper advertisements in 1986 used almost no multi-ethnic models and failed to display properly the equal-opportunity housing logos required by law. Developers were reluctant to address the issue for fear that acceptance of such proposals would open the floodgates for other groups that would demand equal representation in advertising ("Groups Want More," 1987).

In one case involving this issue, attorney Kerry Alan Scanlon of Washington brought charges against the General Services Corporation, one of the largest real-estate advertisers in the Richmond area. At the trial's conclusion, Judge Merhige indicated to the lawyers involved that he was leaning in favor of ruling against the company. As a result, the *Richmond Times–Dispatch* adopted an affirmative-action policy similar to the one used by the *Washington Post*. The *Journal*'s newspaper chain, which publishes five surburban papers in the Washington area, followed the same pattern and implemented a similar policy (Lauter, 1987, p. 12).

At the same time this was occurring, a California civil rights agency was conducting negotiations between a Los Angeles fair-housing group and the Times Mirror Corporation over single-race advertising in the *Los Angeles Times*. Both sides confirmed that negotiations took place that worked out a tentative agreement (Lauter, 1987, p. 12). Bradley Inman, a housing columnist based in Oakland, California, noted that during this time developers were beginning to recognize the fact that multi-ethnic consumers represented a large segment of their market. To remedy the problem, Home Savings of America, based in Los Angeles, went a step further and in addition to showing blacks shopping for housing, one series of television advertisements portrayed black couples and black families moving in. Additionally, Fox Run Estates in West Charles, Maryland, presented print advertisements featuring Asians and African-Americans purchasing homes (Celis, 1988, p. B1).

More recently, the real-estate industry has come under intense scrutiny for its exclusionary practices regarding models from ALANA communities. The impetus for the focus in May 1990 stemmed from Jerome and Renaye Cuyler, who were house hunting in New York City in 1979. Using the *New York Times* as their major source of information, they discovered that most of the models used in the advertisements were white. That experience made an indelible impression on the Cuylers, and ten years later, along with another couple and the New York Open Housing Center, a nonprofit organization that advocates fair housing practices, they filed charges against the *Times* for violation of the 1968 Fair Housing Act. The act prohibits the use of advertisements that discriminate against any racial group. The groups argued that such omissions by the real-estate industry could be compared to "white only" signs imposed by Jim Crow laws (Phillips, 1990, p. 20).

Jerome Cuyler remarked that a white can leaf through and determine that he/she can live anywhere he/she wants, "while a black kid unconsciously gets the message that he can never live there." During December 1989 U.S. District Judge Charles S. Haight cleared the way for the case *Ragin v. the New York Times* to go to trial by rejecting the *Times*'s claim that applying the Fair Housing Act to newspapers would violate the First Amendment. Judge Haight identified "human models as a means by which advertisements may indicate discriminate preference" (Phillips, 1990, p. 20).

The Open Housing Center and the New York City law firm of Shearman and Sterling tried to settle the case 18 months before it went to trial but to no avail. The case filed in January 1988 was expected to go to trial in April 1990.

Renaye Cuyler, a partner in the New York law firm of Gorayed and Cuyler, summarized the situation best when she stated:

I think as a black professional, I have the [responsibility] and the resource to get involved . . . to raise the consciousness of developers in any advertising medium in this minority city. There was a time that you didn't see black models on television advertising toothpaste or Coca-Cola. I have children and friends who have children who will grow up in this city, and they will have a right to see their faces in ads in the *Times*. (Phillips, 1990, p. 20)

On May 14, 1992, a federal district court jury in Washington, D.C., awarded $850,000 in damages against a subsidiary of Mobil Land Development Corporation on a charge that the company used only white models in its real-estate advertising from 1981 to 1986. The suit challenged estate advertising for the Colonial Village complex in Arlington, Virginia. Following a six-day trial, the jury concluded that the advertisements were racially biased and in violation of the Fair Housing Act and opposed the regulations of the United States Department of Housing and Urban Development. The suit was brought by two fair housing groups, the Fair Housing Council of Greater Washington and the Metropolitan Washington Planning and Housing Association, and Girardeau A. Spann, a law professor at Georgetown University. "This verdict sends a clear message to real estate developers and advertisers that even subtle forms of racial discrimination in housing will not be tolerated," said Joe R. Caldwell, Jr., one of the attorneys representing the plaintiffs (Caldwell, 1992). The $850,000 award was by far the largest ever received in a fair-housing case.

In the fall of 1987 United Methodist Communications requested and received a grant of $57,000 from the General Council on Ministries of the United Methodist Church to create materials designed to combat racism in reporting and advertising. In requesting the grant the members of the advisory committee wrote:

We live in a society that is shaped in many ways by the media—by reporting and advertising. When we as a Christian community see our society taking a distorted shape, as projected in the media, it is our responsibility to take action. That is why we are addressing racism in reporting and advertising, because the United Methodist Church must not ignore this vital aspect of the ministry.

In 1968 the Kerner Commission issued a report calling for greater understanding in coverage of the black community and fuller employment of blacks by the media. Yet, today we are still hearing calls from ethnic groups across the nation for greater understanding in coverage of their respective communities and fuller employment of ethnic media professionals. ("New Images for a New Age," 1987)

The advisory committee decided that the development of a training kit, including an advertising manual and a videotape, to be distributed by United Methodist Communications to marketers and advertisers worldwide, would be the most effective means of disseminating information. The videotape, *Racism in Advertising: From the Frito Bandito to PowerMaster,* and the manual were made available in December 1991.[1] They explore the impact of messages that rely on racial stereotypes and characterization. From Aunt Jemima and the Frito Bandito to Power Master malt liquor and Uptown cigarettes, the video and manual offer an eye-opening study of the role racism plays in advertising. They present information about the scope and size of multiracial markets as well as offering practical advice about reaching consumers with advertising that is positive and appealing, rather than demeaning and controversial (United Methodist Communications, 1992).

The purpose of the kit is to empower local groups to impact the decision makers in the news and advertising industries, communications schools/ organizations, and the general public. The kit can also be used to conduct several training sessions as demonstration projects within different communities of United Methodism.

Using the theme "Advertising: New Images for a New Age: Racial Inclusiveness in Reporting and Advertising" as a focal point, the group conducted a focus group in November 1988 with advertising executives in New York. Information received by the advisory committee was used to design the training kit and to assess the perceptions of advertising executives regarding the images of racial groups in campaigns.

The portrayal and use of blacks in advertising were the primary issues addressed during a one-day conference hosted by DePaul University in Chicago in April 1989. The conference more specifically sought to examine:

- The demographic and business forces that are changing multi-ethnic portrayals in advertising, especially the images of blacks and Hispanics.
- The ways nonwhite advertising executives are reshaping the stereotype of racial groups in society.
- The social and cultural implications of the changing images of ALANA in advertising.

Sponsored by a grant from the Leo Burnett Foundation, speakers at the conference raised issues ranging from the growth of multi-ethnic markets to the effects of advertising on children of color. Approximately 100 people attended from the Midwest.

One organization has gone a step beyond just advocating that advertising using blacks be more realistic. CEBA (Communications Excellence to the Black Audience) rewards those whose efforts disseminate positive images of blacks in advertising and public relations. The CEBA national awards program is sponsored by the World Institute of Black Communicators (WIBC). An indication that positive portrayals have increased can be substantiated by the fact that in 1977 only 400 entries were received; in 1989, 1,500 companies submitted advertisements (Beal and Blair, 1990).

During the early 1990s another organization became involved in the fight to make advertising more racially inclusive. In 1990 and 1991 PUSH (People United to Save Humanity, founded by Reverend Jesse Jackson), maligned the practices of *Nike* regarding its lack of black directors or vice presidents, for not using black banks or black advertising agencies. PUSH urged blacks to boycott *Nike*, a leader in the $10 billion a year retail shoe and apparel industry, for these reasons (Hardy, 1991, pp. 1–2; Cox, 1990, p. 7B). In a three-page press release dated July 31, 1990, *Nike* responded to the allegations and *Nike* President Richard K. Donahue noted that "*Nike* is proud of our association with such great black role models as Michael Jordan, David Robinson, Bo Jackson, Spike Lee, and John Thompson, all of whom have been featured in our advertising" (Dolan, 1990, p. 1). In addition, *Nike* donated money to programs directed toward African-American youths, including African-American role models in commercials, and hiring and training African-American employees (Robinson, 1993, p. 8).

The pressures exerted by various organizations, groups, commissions, committees, and other affiliations, coupled with the recommendations of the Kerner Commission, helped in increasing the frequency of black models in American advertising. Although the primary purpose of the civil rights movement was to attain equality in housing, education, employment, voting, and the use of public facilities, there was an intense emphasis placed on what was conveyed in the distorted and pejorative images—and in some cases the lack of images—perpetuated through advertising. Recognizing the important role played by such symbolism in the socialization process, many civil rights leaders were appalled by what they saw and what their children were subjected to on a daily basis. Jesse Jackson was one of the first and most vocal proponents of eliminating racism in the advertising industry. He denounced the practices of Coca-Cola early in his crusade, and later he and other organizations formed coalitions that began to target other companies until a profound and very visible difference was noticed in the portrayal and frequency of appearance of black Americans during the mid- to late 1970s. What occurred as a result is what we now refer to as "integrated advertising."

During the 1960s Civil Rights Movement, black leaders and black organizations and white leaders and white organizations chanted a resounding unison of NO to some of the atrocious images and messages that were being promulgated relative to African-Americans. In essence, we looked up and saw ourselves with that "Aunt-ya-mammy headrag" wrapped around our heads, dressed in our "Uncle Ben Sunday Best" domestic uniform and our Rastus all-teeth-showing grin and asked, "Is that supposed to be me on that TV I see?"

It was a time when blacks in advertising had to be a camouflaged white to be accepted and Ralph Ellison's *Invisible Man* could be used to describe millions of black consumers. It was also a time when Parke D. Gibson looked around in 1969 and said I see beautiful black people who have $30 billion worth of pocket change and then he looked around again in 1978 and said no I see gorgeous black people ranging in every hue of the rainbow with $70 billion worth of pocket change to spend at your Neiman Marcus, Sears, and McDonald's (Gibson, 1969 and 1978). Money to buy Florsheim, Stacy Adams, Gucci, Calvin Klein, Louis Vuitton, and Pierre Cardin. And Madison Avenue, that infamous Wall Street giant, that had been in a notable coma in regard to black consumers for centuries, responded by throwing in one or two black/mulatto models in their television commercials and their print advertisements and integrated advertising was born. Suddenly, blacks were seen holding boxes of *Tide* detergent and proclaiming, "I've got ring around the collar."

General organizations threatened, boycotted and excommunicated companies for their insensitivity toward blacks. And after the threats, the reprimands and the chastisements ceased, black America and the advertising industry reached a compromise. There were more and more blacks gracing our living rooms telling us to buy this or that. The honeymoon, however, was to be short lived as slowly the stereotypical subtleties crept back into integrated advertising. A distorted and unrealistic world evolved. A world consisting of black people using standardized English who did not have families, brush their teeth, wear makeup, or drive away into the wild blue yonder in Cadillacs, Pontiacs or Chevrolets. We were either noticeably absent, irately offended or pigeon-holed into advertising only certain products, and organizations continue to battle the issue on all fronts.

NOTE

1. The videotape and manual are available from Ecufilm, Racism Videos, 810 12th Ave. S., Nashville, TN 37203; 800–251–4091.

REFERENCES

Advertising: New Images for a New Age. 1987. Proposal submitted to the United Methodist Church, Nashville, TN, November.

Baker, Robert, and Sandra Ball. 1969. *A Staff Report to the National Commission on the Causes and Prevention of Violence.* Washington, D.C.: U.S. Government Printing Office.

Beal, Kathleen A., and Marilyn Blair. 1990. "How Are Blacks Portrayed in Advertising?" *The Thomas Report* (June): 14–15.

"Black Image Makers on Madison Avenue." 1971. *Black Enterprise* (February): 15–22.

"Black Media Group Keeps Watch on Ads." 1982. *Editor and Publisher*, December 25, p. 17.

"Blacks in Advertising—A Bigger Share." 1984. *Advertising Age*, November 19, p. 16.

Block, Carl. 1967. "White Backlash to Negro Ads: Fact or Fantasy?" *Journalism Quarterly* 42 (Winter): 258–62.

"Boycott by Negroes." 1963. *Printer's Ink* 284 (August): 5–6.

Boyenton, William. 1965. "The Negro Turns to Advertising." *Journalism Quarterly* 42 (Summer): 227–35.

Caldwell, Joe. 1992. Jury Awards $850,000 against Mobil Company for Publishing All White Ads. Press release issued by Miller, Cassidy, Larroca and Lewin, Washington, D.C., May 14.

Celis, William, III. 1988. "Human Variety Appears in Real-Estate Ads." *Wall Street Journal*, October 10, p. B1.

Cohen, Dorothy. 1970. "Advertising and the Black Community." *Journal of Marketing* 34 (October): 3–11.

Colle, Royal. 1968. "Negro Image in the Mass Media: A Case in Social Change." *Journalism Quarterly* 45 (Spring): 55–60.

Congressional Black Caucus. 1972. A Position on the Mass Communication Media. Mimeographed report, Washington, D.C.

Cox, James. 1990. "Nike: Reebok-PUSH Meetings 'Smoking Gun.' " *USA Today*, August 17, p. 7B.

Dolan, Liz. 1990. Nike Presents Minority Programs to PUSH, press release, Chicago, Illinois, July 31.

Ellison, Ralph. 1952. *Invisible Man.* New York: Random House.

Fisher, Paul, and Ralph Lowenstein, eds. 1967. *Race and the Mass Media.* New York: Praeger.

Fletman, Abbe. 1982. "Charlotte Transit Praised for Ad Featuring Black Driver."
    Charlotte News, December 22, p. 14A.
————. 1983. "Agencies Answer Blacks' Criticisms." *Charlotte News,* March 23, p.
    9A.
Fulwood, Sam, III. 1983. "Advertisers Respond to Black Critics." *Charlotte Ob-
    server,* April 4, p. 9A.
————. 1983. "Watching the Ads for Racial Stereotypes." *Charlotte Observer,* Au-
    gust 29, pp. 1C, 3C.
Gist, Rosalyn. 1982. Black Media Association, press release, November 12.
"Group Tracks Blacks in Ads." 1983. *Advertising Age,* January 3.
"Groups Want More Blacks as Models in Real Estate Ads." 1987. *Editor and Pub-
    lisher,* October 24, p. 44.
Hardy, Thomas. 1991. "PUSH Officials Say NIKE Boycott Wasn't a Mistake." *Chi-
    cago Tribune,* March 18, Sec. 2, pp. 1, 4.
Hartmann, Paul, and Charles Husband. 1974. *Racism and the Mass Media.* London:
    Bristol Typesetting.
Holman, Blan. 1993. "Changing the Face(s) of Advertising: AAF and Its Members
    Seek Solutions to Advertising's Dearth of Diversity. *American Advertising*
    (Fall): 10–13.
Jordan, Vernon. 1975. "Advertising: The Image Is Incomplete." *Opportunities*
    (Fall): 24–25.
Kern-Foxworth, Marilyn. 1992. Speech delivered to Advertising Club of New Or-
    leans, New Orleans, Louisiana, December 15.
Lauter, David. 1987. "Colorblind Ads." *Washington Journalism Review* (January/
    February): pp. 10, 12.
"NAACP Asks FCC to Eliminate Racism in Ads." 1970. *Advertising Age,* October
    5, p. 29.
"NAACP Bids Agencies Ban Mississippi Ads." 1964. *Sponsor* (August): 19.
"Negroes Respond Negatively to Ads." 1963. *Editor and Publisher,* October 5, p. 22.
Phillips, Olivia. 1990. "Times Charged with Running Biased Real Estate Ads." *Black
    Enterprise* (May): 20.
Powers, Ron. 1974. "Changing Faces in TV Commercials." *Tuesday* (August): 4–6.
Pratt, Charlotte A., Cornelius B. Pratt and Mark T. Rumptz. 1993. An Analysis of
    Food, Beverage and Nutrition Advertisements in Three Consumer Magazines:
    Implications for Black Health Risks. Paper presented to the Advertising Di-
    vision, 76th Annual Convention of the Association for Education in
    Journalism and Mass Communication, Kansas City, Missouri, August 11–14.
Report of the National Advisory Commission on Civil Disorders. 1968. Washington,
    D.C.: U.S. Government Printing Office.
Report of the United States Commission on Civil Rights. 1977. Public Law 85–315
    as amended August 1977.
Revett, John. 1978. "Racial Frustrations Unify Black Communicators." *Advertising
    Age,* April 3, p. 32.
Robinson, Velma A. 1993. Corporate America: Adapting to the African-American
    Consumer Market. Paper submitted to the Alan Bussell Student Competition
    sponsored by the Minorities and Communication Division of the Association
    for Education in Journalism and Mass Communication, Kansas City, Missouri,
    August 11–14.

Simmons, Teresa. 1983. "Black Media Association Concerned about Commercials." *Charlotte Post,* March 31, p. 7B.

Snyder, Wally. 1992. "Advertising's Ethical and Economic Imperative." *American Advertising* (Fall): p. 28.

Stearns, James M., Lynette S. Unger, and Steven C. Luebkeman. 1987. "The Portrayal of Blacks in Magazine and Television Advertising." In American Marketing Association Educators' Proceedings, No. 53, pp. 198–203, Susan P. Douglas and Michael R. Solomon, eds.

Stein, M. L. 1972. *Blacks in Communication.* New York: Julian Messner.

Stroud, Daisy Spears. 1983. "Bad Editing." *Charlotte Observer,* May 12.

United Methodist Communications. 1992. *Are You Looking at a Racist?* Nashville: Ecufilm.

"Urban League Exec Charges Ad Industry Neglects Blacks." 1975. *Advertising Age,* March, p. 29.

Vogl, A. J. 1963. "A Face for the Invisible Man." *Sales Management* 91 (December): 30–33, 87.

Wall, Kevin. 1970. "The Great Waste Ignoring Blacks." *Marketing/Communications* 298 (February): 42–50.

Chapter 6 ⸻⸻⸻⸻⸻⸻⸻⸻

SEPARATE AND DEFINITELY NOT EQUAL: FREQUENCY OF BLACKS IN ADVERTISING

> Someone hands you a picture of your high-school class. The first thing you do is look for yourself. Then you look for your friends to see how you look compared to them. Then you settle back and enjoy the picture as a whole. If you missed school that day and you're not in the picture, you'd feel bad. But if someone arbitrarily cropped you out, you'd probably be angry. That's how many blacks feel about much of the advertising presented about them.
>
> Caroline Jones, President
> Caroline Jones Agency

During the 1960s blacks fought for more than integration in housing, education, and employment. Recognizing the power of advertising to influence race relations and to ameliorate the perceptions that blacks held of themselves, they also fought for integrated advertising—"any advertising message using black and white models together or black models alone in a medium directed at a mass audience" (Foote, Cone, and Belding, 1970).

Advertising, operating as the economic support of the mass media, has been a pervasive part of the way we live since the first newspaper advertisement appeared in Germany in 1525, the first American magazine advertisement, for a ferry, appeared in Benjamin Franklin's *General Magazine* on May 10, 1741 (Rankin, 1980, p. 8), and since the first television commercial aired, for the Bulova Watch Company on WNBT in New York, in 1941 (Gardner, 1983, p. 14). Over the years researchers, historians, sociologists, and psychologists have determined that advertising plays a major role in creating values and instilling notions of self-worth in all of us. Gloria Joseph and Jill Lewis, writing in *Common Differences: Conflicts in Black and White Feminist Perspectives* (1981), summarize their view of the role of advertising:

> Advertisements are as essential to American society as life is to death. Billions are spent in order to sell a lot more than products: advertisements sell attitudes, values, goals, and fears. They "sell" a self- and world-concept designed to maintain and ensure the perpetuation of sexual, racial, and economic inequality, which are all necessary to the existence of a patriarchal, capitalistic economic system.

Former Urban League director Whitney Young commented, "It's important that blacks are used more frequently in ads because they serve to educate the masses of viewers that black people, like themselves, have an important role in American life. The situation was awful, is better and has to get better" ("Commercials Crossing," 1968, p. 83).

The following studies give an indication of the frequency of appearance of black models in television commercials, mass-circulation magazines, and newspaper advertisements. Advertising has tremendous influence, and the number of times that African-Americans appear teaches people not only much about themselves but about the status of racial issues in society. According to *Commercial Break Newsletter*, in a typical week in 1987 the average viewer was exposed to 650 television commercials alone, and perhaps 1,000 total advertising messages a day (Muro, 1989). Jean Kilbourne, creator of *Still Killing Us Softly*, suggests that American audiences are exposed to as many as 2,000 advertising messages daily. By the time the average American teenager reaches the age of 18, he or she has viewed nearly 356,000 television commercials. This number rises significantly for African-American children, who watch more television than any other group in their age category. A 1978 study conducted by Michigan State University suggested that:

- Black children believed that television was very true to life.
- Forty-six percent of elementary school children believed that blacks on television were representative of blacks in real life.
- Commercials are more believable for black children than white children.
- Over 50 percent of all black children between the ages of 5 and 12 believe that commercials present true and accurate information. (Browder, 1989)

The primary question then becomes: When watching these commercials, are Americans privy to distorted depictions, distortions, or are presentations of African-Americans in television advertising true to life?

The first study done in this area sampled 292 issues of *Life, The Saturday Evening Post, Time,* and *The New Yorker* during 1949–1950 (Shuey, King, and Griffith, 1953). The researchers found that of the issues examined, slightly more than .5 percent had identifiable blacks. They also found that blacks were nearly always portrayed in the unskilled labor category, the majority being cast as servants, porters, and waiters. Finally, they stated, "The stereotype of the Negro as a servant is vigorously preserved in the advertisements."

The above study was replicated by Keith Cox (1970, p. 287) in 1967–1968, and a small increase in the utilization of black models was noted. Of 11,000 advertisements audited, approximately 2 percent contained black models. However, Cox concluded that "whereas Negroes were predominantly stereotyped as lower skilled laborers such as maids, cooks, and butlers in 1949–50, this stereotyping of Negroes rarely exists in 1967–68."

David Colfax and Susan Sternberg (1972) conducted a similar study and disagreed with the conclusions drawn by Cox. They concluded "that despite the obvious increase in the number of ads which depicted blacks over this period, blacks were being cast in roles which distorted black realities and confirmed racial stereotypes, rather than those which presented a full and more accurate picture of black America." They based their argument on the fact that there was only a shift in stereotypes, from servants to musicians. The researchers pointed out that Cox failed to indicate in his study that half of all the blacks shown in the advertisements appeared on record album covers. To this type of depiction, Goodall (1972) remarked, "Advertisers who depict blacks in these roles symbolically encapsulate them both occupationally and socially, cutting them off from conventional occupation mobility routes" (p. 138).

A longitudinal study was conducted by Harold Kassarjian (1969) of 12 national magazines from 1946 to 1965. Of 150,000 pages examined, only 546 advertisements contained black models—less than .33 percent. Kassarjian found that occupational roles of the blacks changed considerably over the 20-year period, with more being portrayed in higher status jobs in later years. His remark on what Cox (1970) labeled the "Social Effects of Integrated Advertising" was: "The social role of the Negro and the appearance of integrated advertising in which blacks and whites are shown as peers has also tended to increase recently" (p. 39).

The observations made by Kassarjian were questioned by John Wheatley (1971), who argued that Kassarjian should not have counted all the pages in the publications sampled because all did not contain advertisements and all advertisements did not contain people. He further stated:

Based on a sample of 400 pages drawn from the list of magazines used in Kassarjian's study, it appears that approximately 40 percent of the pages did not contain advertising or had ads without models. This means that the incidence of black models in magazine ads was about two-thirds as great again as implied by Kassarjian. (p. 192)

Ronald Geizer (1971) examined advertising content in 1960 and 1969 issues of *Ebony* and found that although "the proportion of advertisements with black models has not changed drastically from 1960 to 1969," (p. 134) there was an increase in the number of integrated advertisements. Such a finding, he concluded, was exemplary of the posture taken by the publication in advocating integrated societal values.

A research team headed by Dr. George Gerbner, professor at the Annenberg School of Communications, at the University of Pennsylvania, analyzed 2,556 TV commercials from 1977 to 1979. The study found the following: "In all commercials, blacks make up only 8 percent of the entire acting cast—while comprising 12 percent of the buying public. Other minorities are rarely seen and Hispanics are especially invisible. Ads with only white actors are shown seven out of 10 times while commercials with black actors only are aired less than two out of 100 times" (Nixon, 1983, p. 20).

A study more specifically targeted at advertising to black women, "The Portrayal of Black Women in the Ads of Popular Magazines" by Juanita Sheperd (1980), examined *Cosmopolitan, Working Woman,* and *Better Homes and Gardens*. The author summarized the results:

When one actually compares the percentage of the black female population to its commercial representation in popular magazines, the figures are disappointing. It is almost as if the black woman is non-existent. Either she is ignored entirely, or she is portrayed in an unfavorable light, which neither improves the knowledge about her or her knowledge about herself. (p. 179)

Sheperd suggested that the dismal portrayal of the black woman in the print media was based on the fact that her physical characteristics are far from those of white women in American culture and some companies view her more as an economic liability than as a consumer because of her limited economic base.

The status of blacks in advertising was examined in another study of white-oriented mass-circulation magazine advertisements during 1959, 1969, and 1979. The primary focus was to determine the extent to which blacks were stereotyped. A total of 1,431 advertisements were coded in sampled issues of *Time, Sports Illustrated, Woman's Day, Newsweek, Vogue,* and *Esquire*. Advertisements with white models constituted 1,373 of the total 1,431, or 95.9 percent. Only 48 advertisements contained identifiable blacks, representing 3.4 percent of the total. There were 39 advertisements with both black and white models and 9 with black models only.

The conclusion of the study was that during the years examined blacks were either eliminated from mainstream advertising or portrayed in stereotypical roles. The study further suggested that without pressures from various civil rights organizations, representation of blacks in advertising would remain dismally low and perpetuation of pejorative images would continue.

More succinctly, the study noted, "It is unfortunate that although statistics show that the mobility of blacks into varied high level occupations has improved since the Civil Rights Movement, this was not reflected in the advertisements analyzed." To correct the problem, the study recommended that more blacks be hired into policy-making positions within the industry (Kern-Foxworth, 1982 and 1988).

A study of the portrayal of blacks in magazine advertisements in 1950 and 1980–1982 (Humphrey and Schuman, 1984) revealed that most advertisers portrayed whites as they would like to think of themselves and blacks as whites would like to think of them. Chi-square tests confirmed that although the proportions of ads with blacks increased in *Time* and *Ladies Home Journal*, blacks were still underrepresented. Additionally, blacks were still depicted as subservient to and dependent upon white authority figures. The researchers concluded that "although blacks in 1980 ads were less likely to be shown in low-skill labor occupations than in 1950, blacks were still overrepresented as sports figures and more blacks than whites were shown in low-skill jobs" (pp. 558–559). The study also showed that between 1980 and 1982 blacks were interacting in ads more informally with whites.

George Zinkhan, Keith Cox, and Jae Hong (1986) examined "Changes in Stereotypes: Blacks and Whites in Magazine Advertisements" from the 1960s to the mid-1980s and discovered that "more ads now have blacks and depict more blacks in professional roles."

A content analysis of the pictorial treatment of African-Americans for all issues of specified years from 1937 to 1988 was conducted for *Life, Newsweek,* and *Time.* One of the areas of focus was advertising. Of the 160,802 pages investigated, 34,238 were devoted to pictures containing people. Of those, 1,149 pages featured African-Americans. The number of advertisements containing black models

were high in the early years, low in 1957, moderate in 1962–1972, gained in 1978, and have declined for all three magazines since 1978. The high percentages reported between 1942 and 1952 for *Newsweek* and *Time* are a result of several full page advertisements that show a butler serving alcohol on a silver tray. The advertising figures in subsequent years are a result of less stereotypical African-American portrayals. (Lester and Smith, 1989, p. 13)

Further analysis revealed that African-Americans appeared in many advertisements in the 1930s and 1940s as porters and train crew workers. Railroad competition was stringent at that time, and the number of advertisements placed by the railroads was very high. The authors concluded that the number of blacks used in advertising during this period was exceptionally high because of the use of blacks in subservient positions. The researchers additionally noted, "In the 1950s, rail passenger travel was replaced by more profitable freight service. The number of African-Americans in the train ads decreased while ads began to appear for airlines with white stewardesses" (p. 15).

The results of the study suggest that "beginning in the 1960s and continuing through the 1980s, African-Americans in advertisements were portrayed in career positions equal to whites and unrelated to their past social stereotypes." This assessment is in contrast to other studies, which acknowledged that the the occupational roles of blacks in advertisements were elevated, but the roles were merely the replacement of one stereotype for another. Being shown as a professional athlete is certainly viewed as more prestigious than being shown as a train porter, but being a natural-born athlete is still stereotypical and plays a pivotal role in limiting the perceived occupations to which blacks can aspire.

Another study examined the use of black models in television commercials for 1967, 1968, and 1969 on CBS, NBC, and ABC (Dominick and Greenberg, 1970). The researchers concluded, "In both prime-time and day, the percentage has more than doubled from 1967 to the 1969 season—from 4 to 10 percent in prime-time and from 5 to 12 percent during the day" (p. 23). This study was replicated by Bush, Solomon, and Hair (1977). Black models appeared in 13 percent of the television commercials shown during the 1974 season.

A study by the New York City Commission on Human Rights in 1967 found that blacks appeared in approximately 2.4 percent of the television commercials surveyed (Shayon, 1968). The study conducted by Churchill Roberts (1970–71) reported four times that amount. Black performers appeared in approximately 10 percent of the television commercials (58 of 588) aired during the week of March 8–14, 1970. By 1973, however, there was a decline shown in the overall frequency of appearance of blacks in television, and they had in fact disappeared from the higher status occupations within the television industry.

Another study that offered a more comprehensive examination of blacks in advertising concluded that it appears that magazine advertising directed toward blacks has experienced very little growth during the 10 years from 1965 to 1975. The extent to which the black consumer is cultivated by advertisers is still small relative to the attempt to influence the white consumer (Stutts, 1982, p. 27).

Subsequently, two other studies also showed a decline in the use of blacks in television advertising. O'Kelly and Bloomquist (1976) and Culley and Bennett (1976) showed frequencies of 7 percent and 10 percent, respectively.

Pierce et al. (1977) sampled 190 different prime-time network commercials during a two-week period in 1972. One hundred-forty were aired during programs with predominantly white characters. Blacks represented 8 percent of the sample, and there was an approximately equal distribution of males and females. Of those characters shown working for wages, 31 percent were black. They ultimately concluded that "although relatively small numbers of characters were depicted dispensing goods or favors or grooming, these behaviors were exhibited exclusively by whites" (p. 82). They illustrated the manner in which commercials reinforced racial disparagement on television by highlighting these conclusions:

1. Blacks are seen less frequently than animals.
2. Blacks never teach whites.
3. Blacks are seen eating more often than whites.
4. Blacks have fewer positive contacts with each other than whites have with each other.
5. Blacks have less involvement in family life.
6. Blacks more often work for wages and are nonprofessional.
7. Blacks do not live in the surburbs.
8. Blacks entertain others.
9. Blacks never initiate or control actions, situations, or events.
10. Blacks evidence less command of technology.
11. Blacks have less command of space.
12. Blacks are more concerned about bodily and/or sexual matters.
13. Blacks are most often used for comedy.
14. Blacks show more teeth.
15. Blacks show wider opening of the eyes. (Pierce, 1980)

Another study by Cynthia Scheibe (1983) examined "Character Portrayals and Values in Network TV Commericals." The sample for the study consisted of 2,604 commercials. A total of 6,500 characters were recorded in the sample, and approximately 94 percent were white. The researcher concluded that all multi-ethnic models were significantly underrepresented and, more specifically, at that time blacks represented 11.7 of the American population, but they were featured in only 5.3 percent of the commercials analyzed. The researcher stated:

In contrast to individual characters, a little more than a third of the crowds shown in commercials contained one or more nonwhite characters. This indicates that while advertisers still are hesitant to place a minority person in the role of spokesperson, they are moving away from using all-white casts. (p. 82)

Fred J. MacDonald (1984) expressed optimism about the treatment of blacks in advertising. He noted an increase in the frequency of black models and wrote, "Television advertisers are now approaching black consumers with sensitivity and relevance rather than stereotypes" (p. 44). He attributed the new attitude in television advertising targeted toward blacks to: (1) Agrowing number of black-owned agencies and companies requiring their services, (2) advocacy groups, such as the National Association for the Advancement of Colored People, and (3) sound business decisions aimed at increased profitability.

Another study examined the use of blacks in commercials from a different angle. Richard Davis (1987) studied the use of blacks in television commercials in terms of "spoiled identity." He defines social identity as participants in social encounters who engage in an exchange of signals about themselves and their state of being. The study also considered one of the factors that must be taken into account simultaneously if the process is to be handled smoothly: stigmas. In the study any visible or perceptible characteristic such as the appearance of one's clothes or the condition of one's skin was considered stigmatizing since they, too, may strongly influence how one is perceived during social encounters. In order to control one's appearance one must have access to what Goffman (1961) called an "identity kit," or those supplies that allow one to make oneself presentable to the public. This study contends that commercials help individuals assemble this kit.

To conduct the analysis 111 half-hour periods containing commercials were selected for viewing during the weeks of March 16–22 and May 11–17, 1980. The researcher observed that 26 percent of all commercials reviewed were stigma-oriented and concluded that stigma-oriented commercials did not seem to be specifically targeted to multi-ethnic audiences, as had been hypothesized. Also, multi-ethnic performers were not steered away from stigma-oriented commercials; on the contrary, they appeared quite frequently in these kinds of commercials. In fact, the results showed that 48 percent of the commercials featuring multi-ethnic models were for stigma-oriented products, compared to only 18.1 percent for white models. The researcher found that "although minority audiences are no longer seen as being in any special need of stigma-management advice, minority performers . . . may be perceived as . . . well suited for passing on this kind of advice" (p. 61).

Yet, Djata's 1987 analysis, "Madison Avenue Blindly Ignores the Black Consumer," asserts (p. 9) that blacks make rare appearances on television commercials.

One of the most recent studies, by Robert Wilkes and Humberto Valencia (1989), conducted content analyses to determine how blacks and Hispanics were portrayed in television commercials. Based upon an examination of three hours of prime-time programming nightly for one week on ABC, CBS, and NBC, commercials with blacks had increased to 26 percent of all advertisements with live models. Keeping pace with trends noted by earlier studies of print advertisements and television commercials, the advertisements using blacks were overwhelmingly integrated. Blacks appeared most frequently in advertisements for food products (24), automobiles (9), beer and wine (8), electronic or high-tech products (8), and drug or health-care products (7). Black men were seen more often than black women. Commercials with blacks also contained more people than those without, with blacks' appearances primarily in minor or background roles.[1] A second analysis using three coders indicated that coder ethnicity, or race, may effect the judgments made in content analysis involving multi-ethnic groups. While the Anglo coder produced essentially the same result as the Anglo coders did in the first study, the black coder saw blacks in more significant roles than did either the Anglo or Hispanic coder. The researchers were quite optimistic with their findings and concluded, "Clearly there are more blacks and Hispanics now in television commercials than has ever been the case" (p. 25).

Another study by Zinkhan, Qualls, and Biswas (1990) examined the frequency of appearance of blacks in magazine and television advertising (see Table 6.1). The authors ultimately investigated more than 13,000 television commercials and 205,000 magazine advertisements from previously published studies. Secondary analyses were made of several major previous content analyses, combined with original data from 1986 issues of *Time, Ladies Home Journal, The New Yorker, Saturday Evening Post,* and *Life.* Additionally, the researchers collected original data by studying prime-time television during the week of February 16–22, 1986. They concluded that the use of blacks increased over the time period studied (1946 to 1986) in a linear fashion for both television and magazine advertising. "Black representation has increased dramatically over time to the point that the percentage of black ads has risen from a low of 0.57 percent in 1949 to a high of 16.0 percent for television advertising in 1986." The researchers did note that their indication that the use of blacks in magazine advertising did not experience the same increase as in television.

A recent study on the use of African-Americans in advertising was conducted by Ronnye Pease (1991), a student at the University of Missouri. Pease examined advertisements in *Good Housekeeping, Harper's Bazaar,* and *Mademoiselle* from 1968 to 1988. The analysis revealed that the use of black models peaked during 1978, shown in 92 of the 1,367 advertisements. Each magazine showed an increase in the number of advertisements that contained black models from 1968 to 1973. The data also showed a decline in the use of black models beginning in 1983. Contrary to earlier studies in which black models had been excluded from advertisements for health and beauty aids, they were shown in advertisements for toothpaste, soap, lotion, bath towels, as well as household cleansers. The author concluded that

the advertising industry did make a concerted effort to enforce Affirmative Action legislation prior to the 1980s. But their efforts have diminished considerably. This phenomenon raises many questions about society and what it accepts and learns to believe about African-Americans. (p. 11)

Table 6.1
Frequency of the Appearance of Blacks in Magazine and Television
Advertising

Medium	Year	Black Ads	Total Ads	Percent	Study (Date)
Magazines	1946	273	43,533	0.63	Kassarjian (69)
Magazines	1949	213		0.57	Shuey et al. (53)
Magazines	1950	25	2,828	0.88	Humphrey & Schuman (84)
Magazines	1956	230	46,244	0.48	Kassarjian (69)
Magazines	1965	305	47,015	0.65	Kassarjian (69)
Magazines	1965	44	3,089	1.42	Colfax & Sternberg (72)
Magazines	1967	45	2,872	1.57	Colfax & Sternberg (72)
Magazines	1967	268	a12,342	2.17	Cox (69 and 70)
Television	1967	71	b1,573	4.5	Dominick & Greenberg (70)
Television	1968	143	b2,023	7.0	Dominick & Greenberg (70)
Magazines	1969	138	2,467	5.57	Colfax & Sternberg (72)
Magazines	1969	335	6,365	5.3	Cox (70)
Television	1969	260	2,363	11.0	Dominick & Greenberg (70)
Magazines	1970	82	3,148	2.6	Colfax & Sternberg (72)
Magazines	1970	246	a11,224	2.19	Cox (70)
Television	1973	288	1,944	14.8	Bush et al. (77)
Television	1974	586	4,534	12.9	Bush et al. (77)
Magazines	1978	72	3,383	2.13	Bush et al. (80)
Magazines	1979	22	b772	2.8	Humphrey & Schuman (84)
Magazines	1980	364	b3,808	9.6	Humphrey & Schuman (84)
Magazines	1981	245	b3,662	6.7	Humphrey & Schuman (84)
Magazines	1982	314	b3,575	8.8	Humphrey & Schuman (84)
Magazines	1984	267	a6,602	4.04	Zinkhan (86)
Magazines	1986	125	a2,863	4.37	Primary data
Television	1986	223	a1,393	16.01	Primary data

aThese figures represent the total number of ads which contained adult models. All other figures
   represent total number of ads that appeared in the sampled media.
bThese represent the total number of ads which were populated.
Source: George M. Zinkhan, William J. Qualls, and Abhijit Biswas. 1990. The Use of Blacks in
   Magazine and Television Advertising: 1946 to 1986. *Journalism Quarterly* 67 (Autumn):
   551.

Another study on this topic was conducted by the City of New York
Department of Consumer Affairs and published in July 1991 (Green, 1991).
The department surveyed 11,391 populated advertisements in 318 issues of
27 different general-interest magazines. There were also 22,685 people
modeling clothes or using merchandise in 157 catalogs mailed by 56 mail-
order companies examined. At least 9 randomly selected issues of each magazine published between July 1988 and July 1991 were reviewed.
The study found that blacks remain nearly invisible in the advertising of

major national magazines, appearing in 4.52 percent of all magazine advertisements and constituting 3.15 percent of the advertisements' characters.
It concluded that "stereotyping, underrepresentation and de facto segregation exist" in advertising, which prompted the authors to ask that publishing companies establish goals for improved representation of black and
other multi-ethnic groups ("The Color of Advertising," 1991, p. 9).

The frequency of African-Americans in several randomly selected magazines did not increase over the past two decades. For example, in 1973 some
1.9 percent of the people in *Vogue* advertisements were African-American,
statistically not more than the 1.6 percent found in this study. Blacks in
Esquire actually declined to 2.4 percent in this study from 2.7 percent in
early 1974. A study of four major magazines in 1970 found that 4.2 percent
of the people in advertisements were African-American and 6.6 percent of
advertisements included African-Americans, appreciably greater than these
findings.

African-Americans in the advertisements were often shown in stereotypical
roles. Thirteen percent of the ads with blacks of the 11,391 reviewed were
for philanthropies, corporate social-message advertisements, or government-
sponsored advertisements, where they were often depicted as objects of social concern and in need of help. For example, 57 percent of the blacks
shown in *Business Week* advertisements were in this category.

The athlete stereotype was especially high in *Gentlemen's Quarterly*, where
27 percent of African-Americans were athletes, compared to under 5 percent
of the whites. And 68 percent of the blacks in *Sports Illustrated* were athletes, compared to only 15 percent of the whites.

The 11 issues of *Esquire* reviewed exhibited all the stereotypes: of the 20
blacks in advertisements, 8 were athletes, 2 were in advertisements for philanthropies, 1 was a jazz musician, 1 was a Caribbean native waiting on
white tourists, and 3 were hotel servants. Only 5 *Esquire* advertisers—
AT&T, Nordstrom, The Gap, Benetton, and a Scotch whisky maker—
showed black adults in non-stereotypical roles.

When African-Americans did appear in non-stereotypical roles in advertisements, their visual impact was often reduced by (a) picturing them with
whites, (b) obscuring them behind whites or in shadows, or (c) disproportionately using children instead of adults.

The report noted that experts say that whites tend to see black children
as less intimidating than black adults, and also noted that if an adult appeared in an advertisement with children, the adult was always white; never
was an African-American adult shown supervising white children.

The frequency of African-Americans in *Time* magazine advertisements declined during the 1980s. The results were quite surprising, considering that
9.8 percent of *Time*'s readers are black. A review of 24 issues of *Time* found
that while 4.8 percent of the people in advertisements were African-
American, if advertisements for philanthropies, like the United Negro Col-

lege Fund and Boys Club, and corporate social-message advertisements were eliminated—because African-Americans were the subject matter—then only 1.8 percent were African-American. Additionally, while African-Americans were depicted in 7.6 percent of *Time* advertisements, this was a third less than the 11.4 percent in 1980.

The report's review of catalogs showed that, on average, African-Americans were seen more frequently than in magazines. Overall, 4.6 percent of the models were African-American. Some major catalogs had virtually no African-Americans, including L.L. Bean, Lillian Vernon, and Tweeds, with fewer than 2 percent or not at all. In 11 Victoria's Secret catalogs, only 1.1 percent of the pictures were of multi-ethnics, and 6 contained no people of color.

Sears and J C Penney catalogs use people of color selectively. The venerable Sears catalog appeared to be more representative than many, with African-Americans comprising 6.2 percent of the people shown in the spring/summer 1991 catalog and 4.9 percent in the fall/winter 1991/92 catalog. On the other hand, blacks in the catalogs were disproportionately juveniles, and no blacks could be identified among pictures of lingerie.

African-Americans with lighter skin tones were often shown. In catalogs African-Americans were usually very light-skinned and, with few exceptions, had straightened hair.

One of the more profound findings of this study was that within the advertising industry "the emergence of the 'ethnic' market has not meant that many more minority images are used in general advertising. Instead, ethnic minorities are used in separate ad campaigns targeted outside the general market, in black and Latino-oriented media" (Green, 1991, p. 42). Green further asserts that, "the data shows irrefutably that the magazine industry is engaged in de facto economic segregation" (Chinyelu, 1991, p. 11).

The notion of separate but equal arose during an interview by the New York researchers with J. Abbot Miller, a professor at the Parson's School of Design, who suggested the following synopsis of the idea:

The separate-but-equal policy arose in the 1960s, when advertisers came up with the concept of "white media" and "black media." At that time, advocacy groups like the NAACP pressured advertisers to represent blacks in mainstream publications. Any results from this effort were short-lived. Advertisers responded that blacks were not used because magazines like *Time* and *Newsweek* were white. . . . By the mid-1970s it became apparent that white models were used only in white media and that black models were used only in the black media. This is true today, with a few exceptions. (Green, 1991, p. 42)

The New York researchers ultimately concluded the following after extensive investigation into the status of people of color in advertising:

The continuing paucity of minorities in magazine advertising . . . also runs counter to what appears to be a trend toward more racial and age diversity in the models seen in magazine editorial layouts. . . .
We also question just how deep have been the changes in white stereotypes of minorities and of African-American in particular. The magazine images of mammies and shoe-shine men have been replaced by a few fashion models and factory workers, but more commonly by athletes and musicians. While these are more desirable images, they're still stereotypes. (Green, 1991, p. 40)

The researchers also concluded that despite the efforts of various organizations, the massive amount of research devoted to the topic, and drastic changes in America's racial composition, African-Americans in magazine advertisements and catalogs are still "invisible people."

One year after the New York Department of Consumer Affairs issued its report *Invisible People,* the Department conducted a follow-up review in *Still Invisible People* of 2,108 advertisements in 10 magazines originally surveyed and noted an increase in African-American models from 3.4 percent in 1991 to 5.2 percent in 1992. The study further noted that, "this improvement in the frequency of African-Americans in magazine ads was undermined by the fact that many of the additional blacks were depicted in stereotypical roles" (Green, 1992, p. 1).

Additionally, a special survey of repeat advertisers in 634 issues of general circulation magazines found that some of the most prominent advertisers rarely depict blacks in their populated advertisements and when they were shown it was in stereotypical portrayals. More specifically, the Department cited *Calvin Klein, Lancome, Cover Girl, Georges Marciano, Gianni Versace, Georgio Armani, Toyota, Perry Ellis* and *NordicTrack,* a company which the Department asserted lived up to its name, as some of those advertisers that they felt should have been more inclusive in using models of color. As a part of their ongoing campaign to make the advertising industry more "diversity friendly," the Department wrote to each of these advertisers adamantly urging them to depict more people of color in their general circulation magazine advertisements. Conversely, there were more African-American models depicted in 1992 than in 1991 in *Esquire, Gentlemen's Quarterly, Better Homes and Gardens* and *Sports Illustrated.*

A survey by *Advertising Age* of 470 marketing and media executives found that a majority do recognize that a problem exists. When asked if they believe there are enough black people in print ads, 54.8 percent checked off "too few." When asked if advertising had an influence on America's current racial problems, 6.1 percent said "extremely influential," 13.8 percent said "very influential" and 36.4 percent said "somewhat influential" ("What Roles Do Ads," 1992, p. 1). The absence of blacks in advertising continues to be noticed regardless of the medium and the situation.

In 1990 Johnnetta Cole, president of Spelman College, became irate when she and five other women were being inducted into the Working Hall of Fame for 1990. During the ceremony at the Pierre Hotel in New York she, the other honorees, a few hundred journalists, editors, and advertisers were serenaded for 20 minutes with a film presentation of the image of women in advertising during the last 50 years. The audience was wowed with images ranging from Rosie the Riveter to Betty Crocker, Betty Furness and the Charlie Girl. What made Cole irate was the fact that during the entire presentation not one of the images included a faint hint of an African-American woman. "Not one!" "Not even Aunt Jemima," noted Cole in an ebullient stance from her seat on the dais to three black women who were seated below at a table directly in front of her (Edwards, 1993, p. 216). Cole's reaction suggests that some blacks would prefer to see blacks at least represented be it favorable or stereotypical. This position was also voiced by one other, who noted:

On a comparative basis, it may be better that minority figures appear as tokens, children or even as stereotypes than not to appear at all. But far more desirable is that they appear as whites appear, as potential customers for clothes, computers and cars, since minorities buy these things too. (Green, 1992, p. 12)

The studies cited above are important because collectively they tell us how much progress has been made and how much work still has to be done to achieve racial equality in the lucrative advertising industry. As evidenced by the studies, there was a dramatic increase in the use of blacks in advertising during the height of the civil rights movement. Blacks had been generally ignored or relegated to negative stereotyped roles until 1969, when a number of black actors and actresses appeared in their own TV shows (Northcott, 1975). With the decline in the use of black actresses and actors in subsequent years, the same is true of the use of African-American models in advertising. In fact, a study published by Yankelovich Partners and the Burrell Communications Group found that almost 60 percent of the nation's 31 million black consumers feel that most commercials and print ads, "are designed only for white people" (Holman, 1993, p. 11).

Researchers should continue to investigate this topic because of the impact that advertising has on formulating images of the black American. Advertising plays an important role with black children who are trying to develop positive images of themselves as well as of their race. "There's been a drastic erosion of self-esteem with young African-Americans—and it's partially because the images they see of themselves are either negative, offensive or not there." (Green, 1992, p. 3; "What Role Do Ads," 1992, p. 1; Gregory and Jacobs, 1993, p. 126). "In a few hours," a report of the House Select Committee on Aging (1977) related, "television can provide greater contact with members of a stereotyped group than one might ordinarily get in a lifetime." The high tech age in which we now live dictates that television is now more pervasive than ever. Blacks make up 10 million television households, while 82 million are white households (Sturgis, 1993, p. 21). This point is further reinforced by the fact that approximately 20 percent of television airtime is allotted to commercials (Achiron, 1986, pp. 35–36).

Thomas Pettigrew (1964), in his investigation of the black self-image, noted that

when the Negro looks around him—except in the spheres of athletics and entertainment—he discovers very few Americans with his skin color who hold important positions in his society. Save for the mass media expressly tailored for Negro audiences, he sees only white models in advertisements. . . . When he does see Negroes in the general mass media, they are likely to be cast in low status roles and appear as "amusingly ignorant." (p. 6)

Advertising also plays an important role with white children who, because of cultural and social alienation, learn about blacks primarily through the mass media. "African-American images impact on not only African-Americans, but European American populations, as well" (Sturgis, 1993, p. 23).

Although there are more blacks appearing in print advertisements and commercials, many companies still do not use black models to tout their products, fearing backlash from white consumers. Surprisingly, this fear has not subsided despite numerous studies, beginning in 1964, that document the contrary: whites do not refuse to purchase products that have been advertised by blacks.

The picture becomes clearer as we examine how much is spent annually by advertisers to reach black consumers. Almost half of all Fortune 1000 companies have some type of ethnic marketing campaign. That contrasts with only a handful in 1980. In 1992 companies spent $500 million on advertising and promotions to reach multi-ethnic audiences, including bilingual billboards, sweepstakes and parades. Interestingly, expenditures on advertising and promotional campaigns targeted at multi-racial groups amounted to $250 million in 1987 (McCarroll, 1993, p. 80).

Ken Smikle, publisher of *Target Market News,* a Chicago trade magazine that provides information on African-American consumers, estimates that as much as $700 million a year is spent by advertisers to target African-Americans (Mabry and Adams, 1989, p. 35). Procter and Gamble alone spends an estimated 5 percent of its $2 billion advertising budget on ethnic-oriented advertising (McCarroll, 1993, p. 80).

The amounts given here may seem adequate, but appear miniscule when it is noted that U.S. advertising expenditures in 1993 were projected at $139.3 billion, according to McCann Erickson Worldwide Insider's Report (Biagi, 1993, p. 2).

NOTE

1. The researchers defined major, minor, and background roles in the following manner:

Major role: very important to the commercial theme or layout; shown in foreground and/or shown holding the product and/or appears to be speaking.

Minor role: average importance to the commercial theme or layout; does not appear to speak or handle product.

Background role: hard to find; not important to the commercial theme or layout.

REFERENCES

Achiron, Marilyn. 1986. "Finding the Perfect Pitch for Women." *Adweek*, July 7, pp. 35–36.

Browder, Anthony T., ed. 1989. *From the Browder File: 22 Essays on the African American Experience*. Washington, D.C.: Institute of Karmic Guidance.

Bush, Ronald, Paul Solomon, and Joseph Hair, Jr. 1977. "There Are More Blacks in TV Commercials." *Journal of Advertising Research* 17 (February): 21–25.

Chinyelu, Mamadou. 1991. "No Color in Magazine Ads." *Black Enterprise* (December): 11.

Colfax, David, and Susan Sternberg. 1972. "The Perpetuation of Racial Stereotypes: Blacks in Mass Circulation Magazine Advertisements." *Public Opinion Quarterly* 36 (Spring): 7–18.

"The Color of Advertising." 1991. *Emerge* 3 (October): 9.

"Commercials Crossing the Color Line." 1968. *Time*, October 25, p. 83.

Cox, Keith. 1970. "Social Effects of Integrated Advertising." *Journal of Advertising Research* 10 (April): 41–44.

Culley, James, and Rex Bennett. 1976. "Selling Women, Selling Blacks." *Journal of Communications* 26 (Autumn): 160–74.

Davis, Richard A. 1987. "Television Commercials and the Management of Spoiled Identity." *Western Journal of Black Studies* 11 (Summer): 59–63.

Djata. 1987. "Madison Avenue Blindly Ignores the Black Consumer." *Business and Society Review* 60 (Winter): 9–13.

Dominick, Joseph, and Bradley Greenberg. 1970. "Three Seasons of Blacks on Television." *Journal of Advertising* 10 (April): 21–27.

Edwards, Audrey. 1993. "From Aunt Jemima to Anita Hill: Media's Split Image of Black Women." *Media Studies Journal* 7 (Winter/Spring): 215–22.

Foote, Cone, and Belding. 1970. Integrated Advertising: A Synthesis of Published Research and Opinion. Foote, Cone and Belding Research Department.

Gardner, Marilyn, and Hy Gardner. 1983. "Glad You Asked That." *Knoxville News-Sentinel*, March 20, p. 14.

Geizer, Ronald. 1971. "Advertising in *Ebony:* 1960 and 1969." *Journalism Quarterly* (Spring): 131–34.

Goffman, Erving. 1961. *Asylums*. Garden City, N.Y.: Anchor Books.

Goodall, Kenneth. 1972. "Blacks in Advertisements in the Post Mammy Era." *Psychology Today* 6 (October): 138.

Green, Mark. 1991. *Invisible People: The Depiction of Minorities in Magazine Ads and Catalogs.* New York: City of New York Department of Consumer Affairs.

———. 1992. *Still Invisible: The Depiction of Minorities in Magazine Ads One Year After the Consumer Affairs Department Study,* Invisible People. New York: City of New York Department of Consumer Affairs.

Gregory, Deborah, and Patricia Jacobs. 1993. "The Ugly Side of the Modeling Business." *Essence* (September): 89–90, 126, 128.

Holman, Blan. 1993. "Changing the Face(s) of Advertising: AAF and Its Members Seek Solutions to Advertising's Dearth of Diversity." *American Advertising* (Fall): 10–13.

House Select Committee on Age Stereotyping and Television. 1977. Washington, D.C.: U.S. Government Printing Office. Communication Publication Number 95–109, September.

Humphrey, Ronald, and Howard Schuman. 1984. "The Portrayal of Blacks in Magazine Advertisements: 1950–1982." *Public Opinion Quarterly* 48 (Fall): 551–63.

Jones, Caroline R. "Advertising in Black and White." *Madison Avenue,* pp. 53–54, 56, 58.

Joseph, Gloria I. and Jill Lewis. 1981. *Common Differences: Conflicts in Black and White Feminist Perspectives.* Garden City, N.Y.: Anchor Books.

Kassarjian, Harold. 1969. "The Negro and American Advertising 1946–1965." *Journal of Marketing Research* 6 (February): 29–39.

Kern-Foxworth, Marilyn. 1982. A Comparative Analysis of the Portrayal of Blacks and Whites in White-Oriented Mass Circulation Magazine Advertisements during 1959, 1969, and 1979. Ph.D. diss., University of Wisconsin, Madison.

———. 1988. "The Kerner Report and the Civil Rights Movement: Implications for the Future of Blacks in Advertising." *Southwestern Mass Communication Journal* 4: 76–92.

Kilbourne, Jean. 1987. "Still Killing Us Softly." Cambridge Documentary Films. Cambridge, MA. (Videotape)

Lester, Paul, and Ron Smith. 1989. African-American Picture Coverage in *Life, Newsweek* and *Time,* 1937–1988. Paper presented at the 72nd annual convention of the Association for Education in Journalism and Mass Communication, Washington, D.C., August 12.

Mabry, Marcus, and Rhonda Adams. 1989. "A Long Way from Aunt Jemima." *Newsweek,* August 14, pp. 34–35.

MacDonald, J. Fred. 1984. "Marketing to Blacks: Stereotypes Fall in TV Ad Portrayals." *Advertising Age* 55 (November 19): 44.

McCarroll, Thomas. 1993. "It's a Mass Market No More: The New Ethnic Consumer is Forcing Companies to Change the Way They Sell Their Wares." *Time,* p. 80.

Muro, Mark. 1989. "Sex in Advertising: Marketers Embrace New Era of Eros." *Bryan-College Station* (Texas) *Eagle,* May 14, p. 4E.

Nixon, Mark. 1983. "Minorities in TV Ads a Hot Topic." *USA Today,* September 29, pp. 1–2D.

Northcott, Herbert, John Segar, and James Hinton. 1975. "Trends in TV Portrayal of Blacks and Women." *Journalism Quarterly* 15: 741–44.

O'Kelly, Charlotte, and Linda Bloomquist. 1976. "Women and Blacks on TV." *Journal of Communications* 26 (Autumn): 179–84.

Pease, Ronnye. 1991. Shades of Gray: The Use of African Americans in Magazine Advertisements. Paper presented at the 74th annual convention of the Association for Education in Journalism and Mass Communication, Boston, August 7–10.

Pettigrew, Thomas. 1964. *A Profile of the Negro American.* Princeton, N.J.: D. Van Nostrand.

Pierce, Chester M., Jean V. Carew, Diane Pierce-Gonzalez, and Deborah Wills. 1977. "An Experiment in Racism: TV Commercials." *Education and Urban Society* 10: 62–88.

Rankin, William Parkman. 1980. *Business Management of General Consumer Magazines.* New York: Praeger.

Roberts, Churchill. 1970–71. "The Portrayal of Blacks on Network Television." *Journal of Broadcasting* 15 (Winter): 45–53.

Scheibe, Cynthia Leone. 1983. Character Portrayals and Values in Network TV Commercials. Master's thesis, Cornell University.

Shayon, Robert. 1968. "Commercials in Black and White." *Saturday Review* (October): 48.

Sheperd, Juanita M. 1980. "The Portrayal of Black Women in the Ads of Popular Magazines." *Western Journal of Black Studies* 4 (Fall): 179–82.

Shuey, Audrey, Nancy King, and Barbara Griffith. 1953. "Stereotyping of Negroes and Whites: An Analysis of Magazine Pictures." *Public Opinion Quarterly* 17 (Summer): 281–87.

Sturgis, Ingrid. 1993. "Black Images in Advertising: A Revolution Is Being Televised in 30-Second Commercials." *Emerge* (September): 21–23.

Stutts, Mary Ann. 1982. "Blacks in Magazine Ads: Are They Growing in Numbers?" *Mid-South Business Journal* 2: 24–27.

"What Roles Do Ad Clubs Play in Racial Tension." 1992. *Advertising Age* August 10, pp. 1, 35.

Wheatley, John. 1971. "The Use of Black Models in Advertising." *Journal of Marketing Research* 8 (August): 390–92.

Wilkes, Robert E., and Humberto Valencia. 1989. "Hispanics and Blacks in Television Commercials." *Journal of Avertising* 18: 19–25.

Zinkhan, George M., Keith Cox, and Jae Hong. 1989. "Changes in Stereotypes: Blacks and Whites in Magazine Advertisements." *Journalism Quarterly* 63 (Autumn): 568–72.

Zinkhan, George M., William J. Qualls, and Abhijit Biswas. 1990. "The Use of Blacks in Magazine and Television Advertising: 1946 to 1986." *Journalism Quarterly* 67 (Autumn): 547–53.

Chapter 7 _____

BLACKS IN ADVERTISING: CRITICS GIVE TWO THUMBS UP

With pressures exerted on advertisers by various organizations, there were significantly more black faces seen selling an array of products during the 1960s. Attention then focused on the response of consumers to such portrayals. One of the chief concerns advertisers had about using black models was the response of white consumers. "Pressure for censorship in television dramatics came from sponsors, networks, advertising agencies and even production personnel. Above all, these elements feared offending the prejudices and the economic strength of their white audiences" (MacDonald, 1983, p. 41). White consumers were the primary purchasers of most of the goods advertised, and alienating them would mean a significant decline in revenues.

One of the first companies to integrate its advertising was Level Brothers (Cohen, 1970, p. 155). A pioneer in this area, the company did not experience any adverse reaction. However, this positive showing was not to continue, and other companies experienced somewhat different outcomes when attempting to integrate their advertising campaigns. One Rheingold beer advertisement showed an integrated beach in a resort area. The scene prompted widespread criticism from both blacks and whites and was ultimately withdrawn. The story did not end there, however, as the absence of a nonwhite finalist in its subsequent "Miss Rheingold" campaigns caused company officials to discontinue the program "since it created the image of 'lily white' in the minds of members of the nonwhite community" (Collier, 1965, p. 134).

Another case occurred during the mid-1950s. Fearing it too controversial for the South, the CBS sales department failed to obtain a sponsor for its documentary on Marian Anderson's operatic tour of the Far East. Not until Edward R. Murrow and coproducer Fred W. Friendly personally found a sponsor did CBS agree to air the feature during prime time. The South's resistance to the televising of blacks in any capacity was eloquently characterized by one author like this: "The South was only an intensified microcosm of national racial attitudes. Its Jim Crow laws were more blatant, its segregation was more developed, and its economic disparity was more apparent than in other regions of the U.S.A." (MacDonald, 1983, p. 44).

On the opposite end of the spectrum, advertisers also were concerned about the response of black consumers to the use of black models in advertisements and commercials. Were the depictions of blacks in advertising merely holographic projections of white advertisers? In other words, would black consumers view the portrayals as the image of blacks seen through white eyes? Interestingly enough, some black leaders did not accept the use of blacks in advertising with open arms. They "regarded integrated advertising as another attempt to remake blacks into imitations of the white bourgeoisie, while some black businessmen viewed social change as the beginning of new economic opportunities" (Atwan et. al., 1979, p. 87).

In March 1970 *Ebony* reacted cynically to the use or nonuse of blacks in advertising when it published an ad with the headline "Why Johnny Can't Read Your Ads" (p. 90). The advertisement maligned the media's use of blond, all-American models to sell everything from cigarettes to automobiles. The ad continued, "Johnny, you see, has trouble identifying with . . . all-American types. They may be all-American in your neighborhood, but not in Johnny's. So Johnny doesn't get past the pictures to the words. He knows they're not meant for him."

As the frequency of blacks appearing in advertising increased, researchers conducted numerous studies during the 1960s and 1970s on the reactions of black and white consumers. However, during the 1980s picking up a magazine or newspaper or turning on the television and seeing a black person selling a product had become passé, and research interest in the reaction of consumers to integrated advertising had waned. For this reason, the number of studies on the topic during the 1980s is minuscule.

So, how did whites and blacks react to seeing a black person selling Coke and Crest? Were the whites irate? Did they stop buying the product? Did they write hate letters to sponsors? Were blacks pleased with how they were represented in the advertisements? The answers to these and other questions can be answered by an examination of the studies outlined below.

REACTIONS OF WHITE CONSUMERS TO INTEGRATED ADVERTISING

Although the socio-economic status of the black population had made it a viable market, advertisers catering to black audiences were fearful that such action would alienate white consumers. Studies were conducted to ascertain the reactions of white consumers to this increase. They asked questions such as the following: If they did not integrate their advertising, what measures would be taken by blacks? Will either the use of black models in advertising or appeals which are basically designed for blacks alienate whites? (Bureau of Advertising, 1970).

Barban and associates (1964, 1965), the first to study this area, used the semantic differential to determine responses of black and white students to integrated advertising. They found no difference between black and white reactions with the exception of those labeled as "integrated." Whites were generally neutral or slightly favorable toward integrated ads, whereas blacks tended to be more favorably inclined.

Stafford, Birdwell, and Van Tassel (1970) also studied this area, showing integrated advertisements to 100 white consumers aged 21 to 50 in New York, Chicago, and Los Angeles. They used both verbal and nonverbal techniques to test the possibility of white backlash.

Advertisements of two very different products, automobiles and lipstick, were used for the experiment, the former for its "low emotional involvement setting" and the latter for its presumed higher level of emotional response. It was hypothesized that the respondents would have a more negative response toward integrated advertisements than to nonintegrated advertisements, and that the degree of emotional response toward integrated advertisements would fluctuate according to product. These were the results:

1. There is some negative response generated toward certain integrated advertisements, but it is not clear if this reaction is a function of race, or the ad being "poor" in a creative sense, or a function of other factors which are not discernible at this point because of the significant interaction taking place.

2. Differences in emotional response do vary across products, but the precise nature and direction of these differences must be examined more closely before accurate response predictions can be made. (p. 20)

A study conducted by Lester Guest (1970) employed five experimental groups to analyze the reactions of white consumers to integrated advertising. Respondents were shown advertisements with white models only, with black and white models, and with black models alone. The conclusion from the study was that "advertisers need not be fearful of adverse effects to the use of Negro models, either by themselves or integrated with whites, especially in view of the expanding market of young and educated consumers" (p. 33). And although a negative response was anticipated, there was none noted when blacks were placed in positions superior to those of whites.

This line of research was broadened by Cagley and Cardozo (1970) when they hypothesized that highly prejudiced whites would respond less favorably to integrated advertising than more liberal whites. Subjects included 34 white college seniors. Degree of prejudice was determined by answers given in questionnaires four weeks prior to the evaluation of the advertisements. With all other factors held constant, the researchers concluded that degree of racial prejudice made a difference in the number of negative responses. The higher the level of prejudice, the higher the degree of negativity to integrated advertisements.

The Bureau of Advertising conducted *A Study of Blacks in Newspaper Ads* (1970), which involved showing a portfolio to black and white females in the New York metropolitan area. An insignificant percentage (4) of white respondents had negative responses to the inclusion of blacks. In fact, 37 percent of the white respondents showed positive reactions toward black models, another 57 percent were neutral, while 15 percent noted no response at all. There also were 7 percent who could not be strictly labeled as positive or negative. However, there was a tendency for these respondents to be more negative than positive. The comments accompanying these reactions were along these lines: "Nothing wrong with it, but I don't like mixed marriages"; "They are pushing their way in but it doesn't bother me." Rejections by white respondents, whether expressed or implied, thus totaled 11 percent. (The percentages add up to more than 100 because of multiple comments; p. 24.)

Contrary to the results of Cagley and Cardozo, signs of rejection could not be ascribed more to prejudiced whites than to nonprejudiced whites in a 1971 study done by Tolley and Goett. Their findings suggested that the presence of black models in advertisements had no effect on the attitudes of whites. Dr. Stuart Tolley, vice president of the Bureau of Advertising Communications Research, reported, "The findings indicate that the store and the merchandise are more [important] factors in motivating purchase behavior than ads with black or white models" (Christopher, 1970, p. 29).

John Gifford (1972) also dealt with the impact of integrated advertising on store image. His purpose was to ascertain the degree to which black and white consumers are capable of formulating store images based upon sample advertisements. The study was also designed to determine the difference in the images formed by black and white consumers. Subjects were students at the University of Colorado. The results were that white subjects were able to interpret store image 100 percent of the time for all-black advertisements, 96.8 percent of the time for integrated advertisements, and 90.3 percent of the time for all-white advertisements (p. 236).

No significant differences were noted between department store images formed by black and white students, whether derived from all-white, all-black, or integrated ads. In fact, white subjects viewed integrated advertisements more favorably than the all-white or all-black advertisements in 80.6 percent of the cases (p. 240).

William Muse (1971, p. 107) conducted research in this area to answer the following questions:

1. How are ads using blacks perceived and received by white audiences?
2. Are ads using black models rated as favorably by white audiences as the same ads using white models?
3. Would the reaction of a white viewer or reader differ across product categories?

The study used both experimental and control groups, formed from students chosen randomly at a midwestern university. One group was shown ads for cigarettes, liquor, feminine hygiene napkins, and beer using white models. The other group was shown similar ads using black models.

In answer to his questions, Muse noted, "One can conclude from these results that white college students tend to rate ads using only black models as favorably as they rate ads using only white models. What indication of unfavorable reaction there is appears to be product-related" (p. 109).

In contrast to the other studies cited, Schlinger and Plummer (1972) investigated television rather than print ads. Black and white females were shown commercials and asked to rate them according to "(1) the company, product, or brand advertised, (2) the ad's content and organization, and (3) thoughts, feelings, and associations that the commercial might have aroused in the viewer's mind" (p. 150). Results indicated that white subjects viewed commercials with blacks as less professional, but the researchers did not see this as indicative of negative feelings toward the models.

Carl Block (1967) tested the hypothesis that "well-known brands of consumer goods are as appealing to white people who have seen them advertised with black models as they are to whites when they are seen in ads using white models." Subjects were representative of white adults from three Missouri communities, who were exposed to 21 different advertisements for soft drinks, cigarettes, and life insurance, and ranked them from "most appealing" to "least appealing." Of the six products studied only one produced significant negative ratings: An advertisement for Coca-Cola was rated lower when using black models than when using whites. There appeared to be a correlation between the prominence of the product being advertised and the race of the model used.

Controversy exists among researchers concerning the capacity of the mass media to influence human behavior. This area of study was applied to advertising when Bush, Gwinner, and Solomon (1974) focused on the actual buying behavior of white consumers after exposure to integrated advertising. Prior studies had focused on the attitudes of consumers toward integrated advertising, assuming that these would be indicative of purchase behavior.

The experiment used three point-of-purchase displays in a supermarket, with all white models, all black models, or black and white models. Sales response of white consumers was hypothesized to be considerably higher for the displays using all white models. The results, however, although focusing on buying rather than attitudes, were no different from those in the studies cited earlier. Negative responses from white respondents were not statistically significant. But since the study was not longitudinal and utilized only a few products, its scope is limited.

A study by Stuart Surlin (1977) attempted to determine the correlation between the degree of authoritarianism exhibited by advertising executives and their use of black models in advertising. The hypothesis was based on a documented parallel between authoritarianism and racism (Kirscht and Dillehay, 1967; Allport, 1962). In 1972 Surlin had found that high-level authoritarian individuals are attracted to careers in advertising. Thus, he thought it logical to assume that advertisers are more apt to be racist authoritarians, and to be reluctant to use black models in advertising directed at a mass audience.

Advertising and business executives were sampled in Atlanta. The researcher concluded that "the low authoritarian advertising executive is significantly more likely to state that he would use a black model in his ad than either the middle or high authoritarian advertising executive" (p. 115).

A 1983 study, "The Effect of Black Models on Magazine Ad Readership," reported that despite the apprehension of advertisers to utilize black models, magazine advertisements with black models, white models, and no models had comparable readership scores (Soley, 1983).

The results of a study presented at the 30th annual conference of the American Council on Consumer Interests supported findings of other studies in this area, and suggested that "with research on black models in advertising, one can easily conclude that the white backlash is a fiction, a paranoia of marketers, that has been upheld in only one old study that yielded the opposite results when replicated" (Pozzi and Rotfield, 1984, p. 14).

REACTIONS OF BLACK CONSUMERS TO INTEGRATED ADVERTISING

Limited research has been devoted to assessing the reactions of black consumers to integrated advertising, even though the advertising industry could suffer very negative repercussions if black consumers reacted negatively. Advertisers generally did not anticipate a negative reaction from black consumers.

Research pertinent to the reaction of blacks to integrated advertising was conducted much earlier than research to test the reactions of whites. In fact, during the 1920s and 1930s tests were conducted to see how advertising appealed to black consumers. Companies would run two advertisements with different illustrations to test response. One would show whites using or discussing a certain product; the other would feature a black person discussing the same product. The advertisements featuring black people gained the attention of most blacks—in fact 80 percent of the respondents showed their approval (Reno, 1986, p. 1). Despite their slowness to heed the advice, these tests did give advertisers some indication that blacks preferred to see blacks in advertising as early as the 1920s.

Many advertisers who did integrate their advertising failed to realize that black consumers were interested in seeing more than just a black face. They wanted to see blacks portrayed in positions commensurate with whites and ads that reflected the upward mobility in the socioeconomic status of the black community.

The study discussed earlier by Barban and Cundiff (1964) also tested the responses of black students to integrated advertising. The researchers noted that black respondents judged ads containing black and white models more favorably than did white respondents.

Schmidt and Preston (1969) surveyed members of the National Association for the Advancement of Colored People to ascertain how the black community felt about integrated advertising. Their findings suggest that the black community was not only interested in seeing black models in advertisements, but wanted to see blacks portrayed in integral positions, socially interacting with whites. The researchers commented, "Ads showing Negroes segregated from whites or, engaging in implausible situations of interaction, may be worse than ads showing no Negroes at all" (p. 16).

Gould, Sigband, and Zourner (1970) surveyed the responses of blacks to integrated advertising. Respondents were chosen from five shopping areas in integrated Los Angeles communities. The interviewers randomly approached consumers and asked them the following questions: "Until just a few years ago, advertisers did not often use black people in their ads. Today we see quite a number of ads in which black and white people appear together. Why do you think advertisers are using ads like this? How do you feel about ads like this?" (p. 24).

Most of the subjects felt that economic and social pressures exerted upon the advertisers caused the increase in integrated advertising. The researchers stated that, "Fewer than 11 percent saw humanitarianism as a motive" (p. 25). The majority of the respondents indicated positive feelings toward integrated advertising. Ambiguous answers were given by more than 7 percent, and negative responses by more than 27 percent.

The substantial number of negative responses prompted the researchers to examine the age, sex, and occupation of the subjects. A significant relationship was noted between age and type of response. Subjects 29 and younger had more negative responses, and subjects 30 and over had more positive responses (p. 26).

The researchers contended that persons 30 and older were more lenient in their acceptance of the ads because any implication of integration was satisfactory to them. However, those 29 and younger were not content with just any level of integration, but would react positively only to integrated advertising that was not exemplary of tokenism.

The investigation by Schlinger and Plummer (1972), cited above, tested the reactions of blacks and whites to integrated advertising. A total of 94 black women were used in the study. After exposure to television commercials, they were asked to express their views by agreeing or disagreeing with 128 statements made about "(1) the company, product, or brand advertised, (2) the ad's content and organization, and (3) thoughts, feelings, and associations that the commercial might have aroused in the viewer's mind" (pp. 151–152). The findings suggested that the subjects were more favorable toward commercials using all black models.

Choudhury and Schmid (1974) investigated the impact on recall of using black models when advertising to blacks. Selected ads from *Life, Look,* and *Ebony* were shown to students from Los Angeles Southwest College. The retention of blacks was much higher when recalling ads with black models. According to the researchers, blacks would be more likely to purchase products advertised by black models or black and white models than by all white models.

Another study examined whether black or white models had a different affect on eliciting product choice behavior on black and white college students. The products used were *Zest* soap and *Annie Green Springs* wine. Major findings were (1) that there were no differences in the behavioral responses of blacks or whites to soap or wine television advertisements that contain either a black or a white model, and (2) that black subjects responded more favorably to black models in wine commercials than to white models in wine commercials (Solomon, 1974).

Data Black Public Opinion Polls, the only black-owned market research firm in 1980, conducted a study to test the reaction of black consumers to the use of blacks in advertising. It was administered by telephone to 1,177 respondents. Of the total sampled, 49 percent said they would be more likely to purchase a product featuring a black model. Twenty-four percent indicated no response either way, 5 percent indicated that they would be less likely to purchase a product featuring a black model, and 10 percent said they would be much less likely to purchase a product advertised by a black model (Rozen, 1980, p. 20).

Percy Sutton, head of Inner City Broadcasting and cofounder of Data Black along with sociologist Kenneth Clark, said of the study results: "They show advertisers that there is a special appeal that can be made to blacks and better results will come of it" (p. 20).

One of the more recent examinations of the responses of black and white consumers to the use of blacks in advertising employed a different strategy. This study by Pitts et al. (1989) used advertisements developed expressly for black consumers. The researchers analyzed the effects of four national television commercials for products that were leaders in their categories: Crest, McDonald's, Ford, and Coca-Cola.[1] Each contained a strong major theme plus secondary themes relevant to the black experience. These secondary themes were more subtle and culturally based, and served the advertiser by creating an emotionally moving, subtextual message that spoke directly to the target audience. The primary objective of the study was to determine the role of values in culturally based advertising.

After black and white responses to the advertisements and the products advertised were compared and examined, the researchers concluded that black respondents displayed a more positive attitude toward a commercial message that featured black actors than did whites. One of the more significant findings was that "when marketing communication utilizes strong cultural orientation, significant difference in black versus white responses may be obtained" (p. 328). The researchers continued their analysis by noting that the "study's subculturally targeted advertisements elicit not only a stronger, more positive response to the brand and the commercial itself from the targeted audience, . . . but they generate a markedly different response in terms of perception of the value message" (p. 328).

The researchers further concluded that at least two interpretations could be made based on the data collected: (1) blacks see more, and (2) whites see less. This point was illustrated by noting that the whites exposed to the Crest commercial observed two values and the blacks observed nine. The whites saw a happy, close-knit family and identified the values of security and warmth. The blacks observed excitement, fun, enjoyment, well-respected, self-fulfillment, self-respect, belonging, and accomplishment. The researchers ultimately surmised that unless the value is dramatically made, as in the McDonald's commercial, white consumers will not receive the message as clearly as black consumers.

Tommy Whittler (1989) reported that white college students reacted the same to advertisements containing white and black models, whereas black college students reacted more favorably to advertisements containing white and black models.

More recent research to examine the reaction of black and white consumers to integrated advertising also was conducted by Whittler (1991) in two tests.

To conduct study number 1 a total of 160 white and 140 black undergraduates rated a professionally prepared storyboard featuring a white or black actor promoting a portable word processor or a liquid laundry detergent. To conduct the second study the researcher measured the reactions of 160 southeastern white adults to a white or black model promoting a fur coat or a liquid laundry detergent.

The results of the studies indicated that black respondents showed an increased likelihood to purchase products featuring black models. Additionally, high-prejudice whites showed less interest in obtaining additional information about the laundry detergent when a black actor was featured in the advertising. The results of study 2 also indicated that low-prejudice whites showed no difference in their ability to identify with white or black models, whereas high-prejudice whites perceived themselves as less similar to black than to white models, and identified more strongly with white than with black models. Whittler concluded that "findings from both studies support the notion that viewers with stronger racial attitudes are more likely to be affected by source characteristics (i.e., whether the actors are black or not) than viewers with weaker racial attitudes" (p. 60).

Whittler (1991) also reports on an unpublished study conducted with a colleague on this topic that suggests that regardless of their attitudes toward blacks, white adults were less likely to purchase the product, and had less favorable attitudes toward the product and the advertisement, when the advertisement featured a black rather than a white model (forthcoming).

Whittler reconciles the differences found between his 1989, 1991, and yet unpublished studies by suggesting that "today's younger whites and blacks have more opportunity for interactions than adult whites and blacks. Thus, younger people may be more willing to accept individuals of different races" (1991, pp. 59–60).

The best answer to whether or not advertisers should be concerned about the presence of blacks in advertisements was summarized in an article by Ronald Bush published in *Advertising Age* in 1978. The author noted that despite all of the studies conducted, most were in agreement that the integration of black models into advertising campaigns would not alienate white consumers. The author did note, however, that "several researchers have suggested that consumer reaction to black models might not be good if the product being advertised is a 'personal care' product . . . [such as for] feminine napkins and bras." The researcher also noted that "an ad containing a black male who, in the opinion of several consumers, appeared 'militant' resulted in low scores." Interestingly, Ron Garner, a heavily bearded black model featured on cigarette billboards during the mid-1970s, reinforced this finding when he was quoted in *Ebony* as saying, "Right now, the problem I'm facing with my beard is that too often it is equated with militancy. I've lost a lot of work because of it, but I have to be me and I think it makes me unique from most other models" (Lewis, 1977, p. 82).

Oddly enough, despite all of the research and the findings suggesting no "white backlash," in 1991 some advertisers were still reluctant to make black models a consistent part of their advertising campaigns. In that year the City of New York Department of Consumer Affairs conducted extensive interviews with modeling and advertising agency executives in an attempt to determine why advertisers and many catalogers still showed so few minorities. Based on their interviews and an analysis of previously published research, they theorized the following in the report *Invisible People: The Depiction of Minorities in Magazine Ads and Catalogs:*

Companies advertise in general-interest magazines to reach the white readership—minorities are an afterthought. To reach black consumers some advertisers use black publications, although not nearly enough do, but those that do do so to the neglect of general circulation publications. There is a flagrant disregard for the large segment of the African-American community that also reads publications intended for the general public.

Much advertising is intended to appeal to the affluent—or to those who identify with the affluent—who are thought of as white. (p. 35)

In advertisements for resorts, expensive hotels, perfumes, and private banking services, only white models are used because they can be more easily associated with wealth, according to Michele Wallace, author of the book *Invisibility Blues.* "The problem is that advertisers think that having blacks in their advertisements would cheapen the look," noted Wallace in an interview (Green, 1991, p. 36). Ken Smikle, publisher of *Target Market News,* a publication that profiles African-American consumers, echoes the sentiments of Wallace and conjectures that featuring a black man in advertisements for certain imported luxury cars might be thought to give the appearance that a thief or drug dealer was using it, and showing blacks in advertisements for luxury apartments warns white consumers that African-Americans live in that neighborhood (Green, 1991, p. 36).

Dr. Carol Moog, head of an advertising consulting firm, told the New York researchers how models are selected. "The facial expression, the position of the model, the gestures, the skin color, ethnicity, and hairstyle are important. If you use a model, it affects the image of the product advertised. So whether or not you use a black model is an important part of the product's image" (p. 36).

The "Procter & Gamble Look" is still king. The Procter & Gamble look, according to Arthur Bonfrin, president of Model Management, Inc., is the all-American, good-looking, girl-next-door look. Susan Jirovec, executive director of Plus Models, described the P&G look as "usually blond hair and blue eyes—although some models with dark hair have been categorized in the P&G look" (p. 37). The researchers assessed the P&G phenomenon like this:

The insistence on this homogenized look in print ads runs counter to the racial diversity seen in the non-ad pages of most magazines. While we did not conduct an empirical analysis of the racial make-up of fashion layouts in magazines like *Mademoiselle* and *Vogue,* we can say generally that we saw much more racial diversity on non-ad pages. *Time, Business Week,* and many of the other magazines we reviewed also had very substantial minority presences in their non-ad pages. (p. 37)

Table 7.1
Summary of Previous Research

Author(s)	Stimuli	Subjects	Dependent Measures	Results
Barban & Cundiff (1964)	1 Integrated Ad	White & Black Students	Favorability	Whites = Slightly favorable Blacks = Very favorable
Barban (1969)	4 @ White, Black, & Integrated ads*	White & Black Midwestern Adults	Preference	White: 1 > W > B Blacks: B > 1 > W
Stafford, Birdwell, & Van Tassel (1970)	2 @ White and Integrated ads	White Adults	Pupil Dilation General Ad Measures	1 < W 1 = W
Guest (1970)	1 @ White and Black ad, 2 Integrated ads	White Students	Overall Evaluation Thoughts	W = B = 1 (see Text for Thought results)
Cagley & Cardoza (1970)	3 @ White, Black, & Integrated Ads	White Students Adults	Message, Ad, Product, & Company Evaluation	For Each Measure: White Actors: Hi Prej = Lo Prej Integrated & Black Actors: Hi Prej < Lo Prej
Bush, Hair, & Solomon (1979)	6 @ White, Black, & Integrated Ads*	White Southern Adults	Same as Cagley & Cardoza	White Actors: Hi Prej > Lo Prej Integrated: Hi Prej = Lo Prej Black Actors: Hi Prej < Lo Prej
Szybillo & Jacoby (1974)	5 Levels of Integrated Ads*	White & Black Students	Attractiveness Purchase Intentions	Whites: B = W = 1 Blacks: B > 1W

Study	Stimuli	Sample	Measures	Results
Bush, Gwinner, & Solomon (1974)	1 @ White, Black, & Integrated P-O-P Displays*	White Southern Adults	Purchase Behavior	W = B = 1
Solomon, Bush, & Hair (1974)	1 @ White, Black, & Integrated P-O-P Displays*	White & Black Southern Adults	Purchase Behavior	W = B = 1
Block (1972)	6 @ White & Black Ads	White Adults	Appeal	W = B
Tolley & Goett (1971)	6 @ White & Integrated Ads	White & Black Adults	Notice Actor's Race Recall Thoughts (+ -0)	For Each Measure: Whites: B < W Blacks: B > W
Muse (1971)	(4) Matched Set of White & Black Ads*	White Midwestern Students	Favorability	For two products, W = B For remaining products, W > B and B > W
Choudury & Schmid (1974)	(13) Matched Set of White & Black Ads	White & Black Students	Recall	Whites: B = W Blacks: B > W
Schlinger & Plummer (1972)	1 @ White & Black Ads*	White & Black Midwestern Adults	General Ad Measures	Whites: W = B Blacks: B > W

*Studies used between-subject manipulation of actor's race.

Perceptions of all African-Americans and all Latinos are lumped together.
Advertisers, like other Americans, have become victims of the portrayals they
see of African-Americans on the six o'clock news—welfare recipients—even
though only 33 percent of the recipients of welfare are black and 61 percent
are white (Ehrenreich, 1991, p. 84). Drug users and drug pushers. Gang
members. Criminals. The black consumer's status is synonymous with poor,
in spite of the fact that only 29.5 percent of African-Americans live at or
below the poverty level, and the majority have middle class incomes.

Subconscious exclusion and "liberal" and "aversive" racism. Bethann Har-
dison, owner of Bethann Management, a prominent African-American modeling agency, defines "liberal racists" as whites who do not deliberately
discriminate but simply never think of hiring black models for advertising
campaigns (Green, 1991, pp. 37–38). Samuel Gaertner and John Davidio
(1986) define "aversive racism" as "the racial attitude that we believe char-
acterizes many white Americans who possess strong egalitarian values." They
regard themselves as nonprejudiced and nondiscriminatory, "but almost un-
avoidably possess negative feelings and beliefs about blacks" (pp. 37–38).

WHAT THE FINDINGS SHOW

For decades advertisers and marketers have used the fear of white backlash
as a reason for not using more African-Americans in their advertising campaigns. As evidenced by the research cited above, there is little or no credence
to this fear (see Table 7.1). Study after study has shown that white consumers
do not base their purchase decisions on the race of the person who advertises
the product. White consumers were oblivious to whether blacks advertised
any certain products or not and didn't hesitate to buy blue Northern toilet paper with the little black girl prominently displayed on it if they had blue bath-
rooms to decorate. There is overwhelming evidence, however, that suggests
that blacks, on the other hand, are more prone to purchase products that use
black models to advertise them. Over the years McDonald's and Burger King
have used a substantial number of black models in their campaigns in very
positive portrayals of African-American culture and life-styles. The rewards for
these companies have been reciprocal and substantial. These two companies
and others like Pepsi and Coke have capitalized on a market that has been virtually ignored by other companies.

As we enter the 21st century other companies, organizations, and institutions will have to become more accountable to their nontraditional customers, patrons, clients, and constituents. In an ever-changing world,
marketers will no longer be able to cloak themselves in the misguided veil
of "white backlash." As America's population becomes more racially and
ethnically diverse, advertisers will have to implement new and innovative
strategies for targeting African-Americans, who will be the majority group
in many major metropolitan areas. The "business as usual" approach will

become antiquated as these astute consumers realize their worth in the global marketplace and systematically and methodically begin spending their money with businesses that recognize every color in the national rainbow.

NOTE

1. The following are the treatments for the commercials used to conduct the study by Pitts (1989):

FIRST COMMERCIAL

Crest Toothpaste

Theme line: "Aren't your kids worth Crest?

Opening Sequence: A telephone conversation between a young boy at home and his father, at work. The son is asking the father if he will be able to attend his concert that night.

Singer: "Sometimes you go through changes for your children's happiness." Family values centrally focused upon the child. "He's your pride and joy, your little boy, he's the reason you switched to Crest."

Sequential Shot: We see the boy getting ready for the orchestra concert and the father at work hurrying to join the family. "Will he make it?" Tension is created as mom and sister are settled in their seats, the boy is poised holding his instrument, scanning the audience for his father. Just as the concert is about to begin Dad slips into his seat, to the joy of the family.

Singer: "Aren't your kids worth it? Aren't your kids worth Crest?"

SECOND COMMERCIAL

McDonald's

Opening Sequence: A weary working mother picks up her small, young boy at the community day-care center.

Singer: "You can't be together till your work is through."

Sequence: Mother and son ride a bus together; Mom falls asleep. Head shots of the boy show his big, beautiful eyes; the wonder of a child.

Singer: "He's only three, so treasure this moment, you know they won't last, time is flying, children grow up fast, take a little break today: at McDonald's."

Sequence: The bus pulls up in front of McDonald's and there's Dad. The family is united at McDonald's: helping the family get together. The commercial ends with Joey sleeping on Dad's shoulder, clutching his McDonald's Kids Meal box.

THIRD COMMERCIAL

Ford

Opening Sequence: A young, handsome man stands looking out the floor-to-ceiling window of a huge, urban office. The furniture is modern; the art is excellent. The background music is hot jazz, the sax voice is bouncy.

Announcer: "I've got the keys to my new office and the keys to my new Thunderbird."

Slow-Mo Sequence: Beaming with joy, he throws his keys in the air. As the keys come down cut to:

Sequence: Exterior shot of a very attractive, very well-dressed young woman waiting anxiously. Cut to the car's interior: the man inspects the details of the instrument panel. Cut to young woman, still in anticipation.

Sequence: Beauty shots of the car driving in a lovely city setting. Cut to the car pulling up to the young woman. She joins him in the car, they kiss, and they drive, in love, in his new Ford.

Singers: "Have you driven a Ford lately?"

FOURTH COMMERCIAL

Coca-Cola

Opening Sequence: Fast paced, high-energy marching band beat.

Singers: (Chanting) "Coke is it!"

Sequence: A dress rehearsal of the Grambling State Marching Band on a dry, dusty field. Fun, and hot summer sun.

Singers: "Your thirst is grand as a big marching band."

Sequence: Quick, funky, highly synchronized band steps, teamwork, and sweat; lots of quick cuts. Intercuts of a hot sun and pan shots of moisture beading on Coke cans and bottles. Coke is shown as the relief from the broiling summer sun as perspiring band members, seeking relief, pull Coke bottles out of tubs of ice. The band's joy is in the music, the dancing, each other, and in Coca-Cola.

Singers: "Coke is it!"

The commercials were produced by the largest black advertising agency, the Uniworld Group of Chicago.

REFERENCES

Allport, Gordon. 1962. *The Nature of Prejudice.* Garden City, N.Y.: Doubleday.
Atwan, Robert, Donald McQuade, and John W. Wright. 1979. *Edsels, Luckies and Frigidaires: Advertising the American Way.* New York: Dell Publishing Company.
Barban, Arnold, and Edward Cundiff. 1964. "Negro and White Response to Advertising Stimuli." *Journal of Marketing Research* 1 (November): 53–56.
Barban, Arnold, and Werner Grunbaum. 1965. "A Factor Analytic Study of Negro and White Responses to Advertising Stimuli." *Journal of Applied Psychology* 49 (August): 274–79.

Block, Carl. 1967. "White Backlash to Negro Ads: Fact or Fantasy?" *Journalism Quarterly* 42 (Winter): 258–62.

Bureau of Advertising. 1970. *A Study of Blacks in Newspaper Ads.* New York: Bureau of Advertising.

Bush, Ronald F. 1978. "Hesitant to Hire Black Models? Don't Be." *Advertising Age,* May 29.

Bush, Ronald, Robert Gwinner, and Paul Solomon. 1974. "White Consumer Sales Response to Black Models." *Journal of Marketing* 38 (April): 25–29.

Cagley, James, and Richard Cardozo. 1970. "White Response to Integrated Advertising." *Journal of Advertising Research* 10 (April): 35–40.

Choudhury, Pravat, and Lawrence Schmid. 1974. "Black Models in Advertising to Blacks." *Journal of Advertising Research* 14 (June): 19–23.

Christopher, Maurine, 1970. "NAACP asks FCC to Eliminate Racism in Ads." *Advertising Age,* October 5, p. 29.

Cohen, Dorothy. 1970. "Advertising and the Black Community." *Journal of Marketing* 34 (October): 3–11.

Collier, James L. 1965. "The Black and White Revolution on Madison Avenue." *Pageant* 20 (January): 134.

Ehrenreich, Barbara. 1991. "Welfare: A White Search." *Time,* December 16, p. 84.

Gaertner, Samuel J., and Davidio, John F. 1986. *Prejudice, Discrimination and Racism.* New York: Harcourt Brace Jovanovich.

Gifford, John. 1972. The Effects of Integrated Advertising on Selected Dimensions and Elements of Department Store Image. Ph.D. diss., Miami University (Ohio).

Gould, John, Norman Sigband, and Cyril Zourner. 1970. "Black Consumer Reactions to Integrated Advertising: An Exploratory Study." *Journal of Marketing* 34 (July): 20–26.

Green, Mark. 1991. *Invisible People: The Depiction of Minorities in Magazine Ads and Catalogs.* New York: City of New York Department of Consumer Affairs.

Guest, Lester. 1970. "How Negro Models Affect Company Image." *Journal of Advertising Research* 10 (April): 29–34.

Kirscht, J. P., and R. C. Dillehay. 1967. *Dimensions of Authoritarianism: A Review of Research and Theory.* Lexington: University of Kentucky Press.

Lewis, Shawn D. 1977. "More Than Just Handsome Faces." *Ebony* (March): 70–72, 82, 84, 86.

MacDonald, J. Fred. 1983. *Blacks and White TV: Afro-Americans in Television since 1948.* Chicago: Nelson-Hall.

Muse, William. 1971. "Product-Related Response to Use of Black Models in Advertising." *Journal of Marketing Research* 8 (February): 107–9.

Pitts, Robert E., D. Joel Whalen, Robert O'Keefe, and Vernon Murray. 1989. "Black and White Response to Culturally Targeted Television Commercials: A Values-Based Approach." *Psychology and Marketing* 6 (Winter): 311–28.

Pozzi, Carl, and Rotfeld, Herbert J. 1984. Blacks in Advertising—Social Criticism and Marketing Paranoia. Paper presented at the 30th annual conference of the American Council on Consumer Interests, April 11–14.

Reno, Dawn. 1986. *Collecting Black Americana.* New York: Crown.

Rozen, Leah. 1980. "Black Presenter Makes a Difference: Study." *Advertising Age,* October 13, p. 20.

Schlinger, Mary, and Joseph Plummer. 1972. "Advertising in Black and White." *Journal of Advertising Research* 9 (May): 149–53.

Schmidt, David, and Ivan Preston. 1969. "How NAACP Leaders View Integrated Advertising." *Journal of Advertising Research* 9 (September): 13–16.

Soley, Lawrence. 1983. "The Effect of Black Models on Magazine Ad Readership." *Journalism Quarterly* 60 (Autumn): 686–90.

Solomon, Paul J. 1974. A Laboratory Experiment to Assess the Aspect of Black Models in Television Advertising. Ph.D. diss., Arizona State University.

Stafford, James, Al Birdwell, and Charles Van Tassel. 1970. "Integrated Advertising—White Backlash." *Journal of Advertising Research* 10 (April): 15–20.

Surlin, Stuart. 1972. "The Attitudes of Prejudiced Individuals toward the Institution of Advertising." *Journal of Advertising* 2: 35–37.

———. 1977. "Authoritarian Advertising Executives and the Use of Black Models in Advertising." *Journal of Black Studies* 8 (September): 105–15.

Tolley, Stuart, and John Goett. 1971. "Reactions to Blacks in Newspaper Ads." *Journal of Advertising Research* 11 (April): 11–16.

Whittler, Tommy. 1989. "Viewers' Processing of Actor's Race and Message Claims in Advertising Stimuli." *Psychology and Marketing* 6 (Winter): 287–309.

———. 1991. "The Effects of Actor's Race in Commercial Advertising: Review and Extension." *Journal of Advertising* 20: 54–60.

"Why Johnny Can't Read Your Ads." 1970. *New York Times,* March, p. 90.

Chapter 8 _____

EPILOGUE: COLORIZING ADVERTISING: A 21ST-CENTURY CHALLENGE

> Mass advertising is color-blind. It approaches the black consumer as if he were somebody's fair-haired boy. It speaks to him in a foreign language. It offers him Great White Hopes. It pictures him in off-color unrealistic settings. Companies aware of this have frantically begun coloring mass advertising black. But the result isn't black. It just looks that way to the people who create it.
>
> (Zebra Advertising, 1970, p. 50)

Zebra Advertising of New York, one of the first black-owned and -operated advertising agencies, offered the above synopsis of advertisers' efforts to target the black consumer market. I have researched the role of multiracial groups in advertising for the past 20 years. Some changes have taken place, but the rhetoric remains the same. The advertising industry has been reluctant to "colorize" its advertisements, its commercials, and its boardrooms because it may alienate white consumers. In other words, the people who visit our homes day in and day out, trying to get us to buy this or that, are still not reflective of the society in which we live.

From all appearances it looks as if the advertising industry is still showing some signs of resistance in reflecting a more diverse society. In the December 1991 issue of *Black Enterprise* John O'Toole, president of the American Association of Advertising Agencies, commented, "It is hard to conceive of advertising's role as depicting the ethnic diversity of American society. Advertising, in general, not only has no obligation, but it has no business trying to depict national diversity" (Chinyelu, 1991, p. 11).

Anyone aware that a book has been published on the history of blacks in advertising might ask why. The answer is that the historical chronicling of blacks in advertising is an important way of gaining a better understanding of what life was like for blacks in earlier years. In other words, advertising documents history. What effect do such portrayals have on people of color if they are not accurate? What perceptions do these portrayals formulate in the minds of others about people of color? African-Americans are not accurately depicted, but the representation of other multi-racial groups is even more distorted. It is often easier to find a needle in a haystack than a Native American, a Latino, or an Asian-American in an advertisement or commercial. If advertising were used to determine what American society was like in the 1990s, a content analysis would reveal few, if any, Native Americans, when in fact there are 1.5 million (Wright, 1989, p. 237). Is this not misleading, and does it not do a disservice to the underrepresented group? The general thesis underlying the entire book is the importance of the messages projected about blacks through advertising. Subliminal, overt, covert, conscious, unconscious, artificial, superficial, and unofficial, they perpetually erode the self-esteem and motivational behavior of African-Americans. Advertising in all of its subtleties has historically, systematically, and methodically alienated and subjugated blacks. This thesis is further developed by discerning what black leaders and organizations have done and continue to do to promote "positive realism" via blacks in advertising.

Advertising projects images that are handed down from generation to generation. These images coupled with others presented through the mass media play a pivotal role in facilitating social change and can be detrimental if not used in a positive manner. Aunt Jemima, Uncle Ben, Rastus, and their other counterparts have been a focus of concern for decades. This concern was explicitly elucidated by Nannie Helen Burroughs (1930), a prominent black woman who headed a school for black girls in Washington, D.C.:

The Gold Dust Twins, Aunt Jemima, and Amos and Andy have piled up millions for two business concerns and two white men. Aunt Jemima and the Gold Dust Twins cook and wash dishes while Amos and Andy broadcast subtle and mischievous propaganda against Negro business. They tell the world that when it comes to business the Negro is a huge joke and a successful failure. . . . They magnify, advertise, capitalize, and broadcast the crude efforts of the most ignorant. Amos and Andy are making an indelible impression upon the minds of the children and young people of the white race. Millions of children are getting their first impression of the Negro from Amos and Andy. Then, too, the Amos and Andy propaganda is not good for the Negro masses. It gives them the wrong impression of their own race and develops an inferiority complex. But there is another Negro in America. Do the American people want to meet him on the air? He keeps a clean cab, does not steal money from his organization, is not a blusterer, a braggart, nor a sham. He has social standards and high ideals and lives up to them. He should be given the same "break" on the air that Amos and Andy have had.

It is important that all aspects of black history be documented because of the importance that history has on determining the future. Clifton Taulbert, author of *Once Upon a Time When We Were Colored* (1989), observed that "it is very difficult to master the present and make a meaningful contribution to the future unless you understand and appreciate the past. . . . To forget our past is to forget ourselves, who we are and what we've come from" (p. 6).

In the past decade blacks have exhibited more interest in their heritage than ever before in history. For years, they fought vociferously to forget slavery, Jim Crow, as well as the stereotypes that they fostered. In an attempt to recapture some of their past, blacks have become avid collectors of black memorabilia, and vintage black advertising is a major component of that effort. In fact, a magazine is targeted to just such artifacts, *Black Ethnic Collectibles* (Ferrigno, 1988). There also exists a Black Memorabilia Collectors' Association. A National African American Museum scheduled to open in Washington, D.C., in 1996 will serve as a major depository for black artifacts and memorabilia (Mercer, 1991; Fox, 1991).[1]

Chronicling the black experience will further expose the images that blacks have held of themselves and that whites have held of them for centuries. In this age of political correctness and diversity, it becomes increasingly more important to scrutinize these perceptions as well as the antiquated stereotypes from which they sprang. Such examination gives us an idea of how far we have come and how far we still have to go. One of the most compelling books to compile information pertinent to the perceptions that many whites retain about blacks is *The Black Image in the White Mind* by George Fredrickson (1971). Fredrickson takes us back in time and offers a macroscopic view of the white nationalism, white supremacy, and Negrophobia that were apparently widespread after the 1830s. These concepts were forged into American society through the widespread distribution of advertising using blacks in derogatory imagery.

Recognizing that many whites have held such views of blacks for centuries, many blacks and whites have sought methods for eradicating them and preventing them from being transferred from generation to generation. To that end, individuals and organizations have attempted to destroy any images or portrayals that further perpetuate the ideologies espoused above.

Images and labels have always been important to black Americans, which is why they have opted to change what they have been called several times during past decades. Race recognition terminology for black Americans has evolved in the following chronology, as outlined in articles by Karen Roebuck (1990) and Dr. Manning Marable (1989): (1) *negro*—the Spanish word meaning black, (2) slave, (3) nigger, (4) colored, (5) Africans, (6) negro, (7) Negro, (8) Afro-American, (9) black, and (10) African-American. In addition, Marshall O. Lee (1991) suggested the name "New African" as a means of unifying all members of the diaspora. Most of these designations have been reflected in American advertising at one point or another. There has been considerable resistance, however, in the transition from the other labels to the designation "African-American" among all American institutions, advertising included.

How people view themselves affects how others view them, and that is why blacks have begun to scrutinize their portrayals in advertising more fervently than before. Advertising serves a social function in society by transmitting social heritage from one generation to the next. It carefully documents the past and gives those who did not live during those times a bird's-eye view of what people were wearing, what their life-styles were, and how they interacted with each other. More importantly, advertising offers a unique perspective on the state of race relations between black and white citizens. Advertising communicates through verbal and nonverbal forms, depending on the medium, and through the years has communicated some important messages about black and white Americans.

Although this book culminates with reactions to the use of blacks in advertising, the participation of blacks in advertising does not end here. A future volume should address the impact of black-owned and -operated advertising agencies upon the industry. The introduction of Burrell, Inc., headed by Tom Burrell, and Uniworld, headed by Bryon Lewis, signaled a significant transitional period in the participation of blacks. Black agencies inspire new concepts about the portrayal of blacks in advertising and introduce African-Americans into American homes in places, situations, and positions in which they have never been shown before. Burrell introduced the concept of "positive realism" which caught on within the industry, and African-Americans could be seen washing their hair, brushing their teeth, driving cars, going to work, and taking vacations like other people. However, a sequel to this book should also describe the conflicts encountered by African-American agencies that do not want to be saddled with the distinction of only being able to do advertising for black people, about black people, for black people. Some of the agencies have viewed being able to "cross over" as a major obstacle. Black agencies were instrumental in bringing a greater understanding of the black consumer market into the advertising arena, but problems still surface from time to time involving blacks and advertising.

Another dimension of a future work should address contemporary issues regarding the black consumer market and advertising. Some of the more relevant topics include, but are not limited to: tobacco and alcoholic beverage advertising and their impact on the African-American community; black athletes and advertising endorsements (are they getting their fair share?); and whether the reluctancy to use black women models still exists, and if so, why?

I think above all, advertisers and marketers are searching for ways to tap the black consumer market, and after a discussion of the reforms brought by black agencies and some of the problems still inherent within the industry, a comprehensive examination of the black consumer market and how to reach it should be addressed. Understanding nuances and idiosyncrasies germane to the black consumer market, and myths that have been and are still being promulgated, will be essential as advertisers prepare for the future. Information relative to what the future holds for the African-American consumer market as it continues to be a formidable force in the American economic structure should provide a completion to this future volume and bring the topic full circle.

Essentially, the present book is historical in content and lets us know where we have been. Its successor should be more of a how-to book on reaching the black consumer market, offering solutions to some of the problems highlighted herein.

As we prepare for the 21st century, this information will be very important in designing advertising targeted to the African-American market. By the turn of the century, if Census Bureau projections are correct, African-Americans, who now represent 12.6 percent of the population, will constitute 13.6 percent of the American public (Wright, 1989, p. 233).[2] Blacks and Hispanics will be the dominant populations in nearly one-third of the United States' 50 largest cities. Blacks alone will constitute the majority in at least nine: Detroit, Baltimore, Memphis, Chicago, Washington, D.C., New Orleans, and Atlanta (The Biggest Secret, 1989, pp. 84, 88). Advertisers, marketers, and promoters will have to take note and listen to African-American consumers, because in many areas they will be the primary mass-media listeners, viewers, readers, and subscribers. Thus, they also will comprise the primary audiences hearing or ignoring "and now a word from our sponsor" (Kern-Foxworth, 1991, p. 29).

To date, advertisers and marketers have not fully tapped this market, which currently has a $300 billion annual disposable income. That equates to $821 million spent daily on goods and services in America. More specifically, ethnic minority shoppers, predominantly African-Americans, Hispanics and Asians, spent $600 billion to purchase everything from toothpaste-to-shoes-to-cars-to-orange juice-to-cigarettes in 1992, an increase of 18 percent since 1990 (McCarroll, 1993, p. 80). The question that desperately needs to be addressed is whether or not these industries will be better prepared to target the black consumer market that is expected to exceed $889 billion in a little more than five years (Black Business, 1985, p. 42). And to target all multi-racial markets with a projected $1 trillion disposable income by the next millennium. By the year 2000, it is projected that advertisers and promoters will spend approximately $900 million targeting ALANA groups (McCarroll, 1993, p. 80).

Finally, colorizing advertising obviously will not be as easy as giving Scarlett O'Hara green eyes and rosy cheeks in *Gone with the Wind*. Which prompts me to ask: Will black consumers have to stop spending their green with companies that consistently act as if blacks don't exist until the firms realize there is a pot of gold at the end of this rainbow?

> I am the emergence of 250 years of slavery
> Picking cotton
>   built my fine body
> Conniving and contriving to save my neck
>   made me highly intelligent
> Clinging to and bragging about my beauty
>   gave me arrogance.
> Therefore,
> I am strong
> I am erudite and
> I am vain
> A member of the "Talenth Tenth"
> And I only answer to Mister.
> For I AM THE REINCARNATION OF BLACK BOY!
>
>   Marilyn Kern-Foxworth, 1988

NOTES

1. Anyone having materials or information to contribute to the National African American Museum should contact Claudine Brown at 202-357-1776.

2. For more information on demographic and economic projections for the African-American consumer market see Marilyn Kern-Foxworth, *Making America Diversity Friendly, A Handbook of Multicultural Materials for Corporations, Organizations, Educational Institutions and Individuals.* Bryan, Texas: Black Fox Productions, 1994. (409) 846–7224.

REFERENCES

"The Biggest Secret of Race Relations: The New White Minority." 1989. *Ebony* (April): 84, 88.

"Black Business in the Year 2000: Going for the $889 Billion Market." 1985. *Ebony* (August): 42.

Burroughs, Nannie. 1930. *Philadelphia Tribune*, December.

Chinyelu, Mamadou. 1991. "No Color in Magazine Ads." *Black Enterprise* (December): 11.

Ferrigno, Robert. 1988. "Racist Memorabilia Now Collectable." *Bryan-College Station Eagle*, July 7, p. 7C.

Fox, Catherine. 1991. "The Making of a Museum." *Atlanta Journal*, August 13, pp. F1, F5.

Fredrickson, George. 1971. *The Black Image in the White Mind*. New York: Harper and Row.

Gibson, D. Parke. 1969. *The $30 Billion Negro*. New York: Macmillan.

———. 1978. *$70 Billion in the Black: America's Black Consumers*. New York: Macmillan.

Kern-Foxworth, Marilyn. 1988. "The Reincarnation of Black Boy." In *Ebonessence: The Expression of a Black Woman through Verse.* Unpublished book of poetry.
————. 1991. "Black, Brown, Red and Yellow Markets Equal Green Power." *Public Relations Quarterly* 36 (Spring): 29.
Lee, Marshall O. 1991. "Nobody Knows Our Name: The New African Option." *Black Issues in Higher Education* 8 (October 10): 30.
Marable, Manning. 1989. "African American or Black? The Politics of Cultural Identity." *Black Issues in Higher Education* (April 13): 72.
McCarroll, Thomas. 1993. "It's A Mass Market No More: The New Ethnic Consumer is Forcing U.S. Companies to Change the Way They Sell Their Wares." *Time* p. 80.
Mercer, Joye. 1991. "The Smithsonian's National African-American Museum." *Black Issues in Higher Education* 8 (October 24): 10.
Roebuck, Karen. 1990. "Identity Will Change until Racism Ends, Black Scholar Says." *Houston Post,* February 24, p. A18.
Taulbert, Clifton. 1989. *Once Upon a Time When We Were Colored.* Tulsa: Council Oak Books.
Van DeBurg, William L. 1984. *Slavery and Race in American Popular Culture.* Madison: University of Wisconsin Press.
Wright, John W. 1989. *The Universal Almanac.* New York: Andrews and McMeel.
Zebra Advertising. 1970. "Mass Advertising Is Color-Blind" (advertisement). *Marketing/Communications,* (February): 50.

APPENDIX: AFRICAN-AMERICAN MUSEUMS AND RESOURCE CENTERS

There are over 120 museums dedicated to providing historical, artistic, and cultural information for, about, and by African-Americans. The list below is a compilation of those depositories, centers, museums, and societies that have exhibits or information pertinent to the evolution of blacks in American advertising or a related area.

African-American Museum
1765 Crawford Road
Cleveland, Ohio 44120
Eleanor Engram, Director
(216) 791-1700

African American Museum and Cultural Center of Western Massachusetts
Amistad Research Center
Tulane University
Tilton Hall
New Orleans, Louisiana 70118
Clifton Johnson, Executive Director
(504) 865-5535

African-American Museum of Nassau County
110 North Franklin Street
Hempstead, New York 11550
Shirly Darkeh, Director
(516) 485-0470

Afro-American Cultural Center
Cleveland State University
Black Studies Program

2121 Euclid Avenue
Cleveland, Ohio 44115
Curtis Wilson, Director
(216) 687-3655

Afro-American Cultural Center
401 North Myers Street
Charlotte, North Carolina 28202
(704) 374-1565

Afro-American Historical and Cultural Museum
7th and Arch Streets
Philadelphia, Pennsylvania 19106
(215) 574-0380

Afro American Historical and Cultural Society of Jersey City
1841 Kennedy Boulevard
Jersey City, New Jersey 07305
(201) 547-5262

Afro-American Historical Society of Delaware
512 East Fourth Street
Wilmington, Delaware 19801
Harmon R. Carey, President
(302) 984-1423

Afro-American Historical Society of the Niagara Frontier
P.O. Box 1663
Buffalo, New York 14216
Dr. Monroe Fordham, Director
(716) 694-5096

Afro-American Resource Center
Founders Library
Howard University
Washington, D. C. 20059
Ethelbert Miller, Director

Avery Institute of Afro-American History and Culture
P.O. Box 2262
Charleston, South Carolina 29403
Lucille Whipper, President
(803) 792-5924

Avery Research Center For African American History and Culture
College of Charleston
Charleston, South Carolina 29424
(803) 792-5742

Balch Institute for Ethnic Studies
18 South 7th Street
Philadelphia, Pennsylvania 19106

M. Mark Stolarik, Director
(215) 925-8090

Baltimore's Black American Mueseum/Third World Museum
1765–69 Carswell Street
Baltimore, Maryland 21218
Frank Richardson, Director
(301) 243-9600

Beck Cultural Exchange Center
1927 Dandridge Avenue
Knoxville, Tennessee 37915
Robert Booker, Director
(615) 524-8461

Black Archives of Mid-America
2033 Vine Street
Kansas City, Missouri 64108
(816) 483-1300

Black Archives Research Center and Museum
Florida A&M University
P.O. Box 809
James N. Eaton, Director
(904) 599-3020

Black Heritage Museum
P.O. Box 570327
Miami, Florida 33257-0327
Prischila Stephens Kruize, President
(305) 252-3535

Black History Museum and Cultural Center
122 West Leigh Street
Richmond, Virginia 23220
(804) 780-9093

Black Texans Cultural Museum And Hall of Fame
1501 East 12th Street
W. H. Passon House
Austin, Texas 78702
David A. Williams, Executive Director
(512) 472-5731

Carter G. Woodson Foundation
P.O. Box 1025
Newark, New Jersey 07101
Phillip Thomas, President
(201) 242-0500

California Afro-American Museum
600 State Drive

Exposition Park
Los Angeles, California 90037
Bridget Cullerton, Acting Director
(213) 744-7432

Carl Swisher Library–Learning Resource Center
Bethune Cookman College
640 Second Avenue
Daytona Beach, Florida 32015
(904) 258-1279

Chattanoogna African American Museum and Research Center
Nolan Estes Educational Plaza
3434 S. R. L. Thornton Freeway
Dallas, Texas 75224
Robert Edison, Director
(214) 375-7530

C. J. Walker Museum and Afro-American Cultural Foundation
c/o Westchester Community College
75 Grasslands Road
Valhalla, New York 10595
(914) 347-2211

Connecticut Afro-American Historical Society
444 Orchard Street
New Haven, Connecticut 06511
George Bellinger, President
(203) 776-4907

Dunbar Hotel Cultural and Historical Museum
4225 South Central Avenue
Los Angeles, California 90011
Bernard Johnson, Director
(213) 462-3475

DuSable Museum of African American History
740 East 56th Place
Chicago, Illinois 60637
(312) 947-0600

First National Black Historical Society of Kansas
601 North Water
Wichita, Kansas 67201
(316) 326-7651

George Washington Carver Museum and Cultural Center
1165 Angelina Street
Austin, Texas 78702
(512) 472-4809

Great Plains Black Museum
2213 Lake Street
Omaha, Nebraska 68110
Bertha Calloway, Director
(402) 345-2212

Harriet Tubman Gallery and Resource Center
United South End Settlements
566 Columbus Avenue
Boston, Massachusetts 02115
(617) 437-3139

Harriet Tubman Historical and Cultural Museum
340 Walnut Street
Macon, Georgia 31208
Dorothy Hardman, Director
(912) 743-8544

Harriet Tubman Museum and Cultural Association
P.O. Box 20178
Cleveland, Ohio 44120-0178
Hanif Wahab, Director/Curator
(216) 663-1115

Harrison Museum and Cultural Association
P.O. Box 194
Roanoke, Virginia 24002
(804) 345-4818

Langston Hughes Institute
Kush Museum
25 Hugh Street
Buffalo, New York 14203
(716) 881-3266

Lillie Carroll Jackson Museum
Civil Rights Museum
1320 Eutaw Place
Baltimore, Maryland 21217
Gail Mitchell, Director
(301) 523-1634

Margaret Walker Alexander National African American Research Center
P.O. Box 17008
Jackson State University
Jackson, Mississippi 39217
Alferdteen Harrison, Director
(601) 968-2055

Maryland Commission on Afro-American History and Culture
Banneker-Douglas Museum

84 Franklin Street
Annapolis, Maryland 21401
Steve Cameron Newsome, Director
(301) 974-2893

Merabash Museum
Museum for Education and Research in American Black Art, Science and History
P.O. Box 752
Willingboro, New Jersey 08046
Mark Henderson, Jr., Executive Director
(609) 877-3177

Museum of African American Life and Culture
P.O. Box 26153
Dallas, Texas 75226
(214) 565-9026

Museum of Afro American History
African Meeting House
Abiel Smith School
46 Joy Street
Boston, Massachusetts 02114
(617) 742-1854

Museum of African American History
301 Frederick Douglass
Detroit, Michigan 48202
(313) 833-9800

National Afro-American Heritage Museum
1875 I Street, N.W.
Washington, D. C. 20006
Barbara Washington Franklin, Executive Director
(202) 554-5100

National Afro-American Museum and Cultural Center
1350 Brush Row Road
Wiberforce, Ohio 45384
(513) 376-4944

Newark Museum
43–49 Washington Street
Newark, New Jersey 07101
Anne M. Spencer, Curator of Ethnology
(201) 596-6550

Northern California Center for Afro-American History and Life
5606 San Pablo Avenue
Oakland, California 94608
Eugene Lasartamay, Director
(415) 658-3158

Old Slave Mart Museum
P.O. Box 459
Sullivan's Island, South Carolina 29482
Judith Wragg Chase, Educational Director
(803) 883-3797

Orchard Street Cultural Museum
24 South Abington Avenue
Baltimore, Maryland 21229
Marguerite Campbell, Director
(301) 669-3100

Parting Ways Museum of Afro-American Ethnohistory
130 Court Street
Plymouth, Massachusetts 02360
(508) 746-6028

Pendleton Foundation for Black History and Culture
116 West Queen Street
Pendleton, South Carolina 29670
(803) 646-3792

Rhode Island Black Heritage Society
1 Hilton Street
Providence, Rhode Island 02905
Linda A'Vant-Coleman, Executive Director
(401) 751-3490

San Francisco African-American Historical and Cultural Society
Fort Mason Center
Building C
San Francisco, California 94123
(415) 441-0640

Schomburg Center for Research in Black Culture
New York Public Library
515 Lenox Avenue
New York, New York 10037
Howard Dodson, Director
(212) 862-4000

Smith-Robertson Museum and Cultural Center
P.O. Box 3259
Jackson, Mississippi 39207
Jesse Mosley, Director
(601) 960-1457

Tuskegee Institute National Historic Site
P.O. Drawer 10
Tuskegee, Alabama, 36830
(205) 727-6390

Vaugh Cultural Center
1408 North Kings Highway
Suite 205
St. Louis, Missouri 63313
Robert Watson, Director
(314) 316-0111

YMI Cultural Center
47 Eagle Street
Asheville, North Carolina 28801
Wanda Henry-Coleman, Executive Director
(704) 252-4614

Your Heritage House
110 East Ferry Street
Detroit, Michigan 48202
(313) 871-1667

SELECTED BIBLIOGRAPHY

This selected bibliography is intended to provide a guide to the critical sources found to be useful in the writing and conceptualization of this book.

Achiron, Marilyn. 1986. "Finding the Perfect Pitch for Women." *Adweek* (July 7): 35–36.

Allen, Bonnie. 1980. In Focus: Blacks in Ads. *Essence* (February): 19.

Andrews, Benny. 1975. "Jemimas, Mysticism, and Mojos: The Art of Betye Saar." *Encore American & Worldwide* (March 17): 30.

Atwan, Robert, Donald McQuade and John W. Wright. 1979. *Edsels, Luckies and Frigidaires: Advertising the American Way.* New York: Dell Publishing Company.

"Aunt Jemima of Pancake Box Fame Dies at 76." 1981. *Knoxville* (Tenn.) *News-Sentinel,* April 2, p. 9.

Baker, Robert and Sandra Ball. 1969. *A Staff Report to the National Commission on the Causes and Prevention of Violence.* Washington, D.C.: U.S. Government Printing Office.

Barban, Arnold and Werner Grunbaum. 1965. "A Factor Analytic Study of Negro and White Responses to Advertising Stimuli." *Journal of Applied Psychology* 49 (August): 274–79.

Barban, Robert, and Edward Cundiff. 1964. "Negro and White Response to Advertising Stimuli." *Journal of Marketing Research* 1 (November): 53–56.

Barnett, Marguerite Ross. 1982. "Nostalgia as Nightmare: Blacks and American Popular Culture." *The Crisis* (February): 42.

Beal, Kathleen A. and Marilyn Blair. 1990. "How Are Blacks Portrayed in Advertising?" *The Thomas Report* (June): 14–15.

Berry, Jon. 1991. "Marketers Reach Out to Blacks." *Chicago Tribune,* May 12, p. 9A.

"Black Image Makers on Madison Avenue." 1971. *Black Enterprise,* (February): 15–22.

"Black Media Group Keeps Watch on Ads." 1982. *Editor and Publisher* (December 25): 17.

"Blacks in Advertising—A Bigger Share." 1984. *Advertising Age,* November 19, p. 16.

Block, Carl. 1967. "White Backlash to Negro Ads: Fact or Fantasy?" *Journalism Quarterly* 42 (Winter): 258–62.

Boskin, Joseph. 1986. *Sambo: The Rise and Demise of an American Jester.* New York: Oxford University Press.

Boyenton, William. 1965. "The Negro Turns to Advertising." *Journalism Quarterly* 42 (Summer): 227–235.

Bureau of Advertising. 1970. *A Study of Blacks in Newspaper Ads.* New York: Bureau of Advertising.

Bush, Ronald F. 1978. "Hesitant to Hire Black Models? Don't Be." *Advertising Age,* May 29.

Bush, Ronald, Robert Gwinner and Paul Solomon. 1974. "White Consumer Sales Response to Black Models." *Journal of Marketing* 38 (April): 25–29.

Bush, Ronald, Paul Solomon and Joseph Hair, Jr. 1977. "There Are More Blacks in TV Commercials." *Journal of Advertising Research* 17 (February): 21–25.

Cagley, James, and Richard Cardozo. 1970. "White Response to Integrated Advertising." *Journal of Advertising Research* 10 (April): 35–40.

Campbell, Cathy. 1989. "A Battered Woman Rises: Aunt Jemima's Corporate Makeover." *Village Voice,* November 7, pp. 45–46.

Campbell, Hannah. 1964. *Why Did They Name It. . . ?* New York: Fleet Publishing.

Choudhury, Pravat, and Lawrence Schmid. 1974. "Black Models in Advertising to Blacks." *Journal of Advertising Research* 14 (June): 19–23.

Cohen, Dorothy. 1970. "Advertising and the Black Community." *Journal of Marketing* 34 (October): 3–11.

Colfax and Sternberg. 1972. "The Perpetuation of Racial Stereotypes: Blacks in Mass Circulation Magazine Advertisements." *Public Opinion Quarterly* 36 (Spring): 7–18.

Collier, James L. 1965. "The Black and White Revolution on Madison Avenue." *Pageant* 20 (January): 134.

Congdon-Martin, Douglas. 1990. *Images in Black: 150 Years of Black Collectibles.* West Chester, Pa.: Schiffer Publishing.

Cox, James. 1990. "Nike: Reebok-PUSH Meetings 'A Smoking Gun.' " *USA Today,* August 17, p. 7B.

Cox, Keith. 1970. "Social Effects of Integrated Advertising." *Journal of Advertising Research* 10 (April): 41–44.

Culley, James, and Rex Bennett. 1976. "Selling Women, Selling Blacks." *Journal of Communications* 26 (Autumn): 160–74.

Dates, Jannette L., and William Barlow. 1990. *Split Image: African Americans in the Mass Media.* Washington, D.C.: Howard University Press.

Davis, Richard A. 1987. "Television Commercials and the Management of Spoiled Identity." *Western Journal of Black Studies* 11 (Summer): 59–63.

Dominick, Joseph, and Bradley Greenberg. 1970. "Three Seasons of Blacks on Television." *Journal of Advertising* 10 (April): 21–27.

Edmerson, Estelle. 1954. A Descriptive Study of the American Negro in United States Professional Radio, 1922–1953. Master's thesis. University of California, Los Angeles.

Edwards, Audrey. 1993. "From Aunt Jemima to Anita Hill: Media's Split Image of Black Women." *Media Studies Journal,* 7 (Winter/Spring): 215–222.

Edwards, Paul Kenneth. 1932. *The Southern Urban Negro as a Consumer.* New York: Prentice-Hall.

Fisher, Paul, and Ralph Lowenstein, eds. 1967. *Race and the Mass Media.* New York: Frederick Praeger.

Foote, Cone, and Belding. 1970. Integrated Advertising: A Synthesis of Published Research and Opinion. Foote, Cone and Belding Research Department.

"For Advertising, Signs of Change." 1969. *The New York Times.* January 6, p. C129.

Fox, Stephen. 1985. *The Mirror Makers: A History of American Advertising and Its Creators.* New York: Vintage.

Garth-Taylor, Mikki. 1988. "Iman: By Her Own Rules." *Essence* (January): 64–65, 97.

Geizer, Ronald. 1971. "Advertising in *Ebony:* 1960 and 1969." *Journalism Quarterly* (Spring): 131–34.

Gibson, D. Parke. 1969. *The $30 Billion Negro.* New York: Macmillan.

———. 1978. *$70 Billion in the Black: America's Black Consumers.* New York: Macmillan.

Gifford, John. 1972. The Effects of Integrated Advertising on Selected Dimensions and Elements of Department Store Image. Ph.D. diss., Miami University (Ohio).

Goings, Kenneth W. 1990. "Memorabilia That Have Perpetuated Stereotypes about African Americans." *Chronicle of Higher Education,* February 14, p. B76.

Gomez, J. 1986. Showing Our Faces: A Century of Black Women Photographed.

Goodall, Kenneth. 1972. "Blacks in Advertisements in the Post Mammy Era." *Psychology Today* 6 (October): 138.

Gould, John, Nomran Sigband, and Cyril Zourner. 1970. "Black Consumer Reactions to Integrated Advertising: An Exploratory Study." *Journal of Marketing* 34 (July): 20–26.

Granda, Megan. 1992. Aunt Jemima in Black and White: America Advertises in Color. Master's thesis. University of Texas.

Green, Mark. 1991. *Invisible People: 1991. The Depiction of Minorities in Magazine Ads and Catalogs.* New York: New York Department of Consumer Affairs.

———. 1992. *Still Invisible People: The Depiction of Minorities in Magazine Ads One Year After the Consumer Affairs Department Study,* Invisible People. New York: New York Department of Consumer Affairs.

Gregory, Deborah, and Patricia Jacobs. 1993. "The Ugly Side of the Modeling Business." *Essence* (September): 89–90, 126, 128.

Guest, Lester. 1970. "How Negro Models Affect Company Image." *Journal of Advertising Research* 10 (April): 29–34.

Harley, Sharon and Rosalyn Terborg-Penn. 1978. *The Afro-American Woman: Struggles and Images.* Port Washington, New York: Kennikat Press.

Harrison, John Thornton. 1933. *The History of the Quaker Oats Company.* Chicago: The University of Chicago.

Hartmann, Paul, and Charles Husband. 1974. *Racism and the Mass Media*. London: Bristol Typesetting Company, Ltd.

"Have Black Models Really Made It?" 1990. *Ebony* (May): 158.

Heller, Steven. 1990. "Advertising Stamps." *Upper & Lower Case* (Winter): 33.

Henderson, Robbin, Pamela Fabry, and Adam David Miller, eds. 1982. *Ethnic Notions: Black Image in the White Mind*. Berkeley, Calif.: Art Center Association.

Holman, Blan. 1993. "Changing the Face(s) of Advertising: AAF and Its Members Seek Solutions to Advertising's Dearth of Diversity." *American Advertising* (Fall): 10–13.

Humphrey, Ronald and Howard Schuman. 1984. "The Portrayal of Blacks in Magazine Advertisements: 1950–1982." *Public Opinion Quarterly* 48 (Fall): 551–563.

Jewell, Karen Sue Warren. 1993. *From Mammy to Miss America and Beyond: Cultural Images and the Shaping of U.S. Social Policy*. New York: Routledge.

Johnson, Robert E. 1987. "Michael Jackson Comes Back." *Ebony* (September): 143–44, 146, 148–49.

Jones, Caroline R. "Advertising in Black and White." *Madison Avenue*, 53–54, 56, 58.

Kaselow, Joseph. 1963. "A Bellwether Ad for Negro Models." *New York Herald Tribune*, May 8.

Kassarjian, Harold. 1969. "The Negro and American Advertising 1946–1965." *Journal of Marketing Research* 6 (February): 29–39.

Kern, Marilyn L. 1982. A Comparative Analysis of the Portrayal of Blacks and Whites in White-Oriented Mass Circulation Advertisements during 1959, 1969, and 1979. Ph.D. diss., University of Wisconsin, Madison.

Kern-Foxworth, Marilyn. 1988. "Aunt Jemima." *Insite* (June): 14.

———. 1988. "The Kerner Report and the Civil Rights Movement: Implications for the Future of Blacks in Advertising." *Southwestern Mass Communication Journal* 4: 76–92.

———. 1989. "Aunt Jemima is 100, but Looking Good." *Media History Digest* 9 (Fall-Winter): 54–58.

———. 1989. "Aunt Jemima: Part I." *Black Ethnic Collectibles* (January/February): 18–19.

———. 1989. "Ads Pose Dilemma for Black Women." *Media and Values* 49 (Winter): 18–19.

———. 1990. "From Plantation Kitchen to American Icon: Aunt Jemima." *Public Relations Review* 16 (Fall): 55–67.

———. 1991. "Advertising and Public Relations: An Educator's Perspective." *Black Issues in Higher Education* 8 (June 6): 42.

———. 1991. "Black, Brown, Red and Yellow Markets Equal Green Power." *Public Relations Quarterly* 36 (Spring): 29.

———. 1991–92. "Colorizing Advertising: What Ad Clubs Can Do To Make the Business More Inclusive." *The American Advertising Federation Magazine* 7 (Winter): 26–28.

———. 1992. "Colorizing Advertising: Challenges for the 1990s and Beyond." *Black Issues in Higher Education* 9 (June 4): 64.

———. 1992. Speech delivered to Advertising Club of New Orleans, New Orleans, Louisiana, December 15.

Kern-Foxworth, Marilyn, and Susanna Hornig. 1992. Aunt Jemima and Betty Crocker: The Infusion of Two American Icons into American Culture. Paper presented to the International Communication Association, Miami, May 23.

Kiefer, Michael. 1988. "Air Attack: Flying High in Points and Profits, Michael Jordan Is the Jam Master of the N.B.A." *Playboy* 35 (April): 80–83.

Lambert, Isaac E. 1976. *The Public Accepts: Stories behind Famous Trade-Marks, Names and Slogans.* New York: Arno Press.

Lemmons, J. Stanley. 1977. "Black Stereotypes as Reflected in Popular Culture." *American Quarterly* 21 (Spring): 103–16.

Levine, Jo Ann. 1968. "Look for Penny Bogan and John Johnston." *Christian Science Monitor,* August 19, p. 6.

Lewis, Alba Myers. 1981. "Beauty, Culture, Fashion and Modeling." In Marianna Davis, ed., *Contributions of Black Women to America.* Columbia, S. C.: Kenday Press.

Lewis, Shawn D. 1977. "More Than Just Handsome Faces." *Ebony* 32 (March): 70–72, 82, 84, 86.

Lippard, Lucy R. 1990. *Mixed Blessings: New Art in a Multicultural America.* New York: Pantheon Books.

Lippert, Barbara. 1988. "Pepsi's 'Chase' Shows Jackson Is a Bad Act to Follow." *Adweek* 10 (March 14): 22.

Mabry, Marcus, and Rhonda Adams. 1989. "A Long Way from 'Aunt Jemima.' " *Newsweek,* August 14, pp. 34–35.

MacDonald, J. Fred. 1983. *Blacks and White TV: Afro-Americans in Television since 1948.* Chicago: Nelson-Hall.

———. 1984. "Marketing to Blacks: Stereotypes Fall in TV Ad Portrayals." *Advertising Age* 55 (November 19): 44.

Malveaux, Julianne. 1993. "Black Women's Images in Women's History Month." *Black Issues in Higher Education* (March 25): 38.

Marquette, Arthur F. 1967. *Brands, Trademarks and Goodwill: The Story of the Quaker Oats Company.* New York: McGraw-Hill.

McCarroll, Thomas. 1993. "It's a Mass Market No More: The New Ethnic Consumer is Forcing U. S. Companies to Change the Ways They Sell Their Wares." *Time* p. 80.

Monroe, William B. 1967. "Television: The Chosen Instrument of the Revolution." In Paul L. Fisher and Ralph L. Lowenstein, eds. *Race and the News Media.* New York: Praeger.

Morgan, Hal. 1986. *Symbols of America.* New York: Viking Penguin.

Morton, Patricia. 1991. *Disfigured Images: The Historical Assault on Afro-American Women.* Westport, Conn.: Greenwood Press.

Murphy, Frederick. 1975. "Black Models Have Their Say." *Encore* (April 7): 33.

Muse, William. 1971. "Product-Related Response to Use of Black Models in Advertising." *Journal of Marketing Research* 8 (February): 107–109.

Nixon, Mark. 1983. "Minorities in TV Ads a Hot Topic." *USA Today,* September 29, pp. 1–2D.

Noel, Pamela. 1984. "'TV Ad Wars' Newest Weapon: Use of Black Celebrities Plays a Big Role in the Wooing of American Consumers." *Ebony* 39 (July): 81–82, 84.

Northcott, Herbert, John Segar and James Hinton. 1975. "Trends in TV Portrayal of Blacks and Women." *Journalism Quarterly* 15: 741–44.

O'Kelly, Charlotte, and Linda Bloomquist. 1976. "Women and Blacks on TV." *Journal of Communications* 26 (Autumn): 179–84.

Parkhurst, Jessie W. 1938. "The Role of the Black Mammy in the Plantation Household." *Journal of Negro History* 23 (July): 349–69.

Patton, June O. 1980. "Moonlight and Magnolias in Southern Education: The Black Mammy Memorial Institute." *Journal of Negro History* 65 (Spring): 149–55.

Patton, Phil. 1993. "Mammy: Her Life and Times." *American Heritage* (September): 79–87.

Peace, Ronnye. 1991. Shades of Gray: The Use of African Americans in Magazine Advertisements. Paper presented at the 74th annual convention of the Association for Education in Journalism and Mass Communication, Boston, August 7–10.

Pierce, Chester M., Jean V. Carew, Diane Pierce-Gonzalez and Deborah Wills. 1977. "An Experiment in Racism: TV Commercials." *Education and Urban Society* 10: 61–87.

Pieterse, Jan Nederveen. 1992. *White on Black: Images of Africa and Blacks in Western Popular Culture*. New Haven, Conn.: Yale University Press.

Pitts, Robert E., D. Joel Whalen, Robert O'Keefe, and Vernon Murray. 1989. "Black and White Response to Culturally Targeted Television Commercials: A Values-Based Approach." *Psychology and Marketing* 6 (Winter): 311–28.

Powers, Ron. 1974. "Changing Faces in TV Commercials." *Tuesday* (August): 4–6.

Pozzi, Carl, and Rotfeld, Herbert J. 1984. Blacks in Advertising—Social Criticism and Marketing Paranoia. Paper presented at the 30th annual conference of the American Council on Consumer Interests, April 11–14.

Pratt, Charlotte A., Cornelius B. Pratt, and Mark Rumptz. 1993. An Analysis of Food, Beverage and Nutrition Advertisements in Three Consumer Magazines: Implications for Black Health Risks. Paper presented to the Advertising Division, 76th Annual Convention of the Association for Education in Journalism and Mass Communication, Kansas City, Missouri, August 11–14.

Presbrey, Frank. 1929. *The History and Development of Advertising*. Garden City, N.Y.: Doubleday, Doran and Company.

Printers' Ink. 1963. *Advertising: Today, Yesterday, Tomorrow*. New York: McGraw-Hill.

Reno, Dawn. 1986. *Collecting Black Americana*. New York: Crown.

Roberts, Churchill. 1970–71. "The Portrayal of Blacks on Network Television." *Journal of Broadcasting* 15 (Winter): 45–53.

Robinson, Velma A. 1993. Corporate America: Adapting to the African-American Consumer Market. Paper submitted to the Alan Bussell Student Competition sponsored by the Minorities and Communication Division, Association for Education in Journalism and Mass Communication, Kansas City, Missouri, August 11–14.

Sacharow, Stanley. 1982. *Symbols of Trade: Your Favorite Trademarks and the Companies They Represent*. New York: Art Direction Book Company.

Scheibe, Cynthia Leone. 1983. Character Portrayals and Values in Network TV Commercials. Master's thesis, Cornell University.

Schlinger, Mary and Joseph Plummer. 1972. "Advertising in Black and White." *Journal of Advertising Research* 9 (May) 149–53.

Schmidt, David and Ivan Preston. 1969. "How NAACP Leaders View Integrated Advertising." *Journal of Advertising Research* 9 (September): 13–16.

Sharp, Saundra. 1993. *Black Women for Beginners.* New York: Writers and Readers Publishing, Inc.

Shayon, Robert. 1968. "Commercials in Black and White." *Saturday Review* (October): 48.

Sheperd, Juanita M. 1980. "The Portrayal of Black Women in the Ads of Popular Magazines." *Western Journal of Black Studies* 4 (Fall): 179–82.

Shiver, Jube. 1988. "Star Struck: The Magical Attraction of Celebrity Families Has Madison Avenue under a Spell." *Black Enterprise* (December): 51.

Shuey, Audrey, Nancy King and Barbara Griffith. 1953. "Stereotyping of Negroes and Whites: An Analysis of Magazine Pictures." *Public Opinion Quarterly* 17 (Summer): 281–87.

Sims-Wood, Janet. 1988. "The Black Female: Mammy, Jemima, Sapphire, and Other Images." In Jessie Carney Smith, ed., *Images of Blacks in American Culture.* Westport, Conn.: Greenwood Press.

Snyder, Wally. 1993. "Advertising's Ethical and Economic Imperative." *American Advertising* (Fall): 28.

Soley, Lawrence. 1983. "The Effect of Black Models on Magazine Ad Readership." *Journalism Quarterly* 60 (Autumn): 686–90.

Solomon, Paul J. 1974. A Laboratory Experiment to Assess the Aspect of Black Models in Television Advertising. Ph.D. Diss., Arizona State University.

Stafford, James, Al Birdwell, and Charles Van Tassel. 1970. "Integrated Advertising—White Backlash." *Journal of Advertising Research* 10 (April): 15–20.

Stearns, James M., Lynette S. Unger, and Steven C. Luebkeman. 1987. "The Portrayal of Blacks in Magazine and Television Advertising." In Susan P. Douglas and Michael R. Solomon, eds., *American Marketing Association Educator's Proceedings, No. 53,* pp. 198–203. Chicago: American Marketing Association.

Stein, M. L. 1972. *Blacks in Communication.* New York: Julian Messner.

Stern, Gail. 1984. *Ethnic Images in Advertising.* Philadelphia, Pa.: Balch Institute for Ethnic Studies and the Anti Defamation League of B'nai B'rith.

The Story of Uncle Ben. 1988. Memo distributed by Uncle Ben's, Inc. Houston, Texas.

Sturgis, Ingrid. 1993. "Black Images in Advertising: A Revolution Is Being Televised in 30-Second Commercials." *Emerge* (September): 21–23.

Stutts, Mary Ann. 1982. "Blacks in Magazine Ads: Are They Growing in Numbers?" *Mid-South Business Journal* 2: 24–27.

Surlin, Stuart. 1972. "The Attitudes of Prejudiced Individuals Toward the Institution of Advertising." *Journal of Advertising* 2: 35–37.

———. 1977. "Authoritarian Advertising Executives and the Use of Black Models in Advertising." *Journal of Black Studies* 8 (September): 105–15.

Thalberg, Jan. 1989. "Cream of Wheat." *Black Ethnic Collectibles,* (January/February): 15.

———. 1990. "Black Advertising: Blotters." *Black Ethnic Collectibles* (Fall): 38.

Tolley, Stuart, and John Goett. 1971. "Reactions to Blacks in Newspapers Ads." *Journal of Advertising Research* 11 (April): 11–16.

Vogl, A. J. 1963. "A Face for the Invisible Man." *Sales Management* 91 (December): 30–33, 87.

Wallace, Michelle. 1990. *Invisibility Blues.* New York: Routledge, Chapman and Hall.

Warren, Nagueyalti. 1988. "From Uncle Tom to Cliff Huxtable, Aunt Jemima to Aunt Nell: Images of Blacks in Film and the Television Industry." In Jessie Carney Smith, ed., *Images of Blacks in American Culture.* Westport, Conn.: Greenwood Press.

Wheatley, John. 1971. "The Use of Black Models in Advertising." *Journal of Marketing Research* 8 (August): 390–92.

Whittler, Tommy. 1989. "Viewers' Processing of Actor's Race and Message Claims in Advertising Stimuli." *Psychology and Marketing* 6 (Winter): 287–309.

———. 1991. "The Effects of Actor's Race in Commercial Advertising: Review and Extension." *Journal of Advertising* 20: 54–60.

Wilkes, Robert E., and Humberto Valencia. 1989. "Hispanics and Blacks in Television Commercials." *Journal of Advertising* 18: 19–25.

Wilson, Clint, and Felix Gutierrez. 1985. *Minorities and Media: The End of Diversity.* New York: Sage Publications.

Wilson, Geraldine L. 1980. "Sticks and Stones and Racial Slurs Do Hurt: The Word Nigger Is What's Not Allowed." In *Children, Race and Racism: How Race Awareness Develops Interracial Books for Children.* New York: Racism and Sexism Resource Center for Education.

Yang, Jeff, Angelo Ragaza, Grace Suh, and Rodney Gonzalez. " The Beauty Machine: The U. S. Is Getting Darker, but the Standard of Beauty Is Still White." *Asian-American Quarterly.*

Young, Jackie. 1988. *Black Collectibles: Mammy and Her Friends.* West Chester, Pa.: Schiffer Publishing.

Zinkhan, George M., Keith Cox and Jae Hong. 1989. "Changes in Stereotypes: Blacks and Whites in Magazine Advertisements." *Journalism Quarterly* 63 (Autumn): 568–72.

Zinkhan, George M., William J. Qualls, and Abhijit Biswas. 1990. "The Use of Blacks in Magazine and Television Advertising: 1946 to 1986." *Journalism Quarterly* 67 (Autumn): 547–53.

INDEX

About the Author

MARILYN KERN-FOXWORTH is Associate Professor in the Department of Journalism at Texas A&M University. In Spring 1994, she was the Garth C. Reeves Endowed Chair at Florida A&M University Department of Journalism, Media, and Graphic Arts. She is the first African-American to receive a Ph.D. with a concentration in advertising. An accomplished, award-winning scholar, in 1993 she became the first person of color to receive the Kreighbaum Under-40 Award from the Association for Education in Journalism and Mass Communication for outstanding performance in teaching, research, and public service. In 1981, she received a Kizzy Award from the Black Women Hall of Fame Foundation and was cited as one of 12 outstanding African-American women in America, in 1993, she was one of several African-American women honored nationwide by the consortium of Doctors, Ltd. for her accomplishments as mass media trailblazer and pioneer.

ISBN 0-313-26798-7

90000>

EAN

9 780313 267987

HARDCOVER BAR CODE